THE FAITHFUL CITIZEN

Studies in Rhetoric and Religion 10

THE FAITHFUL CITIZEN

Popular Christian Media and Gendered Civic Identities

KRISTY MADDUX

BAYLOR UNIVERSITY PRESS

Cover Design by Nicole Weaver, Zeal Design Studio
Cover Image: "Man and Woman Watch 1960s TV" Courtesy of Petrified
Collection/The Image Bank/Getty Images (10064262 [RM])

"The Da Vinci Code and the Regressive Gender Politics of Celebrating Women"
by Kristy Maddux in *Critical Studies in Media Commuunication* 25.3 (2008), 225–
48, copyright © National Communication Association. Reprinted by permission
of Taylor & Francis Ltd, http://www.tandf.co.uk/journals on behalf of The
National Communication Association.

"Playing the Victim: Violence, Suffering, and Feminine Submission in *The Passion
of the Christ*" by Kristy Maddux in *Journal of Media and Religion* 7.3 (2008), 150–69.
Reprinted by permission of Taylor & Francis Ltd, http://www.tandf.co.uk/
journals.

Library of Congress Cataloging-in-Publication Data

Maddux, Kristy.
   The faithful citizen : popular Christian media and gendered civic identities /
Kristy Maddux.
       p. cm. -- (Studies in rhetoric and religion ; 10)
   Includes bibliographical references (p.   ) and index.
   ISBN 978-1-60258-253-8 (alk. paper)
   1. Mass media in religion. 2. Mass media--Religious aspects--Christianity. 3.
Christians--Political participation. 4. Citizenship. 5. Sex role--Religious aspects--
Christianity. I. Title.
   BV652.95.M33 2010
   261.5'2--dc22
                               2009039492

For my grandparents

Robert Paul Bolerjack and Frances Elaine Andersen Bolerjack
and
Marvin Andrew Maddux and Geraldine Jeanette Rowe Maddux

Contents

PREFACE

My maternal grandmother, who tried to teach me manners, would surely be scandalized to know that I have written a book about religion, politics, and gender. Raised the daughter of Danish immigrants in Lincoln, Nebraska, my grandmother learned to put aside such controversial topics so that she could blend into the community, and she encouraged me to do the same. As this book not only seeks out the intersections between religion, politics, and gender, but also commits my arguments to print, my maternal grandmother would worry that I might hurt someone's feelings or offend their sensibilities, and, honestly, I share those worries. But fortunately, I also had a paternal grandmother, a rural preacher's wife with less concern for the social niceties. Known for her feisty disposition, she would sit up late into the night arguing with anyone who would listen. She showed me that sometimes we have to talk about precisely the things that divide us.

Through much of my life, religion, politics, and gender have been the things that divide us. Religion and gender are central battlefields of these "culture wars" that supposedly have polarized American politics at least since the early 1990s. Too often, issues like same-sex marriage, abortion, and evolution become the litmus tests that we use to distinguish our allies from our adversaries. Disputes over these high-profile issues reveal that ours is a culture ruptured along the axes of class, geography, and generation. Not only do the fault lines split Left from Right, but also professional from working class, North from South, and grandkids from grandparents. Navigating this terrain is perilous.

As religion, gender, and politics have loomed large culturally, they have also reigned supreme in my personal life. My firsthand experiences with debates over these issues have admittedly influenced both my scholarly interests and my biases. I came of age as a preacher's kid in the United Methodist Church (UMC) in an era when church leaders could not stop talking about sex. An early flashpoint in my adolescence was the Re-Imagining Conference, when thousands of clergywomen, my mom among them, gathered at an event sponsored by the UMC, the Presbyterian Church (U.S.A.), and other mainline denominations. My mom and her friends returned from the conference inspired and energized, but not shocked or offended, and no one anticipated that months later a controversy would arise and prompt internal investigations of the denominational agencies sponsoring the conference. It seems that participants had affirmed radical and unorthodox theologies: they had used the Greek word *sophia* to refer to God, and they had celebrated communion with milk and honey. The controversy over Re-Imagining revealed, but did not quell, abiding anxiety over the propriety of women in church leadership. It showed me, as a teenager, my church's impulse to curtail ideologies of gender it deemed deviant, an impulse that has not abated in the years since.

Even after the Re-Imagining controversy had run its course, several of the mainline denominations persisted in heated arguments over human sexuality. In my teenage years, as the UMC argued over whether to ordain gay and lesbian clergy and whether to conduct same-sex union ceremonies, my local church declared itself a Reconciling Congregation, signaling its openness to persons of all sexual orientations. Since then, in the UMC, there have been church trials of gay clergy, of clergy who performed same-sex union ceremonies, and of one clergyman who refused church membership to a gay individual. Every four years, when the denomination's General Conference meets and delegates debate these issues, activists stage public demonstrations, which have sometimes included civil disobedience and police arrests. Many of my friends, people I have known my entire life, have provided courageous public witness on both sides of these issues. The denomination seems far from arriving at a happy resolution, and in the meantime, churches are broken, careers are destroyed, and individuals are hurt.

More than just contesting gender, sex, and sexuality, these debates implicate a wide range of theological issues, such as the authority and inerrancy of Scripture, the possibility of God's continuing revelation, the legitimacy of church policy-making processes, the role of the church in dictating individual morality, and the propriety of the church influencing public social positions. One of the most tragic results of the Re-Imagining scandal, in my view, has been an abiding distrust of the Women's Division, the

United Methodist agency that cosponsored the conference. This distrust saddens and concerns me because I understand the Women's Division as a symbol of the church's civic leadership. The Women's Division descends from the nineteenth-century groups, such as ladies' aid societies and foreign and home mission societies, which together revolutionized the roles of both women and the church in civic society. As they provided for mission work, such organizations buttressed their denominations' cultural standing as civic leaders. Moreover, the women who ran these organizations developed leadership skills that translated to the activist causes of the day, including temperance and women's rights in the nineteenth century. When church-women's organizations continue to fulfill these functions today—as they, for instance, raise money for disaster relief around the world—they remind us that we stand in this admirable tradition of civic leadership.

I have great affection for the historic and present social activism modeled by these women's groups, and I am sympathetic to the many other ways that churches work within their communities. In Washington, D.C., I have made my church home at Foundry UMC, a congregation with a long history of civic leadership. Over the last two centuries, Foundry's members have helped found a hospital (Sibley Memorial), a nursing home (The Methodist Home), and a university (American)—institutions that still exist today. Foundry Church continues to exercise civic leadership through both mercy and justice work. Members make sandwiches for day laborers, stock and staff a walk-in mission, and hold an annual fundraiser for AIDS relief organizations, among other efforts. In concert with other area churchgoers, Foundry members also pressure local elected leaders to alleviate the District's homelessness problem that leaves men and women sleeping on the church steps at night. Phone and letter campaigns, as well as citywide advocacy events, are sometimes coordinated from the pulpit (while the church, of course, carefully avoids any legal impropriety associated with mixing religion and politics).

My experiences in the church have led me to form personal opinions on these issues of religion, gender, and civic participation. I am committed, for instance, to the full inclusion of all persons, regardless of gender, sex, or sexuality, in the life of the church. And I choose to participate at Foundry Church because I appreciate being part of a faith community that lives out its calling through such acts of charity and justice. As the research for this book has reminded me again and again, however, Christians are not universally motivated by these same imperatives. And this book is not primarily polemical in nature, and it does not articulate opinions on these specific issues.

Instead, I am concerned with broader questions of Christian ideals of gender and civic participation, and I am interested in the role that entertainment media play in articulating those ideals. Because these issues are contentious, I try to draw on my life's experience in the fractured UMC to approach the diversity of Christian thought with openness and tolerance. As my denomination has struggled with these divisive issues of gender and sexuality, we have faced the looming threat of schism. Trying to avoid the sort of split the Methodist church has not seen since the Civil War, we have worked to listen and speak humbly and respectfully. I have undertaken this book project in that spirit of pluralism, wanting to recognize the diversity of Christian expressions that populate our rhetorical landscape. Even as I find faults in many of these expressions, and even as I expose their limitations, I hope I do so in the spirit of Christian perfection—not because I believe that my understanding of gender, civic participation, and faith is perfect, but because I recognize that we all seek God's perfection in love.

My experiences in the church, especially a divided church, have also driven my inclination toward rhetorical studies as an academic discipline and rhetorical criticism as a scholarly approach. Both enterprises—being a Christian and a rhetorical critic—task us with making sense of the texts around us. I understand religion to be a discursive more than a scientific or objective endeavor, and I have always encountered the Bible as a rhetorical document—a series of well-meaning, divinely inspired texts that reflect their authors' striving, yearning, and ultimately failing to know God and understand God's wisdom. As children of this faith tradition, we inherit this collection of scriptures, along with the extracanonical writings of the great cloud of witnesses throughout the centuries, and we struggle to make sense of these authors, their contexts, their language, and the impact of their ideas throughout the centuries. I study popular media in part because I have been influenced by the Wesleyan quadrilateral, that doctrine that says we find God's continuing revelation in four sources—Scripture, reason, tradition, and experience. Unorthodox though they may be, films, books, and television shows contribute to the ways we experience the divine.

Whether we seek meaning from Scripture or from popular media, however, our interpretations necessarily fall short. After nearly two thousand years of study, theologians, Bible scholars, preachers, and laypeople have not arrived at conclusive interpretations of the Christian Scriptures. Rhetorical critics have fared no better with the popular discourse and media texts we study. Always failing to settle upon the final, definitive analysis of a given rhetorical act, we instead offer the strongest reading supported by the available evidence, and we trust that our readings will be tested by the counter-readings of other critics. I offer the following analyses of contemporary Christian-themed mass media in that spirit; they are intended to be neither definitive nor final, but compelling and provocative. I hope that others interested in these texts, as well as in these questions of Christianity, gender, and civic participation, will engage my analyses and articulate their own responses.

Throughout the process of writing this book, my analyses of these media texts have been tested and refined through helpful conversations with thoughtful people. This project began as a dissertation at the University of Georgia, so I am grateful first for the guidance of my advisor, Bonnie J. Dow. I appreciate her for introducing me to feminist scholarship, nurturing my nascent research program, reading drafts of mediocre essays, encouraging me in the midst of my overwhelming anxiety, and sharing her savvy analyses of academic politics. Because the conceptual framework for this book grew out of my dissertation defense, I am grateful to the participants in that meeting: Celeste Condit, Christine Harold, John Murphy, and Patricia Richards, in addition to Bonnie Dow.

At the University of Maryland, I have been blessed with a group of supportive colleagues in the Department of Communication. I am especially grateful to my colleagues in the Rhetoric and Political Culture area—Robert Gaines, Jim Klumpp, Nneka Ofulue, Shawn Parry-Giles, Trevor Parry-Giles, and, for a time, Mari Boor Tonn. Shawn and Trevor Parry-Giles both read drafts of chapters of this manuscript, and Shawn has been an able mentor during my first few years at Maryland. Our chair, Elizabeth Toth, deserves credit for facilitating a climate that fosters scholarship.

Both the Universities of Georgia and Maryland assisted my research financially. The Graduate School at Georgia sponsored the dissertation phase with a year-long fellowship, and the General Research Board at Maryland provided a stipend for a summer of writing and revision. The staff members at Baylor University Press deserve credit for their helpfulness and professionalism. And I am as grateful to Marty Medhurst for bringing this manuscript to print, as the whole field of rhetorical studies should be for the ways his editorial leadership has increased the reach of our scholarship.

This project and my life as a scholar have also been enriched by my relationships with colleagues at other universities. James Jasinski, of the University of Puget Sound, introduced me to the discipline, helped me identify engaging projects, and trained me out of some of the worst writing habits (but I am sure many of my syntactic choices will still trouble him).

For their friendship, patience, and research consultations, I also thank Jarrod Atchison, Wendy Atkins-Sayre, Jennifer Bevan, Tasha Dubriwny, Shannon Holland, John Jordan, Bethany Keeley, John Lynch, Christina Morus, Kristan Poirot, Gordon Stables, Davi Johnson Thornton, and Dylan Wolfe.

My friends and family have provided the support that makes it possible to finish a big project. In D.C., I have found companionship from the women in my small group, as well as Ned Culhane, Peter Morscheck, and Katie Rush. And, of course, my family has been a steady source of encouragement as well as a distraction from research and writing. I thank my mom, Jan Bolerjack, and Rachel and Riley Klingler.

1

CHRISTIAN MEDIA, GENDER, AND CIVIC PARTICIPATION

Then God said, "Let us make humankind in our image, according to our likeness; and let them have dominion over the fish of the sea, and over the birds of the air, and over the cattle, and over all the wild animals of the earth, and over every creeping thing that creeps upon the earth."

Genesis 1:26

But our citizenship is in heaven, and it is from there we are expecting a Savior, the Lord Jesus Christ.

Philippians 3:20

If you listened to one set of doomsayers at the close of the twentieth century, it seemed that the once-robust American tradition of civic participation had atrophied. Robert Putnam's "Bowling Alone" thesis sounded the alarm: Americans had ceased to volunteer, support charities, and join community organizations—at least at levels rivaling previous generations.[1] In the political arena, citizens showed little interest in legislative debates, they failed to follow the news carefully, and they could not distinguish between one candidate and the next. Studies warned us that America's children seemed poised to continue these trends; even college students reportedly failed the most straightforward civics exams.[2] By the end of the twentieth century, the days of citizen activism, protest marches, and patriotic sacrifice were little more than a distant memory, it seemed.

Amidst this dismal trajectory of civic decline, one demographic stood out for bucking the trend: regular churchgoers. Putnam admitted that Americans in this category were "substantially more likely to be involved in secular organizations, to vote and participate politically in other ways, and

1

to have deeper informal social connections."³ Robert Wuthnow concurred that regular religious participants, especially in mainline Protestant traditions, were more likely to participate in civic life.⁴ But both men identified worrisome trends even among this demographic: Wuthnow agonized about the civic implications of declining membership in mainline Protestant denominations, and Putnam feared that membership was shifting toward the Christian traditions (including evangelicalism) that place less emphasis on community involvement outside the church.⁵ In short, according to both Putnam and Wuthnow, generally positive correlations between religious participation and civic engagement may not ensure vital civic life in the years to come.

At the beginning of the twenty-first century, at least following the 2004 election, it was nearly impossible to escape news coverage narrating the political ascent of "evangelical Christians."⁶ As journalists pored over exit poll data, they concluded that these "values voters" had turned out in record numbers and cast a unified ballot based on the "moral issues," helping guarantee George W. Bush's reelection. Against the widespread tide of civic disengagement, these "evangelical Christians" had seemingly discovered political influence anew. Beyond the ballot box, they donated to candidates, staged public demonstrations, and participated in talk radio shows. Their signature issues were gay marriage and abortion, but they also predictably supported prayer in schools and posting the Ten Commandments in public places, just as they predictably opposed stem cell research and gun control. They arrived at these political priorities through obsequious devotion to the pronouncements made by the figureheads of their movement— James Dobson, Jerry Falwell, and Pat Robertson. Or so the news media taught us.

The 2008 election cycle confounded, complicated, and continued these various narratives about religion and civic participation, as it also foregrounded race and gender as demographic variables. The contest confounded Putnam's civic decline thesis because the primaries and general election alike witnessed an upsurge in political participation by young adults and other previously disengaged citizens.⁷ The day after the Texas primary, the *Austin American-Statesman* called the event a "democracy love fest" for all the enthusiasm it generated.⁸ No one who watched college students pack sports arenas to hear a presidential candidate speak could doubt that we were witnessing a renaissance of political enthusiasm among young voters.⁹

During the 2008 contest, journalists and campaigns alike continued the trend of exalting evangelical Christians as a demographic group. In this case, however, the supposedly unified voting bloc fractured. With the deaths of figureheads like Jerry Falwell and D. James Kennedy, James Dobson inherited the symbolic leadership of their movement, and he used his popular pulpit to offer only intermittent and tepid support for Republican nominee John McCain.[10] Meanwhile, Rick Warren, pastor of the Southern California megachurch Saddleback, hosted both major party candidates at his church for a televised forum prior to any of their official debates.[11] The parties and candidates themselves confounded the assumed affinity between evangelical Christians and the Republican Party. Whereas the Episcopalian-turned-Baptist John McCain sometimes spoke awkwardly about his churchgoing history and never answered questions about his baptism, the mainline Protestant Barack Obama spoke comfortably about his conversion as an adult and his ongoing faith journey.[12] Even controversies over Obama's supposed Muslim heritage and his outspoken pastor, Jeremiah Wright, did not cause irreparable damage to his campaign's relations with faith groups. For its part, the McCain campaign compensated for the candidate's poorly performed religiosity by nominating Sarah Palin, whose unimpeachable Christian and pro-life credentials won her instant popularity with at least some religious conservatives.[13] These shifts within the political parties, in combination with generational transitions among evangelical Christian leaders, made clear that Christian faith did not translate simply into a political platform and a party-line vote.

Although religious voters remained important in 2008, race and gender became the preoccupying demographic concerns of that election. When the Democratic Party presidential primary yielded an African American man and a Euro-American woman as frontrunners, along with a host of Euro-American men also as contenders, it prompted important questions about identity politics and civic participation: would women naturally support a female candidate, and would African Americans lean toward the African American candidate?[14] Primary results quickly belied any easy relationship between female voters and a female candidate, at least; young women's support for Obama distinguished them from older women, who tended to favor Clinton.[15] Some women, however, remained steadfast in their gender-based political decisions; when Hillary Clinton lost the Democratic nomination contest, a group of Clinton supporters, calling themselves PUMA (People United Means Action), protested perceived sexism within the Democratic Party by at least considering supporting the Republican ticket.[16] When the Republicans nominated a female vice-presidential candidate, Alaska governor Sarah Palin, they gave women more reason to consider their party's ticket. The contrast between Governor Palin and Senator Clinton also prompted important questions about women's political leadership. Not only did the two disagree on a host of policy issues, but they offered distinct public images. Palin, of course, played the role of the hockey mom in lipstick, in contrast to the pantsuit-wearing Senator Clinton. Together they suggested that the relationship between gender and leadership style is as complicated as the relationship between gender and voter behavior.

For all the important questions the 2008 election yielded about gender—what women's leadership looks like, what candidates female voters will support—it hardly exhausted the range of questions related to gender and civic participation. For instance, does gender influence other types of civic participation such as volunteering and joining organizations? As part of his civic decline thesis, Putnam considered such gendered questions. He attended, if only cursorily, to the ways that changing gender roles may have contributed to the decline in civic engagement. He presented the hypothesis that as women have attained gainful employment outside the home, they have lost the flexible time that might once have been devoted to volunteer civic work.[17] His data prove this hypothesis to be only partially explanatory because women's civic participation is influenced by a complicated set of variables, including how many hours they perform paid labor and whether or not that work is voluntary.[18]

Surely, however, the twentieth century's revolution in gender roles matters for civic engagement even beyond these patterns of paid labor. After all, many of the behaviors of civic participation that Putnam and others measure—voting, campaigning, and running for office, for instance—were once formally limited to men alone. Conversely, many other behaviors they measure—PTA membership, church attendance, charitable volunteering—have long been dominated by women. Although women now have generally equal access to the legal rights of citizenship, and men are not formally excluded from these other forms of volunteerism, citizenship and civic volunteerism alike are still constrained by powerful social norms of femininity and masculinity.

This book works at the intersection of these competing narratives about civic participation, Christianity, and gender. I am interested, first, in models of faithful Christian civic participation, and second, in the ways that these models of civic participation are defined by gender. I seek out these models in the mediated rhetoric that circulates through our daily lives. If mediated rhetoric shapes the way we see our world, the way we understand and come to interact with the people and institutions around us, then popular media play an important role in articulating civic responsibilities and our avenues, as citizens, for fulfilling those responsibilities. I begin with the premise that popular media offer discursive resources that are available to individual actors as they articulate themselves in relationship to their communities and the state.

To examine the mediated constructions of civic participation, Christianity, and gender, I turn to the Christian-themed mass media texts that, in recent years, have become nearly as inescapable as talk about the "values voters." At about the same time that journalists and politicians alike discovered the power of the evangelical Christian vote, mass media producers discovered anew the power of the evangelical Christian consumer dollar, especially after Christian groups, families, and individuals stormed movie theaters to take in Mel Gibson's 2004 *The Passion of the Christ* during the Christian season of Lent. *The Passion* certainly was not the first mainstream Christian movie—even if news coverage sometimes acted as though it was—as it followed generations of cinematic biblical epics like *The Robe* and *The Ten Commandments* and musicals like *Jesus Christ Superstar*. *The Passion* was not even the first Christian-themed mass media success of its era. By the time it opened, the television show *7th Heaven* was in its eighth season on the WB network, and Tim LaHaye and Jerry Jenkins had published eleven installments of their *Left Behind* series of apocalyptic fiction novels. Moreover, *7th Heaven* shared the airwaves with other religious-themed shows like *Touched by an Angel* and *Joan of Arcadia*, and the *Left Behind* books shared the front tables at the chain bookstores with Dan Brown's *The Da Vinci Code*, Rick Warren's *The Purpose-Driven Life*, and Bruce Wilkinson's *The Prayer of Jabez*. Since then, religious publishing has continued unabated. Rick Warren has developed a purpose-driven empire, including *The Purpose-Driven Church* as well as companion media for the original *The Purpose-Driven Life*. Then, in 2007 and 2008, the Christian media sensation was *The Shack*, a novel by unknown author William Paul Young, which he originally wrote and distributed only informally to his friends and family.

Following on the widely touted success of *The Passion*, the enthusiastic publicity for religious movies only intensified: the spring of 2005 brought NBC's miniseries *Revelations*; December 2006, the movie version of C. S. Lewis' classic, *The Lion, the Witch, and the Wardrobe*, as well as the illustrated gospel *Nativity Story*; and February 2007, the cinematic portrayal of William Wilberforce in *Amazing Grace*. When 20th Century Fox announced plans to create twelve religious-themed films annually, six of which will be released to the theaters, it ensured that such programming will be a mainstay into the near future.[19] In addition to the major studios producing these movies, a small church group based in Albany, Georgia, has turned a profit on two very low-budget films released in wide distribution to movie theaters. In 2006, they released *Facing the Giants*, the story of a small-town football team whose faith in God finds them success in their relationships and their athletic contests. In 2008 the group released *Fireproof*, starring Kirk Cameron as a firefighter struggling to save his marriage.

This project takes just five of these texts—*The Passion of the Christ*, *Left Behind*, *7th Heaven*, *Amazing Grace*, and *The Da Vinci Code*—as case studies of how these mediated discourses model Christian civic responsibility, and how they do so in gendered terms. Surely these entertainment media were influential in much larger senses; they popularized particular theologies and eschatologies, for instance. My analysis, however, largely eschews these other topics, which merit attention on their own terms, in favor of close textual analysis of notions of civic engagement and its gendered bases. In each case, I articulate and interrogate the text's model of civic participation and gender ideology in light of a contemporary dispute over theology, politics, or feminism. My treatment of *The Passion*, for instance, reads that film in light of feminist critiques of liberation theology and its potential for political activism. The chapter about *7th Heaven* considers that program's implications in terms of the political debate over government funding for charity programs. In the five case studies, I find five conflicted images of civic engagement with five different ideologies of gender, which, taken together, suggest the richness of contemporary ideals of civic participation. In the conclusion of each chapter, I try to illuminate the contemporary political implications of the text's model of civic engagement.

In the remainder of this opening chapter, I advance a few simple claims that lay the groundwork for the analysis that follows in subsequent chapters. Through these five claims, I suggest the relationships between the key terms of this analysis: civic participation, Christianity, gender, and media. First, I argue that recent narratives of civic decline have been constrained by unnecessarily narrow definitions of citizenship or civic participation. Second, I make two points about gender: that citizenship has always been defined by gendered norms, and that, since the early church, Christianity has always influenced cultural ideologies of gender. Third, I show how American Christianity's civic outlook has long alternated between competing impulses that advocate moral reform and social justice. Fourth, I demonstrate the history Christian faith communities have of adopting new media technologies, and I argue that popular media remain influential within Christianity. Finally, I demonstrate how the rhetorical critical approach, and especially the constitutive rhetoric perspective, adds a useful layer to a scholarly conversation that has otherwise been dominated by social scientific survey research.

CITIZENSHIP AND CIVIC PARTICIPATION

If the many and varied accounts of civic health or decline prove one thing, it is that citizenship is not a static concept. Citizenship proves difficult to track or measure across time precisely because the attendant rights and behaviors have changed. Citizenship on a formal, legal, and technical level can be traced back at least as far as the foundations of democracy in the Athenian polis and Aristotle's *Politics*. Michael Ignatieff notes that it can then be traced through Rome, thirteenth-century Italy, the English civil war, and the Enlightenment ideology spelled out in the Declaration of Independence and the Declaration of the Rights of Man, making even more stops along the way.[20] The notion of citizenship at which this intellectual trek arrives is one that finds citizens much as Aristotle understood them: as the men (and later women) naturally inclined to self-rule. It is, as such, fundamentally intertwined with the concept of a democratic nation state because, as J. G. A. Pocock explains, "the citizen rules and is ruled; citizens join each other in making decisions where each decider respects the authority of the others, and all join in obeying the decisions (now known as 'laws') they have made."[21] When this Aristotelian concept of a citizen reemerged in early modern Europe, it distinguished citizens in the new political orders from subjects in the previous ones. Whereas subjects submitted to the rule of a sovereign, citizens submitted only to laws of their own collective design.[22] These definitions commonly lean to the republican over the liberal—treating citizens as political beings primarily, rather than economic or market-oriented ones.

In contemporary American democracy, citizenship is commonly construed as the set of rights conferred upon member constituents of the state, whether by birth or by naturalization, including the rights to vote, serve on juries, run for political office, and carry an American passport, along with the simple right of inhabitance. However, as Rogers Smith and Michael Schudson both remind us, those defining rights of citizenship have not been stable across American history.[23] Smith argues that "through most of U.S. history, lawmakers pervasively and unapologetically structured U.S.

citizenship in terms of illiberal and undemocratic racial, ethnic, and gender hierarchies,"[24] tendencies that have unraveled slowly. By his historical narrative, concepts of citizenship have progressed through "three great eras of democratizing American civic reforms: the Revolution and Confederation years, the Civil War and Reconstruction epoch, and the civil rights era of the 1950s and 1960s," each of which won legal citizenship rights for a new segment of the American population.[25] Schudson also traces a progression in American citizenship, specifically in terms of participation in elections and the judiciary system.[26] His narrative begins with the colonial era, where the property-holding men who had citizenship rights made their political decisions based on interpersonal trust. That era gave way to the era of party politics, where party machines orchestrated elections, which then gave way to the progressive era, which introduced our current appreciation for the educated, literate citizen as a rational decision-maker. The twentieth century also saw the rise of the judicial system as an arena for citizen participation, and the lawsuit became a critical tool of citizenship.

These legal and political definitions—even traced all the way from Aristotle's rational man to the twenty-first-century litigant—still form an incomplete understanding of citizenship. As George Armstrong Kelly urges, "we must realistically allow that the citizen's activity is pluralistic and not exclusively state-oriented."[27] These definitions have commonly accounted only for what Will Kymlicka and Wayne Norman call "citizenship-as-legal-status, that is, as full membership in a particular political community," but not what they call "citizenship-as-desirable-activity, where the extent and quality of one's citizenship is a function of one's participation in that community."[28] The latter performance of citizenship, because it is not oriented toward the state, is operative in the civic sphere, a unique space separate from the state, the market, and the family, which is presumably capable of mediating between these sectors.

When social theorists lament the decline of citizenship, they are typically referring to the loss of this civic sphere and the civic behaviors historically performed there. In his dire narrative of the "structural transformation of the public sphere," Jürgen Habermas bemoans the loss of just such a space that he argues existed in bourgeois Europe. Clearly a product of his Frankfurt School mentors—Theodor Adorno and Max Horkheimer— Habermas attributes this disappearance to the development of private interests, especially the media, and their collusion with the state. Because of this interlocking between the state and the market, "the public sphere, which must now mediate these demands, becomes a field for the competition of interests, competitions which assume the form of violent conflict."[29]

Other accounts find a vital civic sphere operative more recently than bourgeois Europe. Although he does not specify exactly when, Benjamin Barber asserts that "once upon a time" civil society was a cornerstone of the American model of democracy. Then, "there was a vital idling choice for Americans between the opposing poles of government and market, state and individual, contract association and community, and it was admired and imitated elsewhere in the world . . . it held the key to our country's early democratic energy and civic activism."[30] He alludes to Alexis de Tocqueville's famous account of the young republic, which claimed that civic associations distinguished the United States from the visitor's native Europe.

These critics especially decry the loss of the modes of citizenship that were characteristic of that public sphere. For Habermas, the disappearance of the public sphere is lamentable precisely because it was once the space where citizens bracketed their private interests and participated in rational-critical deliberation about matters of common concern.[31] He is dismayed to find that citizens are now passive consumers of information marketed by private interests and the state, rather than active participants in rational-critical deliberation.[32] Habermas' yearning for rational-critical discourse in place of passive consumption resonates with the images of political deliberation popular in the field of communication studies. Many rhetoricians also long to reinvigorate the democratic polis with deliberative rhetoric, which we trace as our heritage though the sophists, Aristotle, and Cicero, right up to the American lyceums and the forum and discussion movements.[33] These images of deliberative rhetoric hearken back "to a more local, popular democracy, reminiscent of the New England town meeting,"[34] where citizens gathered together in good faith to deliberate over the issues facing their communities. When rhetoricians invoke these bygone eras of public deliberation, they reinvest faith in the common assumption that talking, arguing, and persuading comprise the virtuous route to political truth.

For other social theorists, however, the types of civic participation lost are bigger than just rational-critical deliberation. Putnam, for instance, surveys what seems like an exhaustive breadth of more contemporary civic activities—bowling leagues, PTA projects, electoral campaigning, church services, charity work—far beyond rational-critical public deliberation.[35] Yet Putnam also finds contemporary civic life wanting. Americans, he claims, no longer vote, join community groups, campaign for candidates, or participate in league sports and the like, at least not at the levels their parents and grandparents did.

These declines in civic participation are especially troubling for social theorists who assume that vital democracy is premised on a vital civic sphere. According to Michael Walzer, a democratic state is intertwined with the civic sphere because "only a democratic state can create a democratic civil society; only a democratic civil society can sustain a democratic state."[36] Furthermore, Walzer suggests that the civic sphere provides the training grounds for state-oriented democratic citizenship. He explains, "The civility that makes democratic politics possible can only be learned in the associational networks" of the civic sphere.[37] Benjamin Barber echoes Walzer on this point, and he dwells especially on the lessons conveyed by volunteerism. In its ideal, non-coerced form, volunteerism brings individuals, especially young adults, into civic life and provides training in the skills necessary for lifelong citizenship.[38] Putnam sees the significance of civic associational life in the social capital it creates. Civic engagement facilitates "bridging," or making connections between groups, and "bonding," or strengthening connections within groups, which in turn create "social networks and the norms of reciprocity and trustworthiness that arise from them."[39] The social trust that results, Putnam claims, fuels cooperative democracy.

Citizenship may be in part a set of legal and political rights, and in part an inclination toward participation in a civic or public sphere, but Robert Asen has pointed out how both of these perspectives are inadequate. Invoking the spirit of social theorist John Dewey, Asen indicts Putnam in particular for trying to delimit what might "count" as civic engagement. Dewey conceptualizes the public as an entity prior to and bigger than the state, which means that citizenship cannot be defined by narrow acts like voting and legislating. Instead, democracy is a "way of life"—less a formal end and more a means to public engagement.[40] When Asen then introduces a "discourse theory of citizenship," he "conceives of citizenship as a *mode of public engagement*." Asen elaborates, "In drawing attention to citizenship as a process, a discourse theory recognizes the fluid, multimodal, and quotidian enactments of citizenship in a multiple public sphere."[41] Rather than just asking the *what* questions, like Putnam does, more fruitful analyses of civic participation would also ask the *how* questions. Such analyses should shift "our attention from acts to action," distinguishing "the manner by which something is done from what is done."[42] What is done does not become unimportant, but it can be read most profitably in relationship to the "dispositional factors" that define any practice of civic engagement.[43]

Asen's framework is certainly provocative, and it provides impetus for this project.[44] Like Asen, I assume that civic engagement is a disposition as much as it is a set of acts, and that the possibilities for this disposition are expansive. The latter has been amply proven by rhetorical critics whose case studies of citizen activism—from WTO protesters who smash storefronts to environmentalists who traverse toxic sites to AIDS activists who participate in the rational deliberation of congressional hearings—demonstrate that these contemporary performances are far too diverse to be accounted for by either Habermas' or Putnam's perspective.[45] In seeking out the models of civic engagement made available through mass media texts, this project differs from these earlier analyses of anti-WTO, environmental, and AIDS activists, however. Whereas those analyses examined the rhetoric produced by those activist groups, I am interested, instead, in the discursive resources that make such activism possible and intelligible. Looking at popular culture artifacts, I am asking, how do these movies, books, and television shows construct the multiple possibilities for dispositions of civic engagement? How do they situate the possibilities for civic engagement within the social worlds in which Christians live and work? And how are these dispositions of citizenship, or civic participation, defined by social norms of gender?

GENDER, CITIZENSHIP, AND CHRISTIANITY

Throughout its conflicted history, the concept of citizenship—both as legal status and civic responsibility—has been marked by gender. Certainly Aristotle's political man was just that—a man—and this gendered exclusion would be taken for granted for many centuries. Citizenship's maleness was codified in the modern era first with the 1791 French Declaration of the Rights of Man and Citizen and then in the United States with the 1869 Fourteenth Amendment to the Constitution, even if it had been unambiguous, if implicit, prior to that.[46] In the United States, not only was the citizen's franchise restricted to men until 1920, women had neither the right to sit on juries, which left female defendants with all-male juries of their peers, nor the right to bring lawsuits, which restricted women's ability to file for divorce.[47] Thus, women had no influence on the laws that governed their lives; only men were the self-governing political animals that Aristotle called citizens. Women have also been legally and formally excluded from other state-oriented expressions of citizenship, such as military service, where women's participation was severely curtailed as recently as the 1948 Women's Armed Services Act.[48] Indeed, a common argument against women's enfranchisement linked military service to the right to vote, suggesting that as long as women did not fight for their country, they did not earn the level of citizenship necessary to influence lawmaking.[49] At least in legal terms, through most of American history, citizenship has been defined by rights—the franchise, jury service, military enlistment, etc.—commonly restricted to men.

Because citizenship has been limited to men, these practices of citizenship are commonly defined by characteristics associated with masculinity. Masculinity is a set of behaviors that, although not limited to individuals with male bodies, have historically been performed by men.[50] Femininity is, likewise, a set of behaviors not limited to individuals with female bodies, but traditionally performed by women. Although masculine and feminine behaviors are not essential or exclusive to male and female bodies, respectively, they have been so frequently and convincingly performed by these sexed bodies that the connections have come to seem natural. By extension, masculine traits may seem "unwomanly" or inappropriate when performed by female bodies, just as feminine traits may seem unnatural when performed by male bodies. In the case of citizenship, because the associated legal rights were so long restricted to men, the characteristics associated with citizenship are overwhelmingly masculine, such as rational deliberation and public speaking.[51] Women who now exercise the privileges of citizenship must negotiate these masculine characteristics and risk being labeled "unfeminine" as they do so.

Beyond legal, state-oriented citizenship, civic participation in the public sphere has also often been restricted to men and thus defined by the standards of masculinity. The vibrant American civic life that so inspired Tocqueville was almost entirely restricted to men; Smith indicts the French observer for "endorsing a slightly modified ascriptive hierarchy that denied American women full democratic citizenship."[52] These exclusions were only partly based on an ideology of gender hierarchy; Elisabeth Clemens notes that organizational and associational logics played a role as well. "To the extent that political associations were based on workplace identities, the different patterns of men's and women's involvement in the labor market ensured that these associations would be primarily single-sex groups," Clemens explains. "Similarly, insofar as turn-of-the-century political mobilization built on the fraternal organizations of nineteenth-century America, it perpetuated that period's distinctively male and female political cultures."[53] Thus, especially with industrialization, urbanization, and professionalization, men and women increasingly worked in such distinct spheres that it is no surprise that they also maintained unique civic spheres.

Because civic life historically has been so gendered, one way of reading recent calls to reinvigorate civic life is to see them as pleas to reinstitute a form of patriarchy. Helen Irving, for instance, explains, "Because the social role historically performed by women has tended to be excluded from definitions of the civic or public sphere, normative theories that tie citizenship to a particular notion of public activity, conduct, or qualities need to be treated with caution."[54] She goes on to lament how these normative definitions "reproduce the dichotomies that assume women's traditional contribution to social life as caregivers and nurturers to be insignificant and not 'citizenly.' "[55] These normative theories of citizenship, in short, are problematic for women in part because they ignore women's historic contributions to public life and in part because where they do recognize women's contributions, they tend to view them as inferior to men's.

Women have, after all, not been entirely absent from civic life in American history, even if their participation has been constrained by powerful legal and social sources. Most often, when women have been excluded from the dominant forms of civic participation, they have developed socially acceptable alternatives, which have resulted in distinctly feminine modes of civic participation. Upon the nation's founding, when women were formally excluded from citizenship, they took up the mantle of "republican motherhood" instead, winning the valuable role of inculcating in their sons the ideals of democratic life.[56] Women increasingly expanded the possibilities for combining domesticity and democracy, transforming the home into a locus for social reform. According to Mary Ryan, "While menfolk flocked to public meetings, American women, especially of the urban middle classes, worked just as frantically to infuse the home with social functions."[57] Ryan is careful to note that women's development of domesticity as a public reform strategy was not a lesser form of activism; instead, it "invested the social practice of bourgeois wives and mothers with public significance."[58]

As the nineteenth century progressed, women added associational life to their civic portfolio, forming organizations that advocated not only for women's rights but also for other social and political goals, such as temperance.[59] In those organizations, women developed activist tools congruent with femininity, especially working around social norms that discouraged women's public speaking. For instance, abolitionist women put the petition to great use, sending hundreds of thousands of signatures to Congress beginning as early as 1834.[60] Susan Zaeske describes women who "produced needlepoint and other material objects that promoted . . . candidates, employed interpersonal influence to sway voters, conducted political meetings, wrote pamphlets, and gave speeches."[61] Their speeches commonly deployed what Karlyn Kohrs Campbell has called "feminine style," a rhetorical form distinct from men's.[62] In this mode of discourse, which allowed them to navigate attempts to censor their speech, women characteristically employed inductive reasoning, example evidence, a personal tone, and audience participation.[63] Although the feminine style of rhetoric never characterized women's rhetoric exclusively, nor did it characterize all women's rhetoric, it still formed an alternative to the otherwise male-dominated, masculine styles of participation in the public sphere.

Because men and women, through most of American history, have maintained separate civic spheres that relied on separate modes of civic participation, these gendered characteristics surely continue to linger today. Running for office, for instance, is still clearly characterized by masculine norms, such as public speaking, aggressive attacks on the candidate's opponents, and self-promotion of personal accomplishments—all of which can be troublesome for female candidates who perform them too well (and seem unfeminine or unnatural) or who perform them not well enough (and seem inadequate as leaders).[64] And club and organization work may still exemplify the feminine traits inherited from the nineteenth century.

Just as surely as civic participation has been characterized by gender norms, so too has Christian discourse played an important role in defining gender ideology. Biblical rationales have been integral in arguments against women's public participation throughout American history. Popular readings of the second creation story in Genesis, where woman is designed as man's "helpmeet" and blamed for the fall of humanity, have commonly consigned women to an inferior lot in life.[65] The apostle Paul's epistles in the New Testament are equally damning. In the first letter to the Corinthians, he asserts that women are to keep silent in the church, and in his letter to the Ephesians, Paul instructs women to submit to their husbands.[66] Early American women's rights advocates, such as Sarah Grimké and Elizabeth Cady Stanton, recognized the Bible as one of the greatest obstacles to women's emancipation, and they argued forcefully against the ways it was deployed by Christian leaders bent on restricting women's public role.[67] In Grimké's and Stanton's lifetimes, however, Christian theology also did important work to reduce social barriers between men and women. It was in evangelical Protestant and Quaker meetings that women first found the freedom to speak in front of a mixed audience, for instance.[68] Scripture passages such as Joel 2:28, which promises "your sons and daughters shall prophesy," and Galatians 3:28, in which the apostle Paul announces that there is no longer "male nor female," provided rationales for eliminating gender differences.[69]

In the twentieth century, Christianity maintained its influence over popular gender ideology. When the movement against women's suffrage became a public force in the 1910s, its leaders again drew heavily on theological rationales to make their separate spheres argument, claiming that the Bible consigns women and men to the private and public spheres, respectively.[70] Then, in the 1970s and 1980s, Phyllis Schlafly's StopERA campaign depicted a divinely ordained order, "manifest in nature, and sanctioned by tradition," that assigned to women a lower and separate sphere.[71] In 1998, the Southern Baptist Convention, the largest Protestant body in the United States, capitalized on the sentiment popularized by the Promise Keepers and codified this separate spheres ideology in its church doctrine. The convention adapted the language of the apostle Paul to amend its doctrinal Faith and Message, so that it explained, "The husband and wife are of equal worth before God," but then went on to admonish that the "wife is to submit herself graciously to the servant leadership of her husband even as the church willingly submits to the headship of Christ. She . . . has the God-given responsibility to respect and to serve as his helper."[72] At the same time, however, other denominations have loosened gender expectations, and most Protestant bodies now even ordain women to the highest ranks of their clergy.[73] The fact that so many of those same denominations now fixate on issues of gender and sexuality should suggest that they are bent on maintaining their preeminent influence on cultural gender ideology.

CHRISTIANITY AND CIVIC PARTICIPATION

When contemporary Christian media send strong messages about faith-based civic participation, they resonate with the long-standing Christian effort to discern the believer's responsibility to his or her earthly life. Christians, like members of other faith traditions, have struggled to balance and reconcile their temporal and spiritual obligations since the writers of the New Testament Gospels and Epistles wrestled with Jesus' teachings on the subject.[74] On the one hand, there is the Jesus portrayed in the Synoptic Gospels, who was deeply invested in the concrete matters of life in his earthly community. This Jesus instructed his followers to feed the hungry and care for the sick, and he challenged the social and political norms of his day when he angrily turned over the tables at the temple.[75] On the other hand, the Gospel of John and the Epistles of Paul commonly recall that Jesus promised his believers life in another realm. Paul told them that their citizenship was in heaven,[76] and the book of Revelation promises that God will bring a new heaven and a new earth.[77] The Gospels record the Pharisees trying to trick Jesus on this very issue. They questioned him about his followers' obligations, asking Jesus whether or not his followers should pay taxes. Jesus responded by holding up a coin; "Give therefore to the emperor the things that are the emperor's," Jesus explained, "and to God the things that are God's."[78]

It is surely little wonder that Christians have remained conflicted about where their loyalties lie. American Christianity has incorporated both strains of the tradition—the one fiercely committed to engaging with the earthly realm and the other endlessly drawn to individual spiritual development—but has found the two strains often at odds. They came into sharp relief, Martin Marty has famously argued, at the turn of the twentieth century, when a "two-party system" emerged.[79] In that era, the developing Social Gospel movement became what Marty identifies as "public Protestantism," and it inspired a pronounced backlash by "private Protestantism." The latter, Marty explains, "accented individual salvation out of the world, personal moral life congruent with the ideals of the saved, and fulfillment or its absence in the rewards or punishments in another world in a life to come."[80] Public Protestantism, on the other hand, "was public insofar as it was more exposed to the social order and the social destinies of men . . . They pursued a Social Christianity, the Social Gospel, Social Service, Social Realism, and the like."[81] David Moberg shows how the two groups differed in their approach to sin. The Christians he calls "soul-winners" believed that because sin was individual, converting and reforming individuals would eliminate criminality, corruption, sexual perversion, improvidence, laziness, greediness, and other sins.[82] Other Christians, whom Moberg calls "social gospelers," believed that because evil was "deeply entrenched in man's social systems," challenging those very systems was the only way to eradicate sin.[83]

The "two-party system" developed in concert with other social changes, such as the industrialization, urbanization, and immigration that created the inner-city poverty that, in turn, inspired Social Gospel activism.[84] Confronted with these social problems, clergy like Walter Rauschenbusch and Washington Gladden articulated the Social Gospel, which was then institutionalized in 1908 when, at their Philadelphia convention, the thirty-three member denominations of the Federal Council of Churches unanimously adopted the Social Creed of the Churches.[85] At the same time, scientific and social Darwinism, as well as historical-critical biblical criticism, had been making their way to the United States from Europe, where they revolutionized the ways that Christians read and interpreted the Scriptures.[86] Fundamentalist Christianity formalized itself in response to these trends with the publication of a series of pamphlets called *The Fundamentals* in the 1910s and the organization of the World's Christian Fundamentals Association in 1919. Since that time, the two parties—private and public, soul-winners and social gospelers, moral reform and social justice—have defined American Christianity.[87]

This division within Protestantism has largely persisted since its advent, but it reemerged visibly in the tumultuous heyday of American social protest, the 1960s, when Protestants again disagreed over the most suitable means of effecting reform. Protestant clergy throughout the United States advocated the Social Gospel, but its most visible proponents were social movement leaders, such as Rev. Dr. Martin Luther King Jr. and Rev. William Sloane Coffin. King famously used his pastoral pulpit to make civil rights a moral imperative, and he rendered the movement in biblical terms, such as his analogy to the Exodus narrative.[88] When King expanded his moral purview to include opposition to the Vietnam War, he explained that his critique grew out of his "commitment to the ministry of Jesus Christ."[89] Coffin, the chaplain at Yale University, also lent his moral authority to both causes. He rode through the American South with the Freedom Riders[90] and argued that Christians "must make peace our major religious responsibility, and Viet Nam our immediate one."[91] Both men, advocating civil rights and opposing U.S. military involvement in Vietnam, articulated faith-based positions on political issues, and they treated democratic politics as an appropriate avenue for their moral concerns.

Their very public activism came into sharp relief with the ever-present strain of "private Protestantism" when a young Reverend Jerry Falwell criticized their tactics. In a sermon called "Ministers and Marches," the emerging fundamentalist leader proclaimed, "Preachers are not called to be politicians but to be soul winners."[92] He found in Matthew 28:18-20 (the Great Commission) Christians' entire calling for their earthly lives: to bring the gospel of Jesus Christ to the world. This evangelism, he argued, would be more transformative than any political activism. According to Falwell,

> If the many thousands of churches and pastors of America would suddenly begin preaching the old fashioned gospel of Jesus Christ and the

power that is in His atoning blood, a revival would grip our land such as
we have never known before. If as much effort could be put into winning
people to Jesus Christ across the land as is being exerted in the present
civil rights movement, America would be turned upside down for God.
Hate and prejudice would certainly be in a great measure overcome.[93]

Falwell did not promote evangelism simply for the purpose of guarantee-
ing salvation for more people. He argued that evangelism itself was a social
reform program: bringing more people to Christ would make the world
a better place by, in part, reducing hate and prejudice. And Falwell was
hardly alone; Dean Hoge identifies Billy Graham and Norman Vincent
Peale as evangelical leaders who articulated "private Protestantism" in the
mid-twentieth century.[94]

The definitive scholarly explanations of the two-party system, Marty's
Righteous Empire and Moberg's *The Great Reversal*, both appeared in the 1970s,
in the wake of conflicts such as the one between Falwell and the Freedom
Riders. Marty and Moberg both endeavored to show the constancy of these
conflicts between public and private, Social Gospel and evangelism, this
world and another world, at least since the fundamentalist-modernist split.
Although these tensions have been constant, however, the two sides have
not always been polarized, and many Christians have found ways to reconcile them. Donald Gorrell explains, "Contrary to common interpretations
that often polarize the social gospel and revivalism, many leaders of social
Christianity thought, wrote, and spoke as evangelicals who valued campaigns
for conversion. Their conceptions of social awakening, social salvation, and
social evangelism were expressed in revival terms; what they did was to add
a social dimension to the prevailing emphasis on individual salvation, not
deny it."[95] Even Marty agrees: "The social gospel spokesmen and other social
Christian advocates did not abandon the old reform causes of the first half-
century. They still opposed intemperance, profanity, prostitution, and other
vices." Instead, they simply "rejected the individualists' preoccupation with
these personally controllable faults to the exclusion of an address to the soci-
etal faults over which the single individual had little control."[96] On some
issues, "public" and "private" Protestants could agree; they all opposed intemperance, for example. Public Protestants were more likely to see the solution
to intemperance in legal and structural change, whereas private Protestants
sought its solution in individual conversion.

In the years since Marty and Moberg identified the two parties in
American Protestantism, the tension between public and private has

remained, while the party lines have undergone radical transformation. Whereas conservative evangelical Christians were once content to save souls while liberal and mainline Protestants pursued social activism, evangelical Christians have since adopted political means for their reform goals. James Guth explains, "We find that Evangelical Protestants have indeed formulated a new social theology, one that incorporates the old individualist model of social change but superimposes on it new (or perhaps renewed) expectations for government's role in fostering moral transformation," while "mainline Protestants still persevere in the old Social Gospel tradition . . . with even greater expectations about the role of government in bringing about social justice."[97] In short, according to Guth's research, American Protestants still hold two distinct issue agendas—the one focused on moral reform and the other on social justice—but both now seek government solutions to these problems in this earthly realm. Ram A. Cnaan similarly challenges the common association between mainline and public Protestantism and evangelical and private Protestantism. This assumption draws linkages between theology, social theology, and institutional/denominational history, which Cnaan's research does not bear out.[98] According to his survey data, liberal and fundamentalist theologies are not determinative of either approach to social engagement. Christian leaders of all stripes, it seems, remain divided over the propriety of faith-based worldly engagement, and especially faith-based political engagement.

CHRISTIANITY AND POPULAR MEDIA

Christian-themed media are an important source for the ideologies that circulate through faith communities, including beliefs and assumptions about civic participation. Because Christian leaders have long recognized the religious benefits of adopting new media technologies, and media executives have identified the economic potential of religious audiences, Christians are accustomed to integrating mass media into their faith lives.[99] These mass media have enjoyed such popularity because they fulfill at least two purposes central to Christian faith. First, the Christian gospels call believers to spread the faith by winning new adherents. Jesus taught his disciples to be "fishers of men," and he instructed them to "go therefore and make disciples of all nations, baptizing them in the name of the Father, the Son, and the Holy Spirit."[100] Because the mass media, simply by their mass nature, afford the possibility of reaching potential disciples in the greatest numbers, they are an indispensable tool for satisfying Jesus' call to evangelize.

Second, Christianity, especially Protestantism, prizes an intimate relationship between the believer and the deity, typically mediated through the Christ figure.[101] Any mass medium—books, pamphlets, radio, music, television, film, or Web sites—that allows the believer to bring artifacts of the faith into his private space affords the possibility for developing this personal relationship. Moreover, the visual nature of more recent mass media, especially film and television, has increased the intimacy and familiarity possible.[102] By watching Jesus movies, for instance, believers and nonbelievers alike can come to know a personal savior in both sight and sound, as he walks and talks and preaches and heals the sick. So, too, can believers come to know the heroes of their faith—Moses of *The Ten Commandments* fame and the disciples portrayed so vividly in *Jesus Christ Superstar*, for instance.

Although the mass media have not been universally popular among Christian leaders,[103] these inherent advantages still won the early adoption of each new technology—including the printing press, film, radio, television, video, and the Internet—by faith communities. In the nineteenth century, the American Bible Society and the American Tract Society took advantage of developing printing and papermaking technologies, and in just the 1820s and 1830s, those two organizations were responsible for distributing almost half a million inexpensive Bibles and more than ten million tracts nationwide.[104] The twentieth century saw Christian themes emerge in the developing film industry, driven at least as much by producers' desire to capitalize on the Christian imperative to know the divine personally as by Christian imperatives to evangelize. Religion made its way to the big screen as early as the 1901 adaptation of the novel *Quo Vadis?*, and religious-themed films would dominate the industry for a few decades. Gerald Forshey notes, for instance, that in the 1950s, five religious films were the most popular of their year—*Quo Vadis* and *David and Bathsheba* in 1951, *The Robe* in 1953, *The Ten Commandments* in 1956, and *Ben-Hur* in 1959—and that religious themes have continued to emerge in films like *Elmer Gantry* (1960), *The Exorcist* (1974), and *The Last Temptation of Christ* (1989).[105]

Radio and television, more so than film, have been technologies accessible to a wide range of Christians eager to put them to their own uses. Popular evangelists like Aimee Semple McPherson and Oral Roberts built their ministries over the radio airwaves; Roberts went from one local broadcast in 1947 on KCRC in Enid, Oklahoma, to a contract with ABC in 1953, by which he reached more than five hundred stations.[106] Today, Christian radio stations broadcasting around the clock feature mixed formats that include not only preaching but also talk shows and popular music. Many of these radio stations are affiliated with Salem Communications, which owns 103 stations and broadcasts to more than 1,900 affiliates.[107] The development of Christian television has been similar: by 1957, Oral Roberts' televangelism program was shown on 135 stations (of the nation's 500), reaching 80 percent of the nation's television audience.[108] By televangelism's 1980s pre-scandal heyday, Sunday morning preaching claimed an audience of 13 to 15 million Americans, while another 4.5 million tuned in to see Pat Robertson's *700 Club*.[109] At that point, Christians did more than just preach on television; they produced more than sixty syndicated programs and owned five religious television networks, such as Robertson's Christian Broadcasting Network and International Family Entertainment.[110] Finally, the Internet has facilitated other Christian media projects: a Web site called Tangle provides a Christian social networking alternative to the secular video-sharing Web site YouTube; older print media, such as *Sojourners* and *Christianity Today*, make their content available online; and some churches engage in "Godcasting," posting weekly sermons available for download in MP3 format.

It is important to note that although the Christian imperatives to evangelize and to know the divine personally may explain the popularity of these mediated texts, these texts have always done ideological work beyond promoting the gospel. They have routinely articulated positions within national and international conflicts, alternately promoting nationalism, militarism, and pacifism. And they have often reinforced gender roles and popularized ideals of family life. For instance, Stephen Prothero's analysis of the images in nineteenth-century Christian tracts suggests that their depictions of Jesus Christ first as "sweet savior" and later as "manly redeemer" reinforced popular beliefs about masculinity and femininity.[111] Similarly, James Dobson's multi-million-dollar Focus on the Family industry continues to produce and distribute books and videos that define Christian standards for family life including traditional and nostalgic ideals of the nuclear family.

Like the pamphlets, films, television shows, and Web sites that have been popular throughout American Christian history, the films, books, and television shows considered here simultaneously promote a religious message, espouse associated ideologies, and generate revenue for their producers. These motives and outcomes are inextricable in each case. *The Passion of the Christ, Left Behind,* and *Amazing Grace* were all written and produced by avowed evangelical Christians who may have been happy to share their faith, but who also reaped economic rewards for their efforts (especially in the first two cases). *7th Heaven* and *The Da Vinci Code* were produced and publicized by secular organizations, which is not to say that the authors of these texts did not have faith-based messages they hoped to share with their audiences. Regardless of their authors' intentions, however, these popular media texts reached broad audiences and popularized religious narratives while they also made money.

CIVIC PARTICIPATION IN MEDIATED RHETORIC

Given the long-lasting resonance of popular media in American faith communities, I turn to a handful of these texts in order to consider the images of civic participation widely available to contemporary Christians. In doing so, I break from the dominant trends in scholarship on civic participation and faith-based civic participation. Most of this research has relied heavily on social scientific analysis of survey results "as scholars mine survey data since the mid-1970s to explore whether and why Americans have become more distrustful of government and their fellow citizens and less likely to join voluntary groups."[112] Even Theda Skocpol and her colleagues, who lament this singular focus on survey data, make reparations only by adding their own social scientific analysis of historical and institutional data.[113] Research on Christianity, politics, and civic participation has followed these methodological trends. Major national surveys have given social scientists plenty of data to probe for relationships between theological worldviews, political orientations, and attitudes toward social welfare.[114] When Hoge wanted to test Marty and Moberg's "two party" and "great reversal" theses, for instance, he turned to just this type of data, using local surveys in Philadelphia and New Jersey, as well as a national survey of Presbyterians, to prove that the two parties did exist.[115] Recently, Rodney Stark and his collaborators replicated and expanded upon the survey of American religious life they first published in 1968.[116] Their study measured civic participation specifically by asking respondents which types of community organizations they belonged to and which forms of political activism they had performed.

Individuals and their survey responses, however, are hardly the only available sources of information about shared cultural models of civic participation. I turn to popular media, as others have done, because these texts construct, popularize, and disseminate all sorts of ideologies, including notions of civic participation. In their recent analysis of print and television news sources, Justin Lewis, Sanna Inthorn, and Karin Wahl-Jorgensen have turned to the news media for much the same reason. They ask,

Since most of us learn much of what we know about politics and politicians from the news media, what do the news media tell us about *our* role,
as citizens in a democracy? Are we encouraged to be active, informed
citizens, contributing to public discussion and debate? Or is politics presented as something that is irrelevant to our daily lives? And if we do have
opinions, is it suggested that we can influence the political process or are
we portrayed as powerless?[117]

Their analysis reveals that the news media depict citizens as passive and
apolitical far more commonly than as active and deliberative. News stories often quote individual citizens who speak about their personal experiences and interests rather than deliberating about the public good. In the
British and American news media, Lewis et al. conclude, ordinary people
are constructed as consumers rather than citizens.

These mass media texts, whether news or entertainment, are rhetorical;
that is, they give meaning and definition to the ways that audience members
understand their social worlds. According to Kevin Michael DeLuca and
Anne Teresa Demo, rhetoric is "the mobilization of signs for the articulation of identities, ideologies, consciousnesses, communities, publics, and
cultures."[118] Thus, as rhetoric, media texts carry a constructive, constitutive
capacity for shaping worldviews, defining identities, and influencing behavior. Rhetoric defines identities when it provides audience members resources
for cobbling together and articulating their own identities. These media
texts become the discursive forces that, in Louis Althusser's familiar terms,
"hail" subjects and "interpellate" them into subject positions. This hail-
ing is hardly a momentary interaction, however. Instead, rhetoric's powers
of interpellation are dynamic and continuous, and, in Maurice Charland's
words, "this rhetoric of identification is ongoing, not restricted to one hail-
ing, but usually part of a rhetoric of socialization."[119] Every subject is situated
amidst multiple dynamic, conflicting, competing, and shifting rhetorical
fragments, which all serve as resources for the individual as she articulates
her identity. For instance, an audience member watching *The Passion of the
Christ* might have identified with the model of civic participation therein,
which I identify as "feminine submission," while she may simultaneously
identify with the "masculine aggression" modeled by the *Left Behind* books,
while she is also influenced by the images she sees on the nightly news,
hears from the pulpit on Sunday morning, and remembers from her parents' lessons when she was a child. All of these rhetorical fragments may be
available simultaneously to the individual whose identity, as a result, is as
rich, conflicted, and unstable as the discourses that constitute it.

I treat these media texts not as a repository of ideas, a place where we might look to discover what notions of civic participation, for instance, were operative in a given cultural moment. These texts do not merely reflect those notions; they construct, disseminate, and popularize these ideologies and identities. As such, I ask questions that probe what these texts *do* in their social world, not simply what they *mean* about their social world.[120] I ask, how does each text shape a Christian worldview: what theologies does it draw upon, what role does it allow for the divine in orchestrating human affairs, how does it distinguish good from evil? How does each text construct the identity of a faithful Christian and the nature of a faithful Christian's civic responsibility? How does the text tie that model of civic participation to gender identity?

The close textual analysis found in each of the subsequent chapters endeavors to answer these questions about each of the five media texts in turn. These analyses focus narrowly on the texts themselves so as to illuminate the models of civic participation they make available to audience members, along with the theologies and gender ideologies that encumber those models.[121] I attend to the conventions of images, language, and media that make those depictions of civic participation possible. This narrow focus on the texts themselves comes at the expense of interpretation of their production, dissemination, or audience reception.[122] Surely these other components would prove interesting; the popular press coverage of *The Passion*, for instance, endlessly demonstrated just how irresistible speculating about Mel Gibson's intentions and psychoses can become. I attend to the text itself instead of these other components, however, not because they are unimportant, but because a close reading of these texts answers questions that are important on their own terms. It does not make claims for how audience members necessarily have read or will read these texts or behave in response; rather, a close reading of the text itself reframes the question of audience effects, asking instead what discursive resources each text makes available to its audience members.[123] This focus on close textual analysis allows me to draw out visual and discursive details that might otherwise be lost; such nuances are rendered invisible, for instance, in the qualitative coding scheme that drives Lewis et al.'s analysis.

I assume that these texts have constitutive value, but I do not assume that they operate alone, nor do I assume that they assert total ideological control over their audiences.[124] These texts are not purveyors of dominant ideology that necessarily represses audience members. And audience members are not necessarily passive consumers who mindlessly accept the text's strategic messages (the approach that skeptics have called the "hypodermic needle" model of media influence). Instead, as I read media discourses for their constitutive function, I assume that individual consumers read these texts and adopt these discourses as their own in more and less passive ways.

Finally, my close textual analysis is sympathetic to the ideological turn now commonplace in the field of rhetorical studies.[125] Critical rhetoric projects, in particular, adopt the Foucauldian framework that assumes that rhetoric constitutes our shared "grids of intelligibility," which makes it a mechanism of power—that simultaneously constructive and repressive force.[126] From this perspective, rhetorical criticism becomes a political act when its careful analysis of texts illuminates these grids of intelligibility. This project is political in two respects because it brings into sharp relief two axes within this grid. On one level, I highlight models of faithful citizenship that encourage and discourage civic participation, which has surely been a divisive issue within American Christianity. I show how these models are operative in these texts, and I also suggest the implications of each model for contemporary politics. On another level, this project is a feminist intervention because it illuminates the gendered ideologies reconstituted by these models of civic engagement.

CHRISTIAN MEDIA, GENDER, AND CIVIC PARTICIPATION

Each of the chapters that follow takes a close look at one recent Christian-themed mass media text—one novel, one series of novels, one television show, and two films. Not only do these popular culture artifacts rely on distinct media technologies, but I suggest that each one celebrates a unique model of civic participation. I situate each case study in a recent or current dispute—some popular, some scholarly—and I show how that text's model of civic participation fits within that debate. In every case, I show how this model of civic participation grows out of a particular construction of the social order, divine will, and Christian theology. And in every case, the chapter's conclusion links these models of civic engagement to forms of activism readily visible in the public sphere. I never, however, draw direct or causal linkages between these texts and those public performances. That is, I do not assert that Christians whose disposition toward civic participation might be characterized as "masculine aggression" are so disposed because they have read the *Left Behind* books. Media influence is never so simple. Instead, by linking these models of civic participation to contemporary practices of activism, I try to suggest some of the implications of these models for American civic life. I also acknowledge that these five texts rely on three different media technologies, and I show how their constructions of civic participation are enabled by the unique constraints and resources of each medium.

Taken together, these case studies argue that the possibilities for faith-based civic participation are much richer than previous analyses have been able to measure. Cobbling together their civic identities, American Christians have at their disposal fertile resources that articulate sharply contrasting visions of Christian civic responsibility. Certainly, the remnants of the "two-party system" remain influential within American Christianity, but Christian attitudes toward civic participation are more complicated than simply evangelicalism versus social concern. These basic orientations are further nuanced by apocalyptic theologies, for instance, as well as pragmatic distinctions in the way that social concern is articulated (such as social welfare versus social activism). And, of course, these dispositions are defined by gender in a way that early proponents of the two-party thesis did not consider.

Chapter 2 considers the film *Amazing Grace* within the context of the recent faith-based backlash against the Christian Right. As a result of all the public notice that the Christian Right's political influence has won, conservative and liberal Christians alike have reopened the question of the propriety of faith-based influence in politics. I suggest that this dispute reanimates the age-old two-party split, and then I show how *Amazing Grace* offers a resounding endorsement of Christian social concern, as well as politics as an appropriate venue for realizing social change. The film does so through its depiction of William Wilberforce, long a celebrated hero among conservative Christians, thus making this model of political participation especially palatable for conservative Christians. In the film, Wilberforce's political activism is characterized by genteel masculinity and a prophetic posture, and these traits become the film's celebrated disposition of civic participation.

Chapter 3 analyzes *The Passion of the Christ* with regard to ongoing debates over liberation theology. I argue that, like liberation theology, the film valorizes suffering, even in the face of great evil and violence. Through its portrayal of the final hours of Jesus' earthly life and especially through its extreme graphic violence, *The Passion* sets up a world order wherein the followers of Jesus—who we now recognize as early Christians—are the victims of tyrannical Jewish high priests and a brutal Roman regime. The film takes as its heroes Mary the mother of Jesus, Mary Magdalene, and the disciple John, all of whom are depicted as patiently, if painfully, acquiescing to the violent torture directed at Jesus. Importantly, all three of these characters are coded as feminine, making feminine submission the model of exemplary discipleship within an oppressive civic life.

Chapter 4 finds a model of civic engagement in the *Left Behind* books that is almost exactly the reverse: these books privilege brutish masculinity as the faithful performance of Christian discipleship. I consider *Left Behind* in light of scholarly and popular debates over the civic implications of premillennial and postmillennial Christian theologies, and I show how the *Left Behind* books make space for civic engagement even within premillennialism, which is usually considered to be an entirely otherworldly system of thought. Within the *Left Behind* narrative, the world situation in some ways echoes the one in *The Passion*: faithful Christians are again the victims of a brutal tyranny, in this case the one-world government run by the antichrist. The heroes of this speculative futuristic story, however, actively fight back against the regime that represses them, using guns, tanks, and whatever other weapons they find available. In this case, the story's heroes are coded in overtly masculine ways—and the most valorous characters are exclusively men—making brutish masculinity *Left Behind*'s celebrated disposition of Christian civic participation.

Chapter 5 examines the television show *7th Heaven* in the context of recent political debates over welfare reform and the role of faith communities in providing social welfare. Unlike the first three case studies, *7th Heaven* depicts a social order that might seem familiar to contemporary audiences: it portrays a middle-class, suburban Christian minister and his family, who only find themselves at odds with the surrounding culture in minor ways. Because its characters, especially the minister-father, play an integral role in providing social welfare for members of their community, *7th Heaven* invests faith in churches as civic institutions capable of providing for social welfare. The minister doles out charity in typically feminine, individual, and secular ways.

Chapter 6 analyzes *The Da Vinci Code* in terms of the popular debates over its purported "radical feminist agenda." Close attention to the novel's gender politics, I maintain, highlights its affinity for the private sphere and its model of civic nonparticipation. As the novel celebrates heterosexuality and gendered biology, it makes domestic life, at the expense of public or civic life, the proper venue for expressions of faithfulness. Ironically, the novel's conservative gender politics set it apart from the tradition of American feminism, and its preference for the private sphere gives it kinship with the conservative moral reform traditon, or "private Protestantism."

Although each chapter argues that individually, each of these texts disciplines one model of civic participation as faithful discipleship, considered together they show larger connections between civic participation, faith, and gender. They show that American civic life is rich with competing ideologies of civic participation that circulate through our shared discursive space and, as they do so, become resources for individuals as they articulate their public identities. Chapter 7 considers the implications of these competing ideals circulating through popular culture. It explores the limitations of these models of civic participation in terms of gender and race, as well as the limitations of the media technologies that produce them. It also, however, explores the fecund possibilities of religion serving as a locus for social activism.

2

Genteel Masculinity, the Prophetic Posture, and Legislative Politics

Amazing Grace

Then he said to them, "Give therefore to the emperor the things that are the emperor's, and to God the things that are God's."

Matthew 22:21

So faith by itself, if it has no works, is dead.

James 2:17

Following the 2004 election, journalistic narratives made religious influence in electoral politics seem simple: Christian beliefs translate naturally into political platforms that translate naturally into electoral votes. The remarkable backlash that greeted the "values voters" and their evangelical leaders, however, suggests that Christian political activism is hardly so simple or unanimous. The evangelical Christians who supposedly won the White House for George W. Bush, and whose agenda he was expected to use his office to promote, were not a voting demographic that arose spontaneously or uncontroversially. They were, instead, the end result of a mobilization effort that dates back at least to Jerry Falwell's founding of the Moral Majority in the 1970s, Pat Robertson's presidential bid in the 1980s, and Ralph Reed's leadership of the Christian Coalition in the 1990s, each of whom had incited controversy in his own time. The recent emergence of evangelical Christians as a political force has been no different; it has inspired a passionate debate involving religious leaders, academics, journalists, and elected officials, all of whom are asking, what role can and should religion play in democratic politics?

When legal and political theorists question the propriety of the Christian Right's political involvement, they do so on constitutional and theoretical grounds.[1] They ask, what role does the First Amendment allow religious organizations, leaders, and rationales to play in public policy making? Moreover, do the basic requirements of liberal democracy allow for these types of religious influence? Religious leaders are equally passionate in challenging the propriety of the Christian Right's organizing, but they do so on theological grounds. Are Christians called to participate in earthly politics? they ask.[2] Does God's vision for humanity entail particular political positions? How should Christians engage in earthly politics? Although these are the same questions that have reverberated through two centuries of American Christianity, they have reemerged with a new urgency since the arrival of the "values voters" at the beginning of the twenty-first century.

Opening on nearly eight hundred screens in February 2007, *Amazing Grace* arrived in movie theaters at the height of this debate, and it offered a clear example of religious influence in institutional politics. Narrating the life and work of the eighteenth-century British reformer William Wilberforce, *Amazing Grace* takes audience members to a historical time and place where one of the most significant legal reforms in human history was driven by a small band of religiously motivated activists who achieved their objectives politically. The film's Wilberforce expresses a clear divine calling to political activism, and the men and women who join his abolition work are similarly motivated by religious principles. They take their inspiration from the Christian hymn "Amazing Grace," penned by the repentant slave ship captain and Wilberforce's former pastor, John Newton.

Amazing Grace opens in 1797, when a broken, exhausted William Wilberforce retires to his cousin Henry Thornton's country home in order to recuperate. While there, he meets Barbara Spooner, and their abbreviated courtship affords Wilberforce the opportunity to recount his fifteen years of work to legislate the end of the slave trade. In those years, Wilberforce's effort is characterized by relative weakness against the strength of the established slave industry and the members of Parliament who hold personal interests in slavery. These are men so comfortable with slavery that William, Duke of Clarence, even tries to bet his own slave against Wilberforce in a game of cards. In his initially feeble efforts, Wilberforce's only allies in Parliament are his close friend Prime Minister William Pitt and Charles Fox. Outside of Parliament, his supporters include activists Thomas Clarkson, Hannah More, James Stephen, and Olaudah Equiano.[3]

Wilberforce, his colleagues in the House of Commons, and this small band of abolitionists use all the resources at their disposal to win support for their cause. The tireless Wilberforce offers one bill after another in the

Commons and engages his hostile colleagues in sharp debates over each one. As Spooner describes it, for many years, "it seemed that every spring, the daffodils came out, every summer the cherries ripened, and every autumn, William Wilberforce would present his bill to the house." In addition to making his case on the floor of the Commons, Wilberforce also appeals to his colleagues interpersonally. At a particular point of frustration, he even tries singing the hymn "Amazing Grace" to a drunken, rowdy group of legislators. For his part, William Pitt steps in to play a hand of cards with a member of Parliament who is planning to speak in opposition to abolition. Applying personal pressure to the man, Pitt convinces him to take a more neutral stance in the impending debate.

Although Wilberforce's and Pitt's parliamentary maneuvering drives the plot's action, *Amazing Grace* also depicts the alternative forms of activism pursued by many of the minor characters. For instance, the activists, led by the lawyer James Stephen, travel the countryside gathering evidence of the horrors of slavery. The former slave, Equiano, introduces Wilberforce firsthand to the horrors of a slave ship, and Wilberforce in turn shares that experience with other legislators. Equiano also writes an autobiography and itinerates from town to town sharing it. John Newton, in addition to composing the hymn that inspires the movement, writes his own narrative of his time as a slave ship captain as well. Women throughout the country, including Spooner, boycott sugar, wear abolition pins, and sign petitions. Ultimately, Wilberforce and his allies are able to unveil, on the floor of Parliament, a scroll containing a petition with more than 390,000 signatures. Fox adds his own name while the members of Parliament watch.

Finally, the abolitionists' legislative victory comes only as the result of cunning deception. While unsuspecting legislators forgo a day's work in favor of free tickets to the races, Wilberforce and his allies pass what seems like benign legislation to allow French and British ships flying under the neutral American flag to be boarded by privateers. This law, which appears patriotic in light of heightening tensions across the Continent, will effectively end the slave trade by increasing the danger of sailing slave ships. On the verge of this legislative victory, the film's flashbacks arrive at the present. The story line progresses into the future, and Wilberforce marries Barbara Spooner, with whom he ultimately has two children. Although Wilberforce still struggles with his health, the film's closing narrative promises that he continued to fight throughout his life for the causes he believed important—education, health care, and prison reform. *Amazing Grace* closes with the hymn being played by bagpipes and a marching band in front of

Westminster Abbey, where, the written narration explains, Wilberforce and Pitt are both buried.

For all its merits, *Amazing Grace* did not garner box office receipts competitive with other recent religious films, such as 2004's *The Passion of the Christ* and 2005's *The Chronicles of Narnia*. In twelve weeks in the theaters, *Amazing Grace* brought in just $21 million in gross revenue, and it inspired no associated merchandizing or other forms of supplemental income. It did, however, inspire generally positive reviews in the mainstream press, and it received special attention in Christian and evangelical Christian outlets. For example, the editorial board of the widely circulated mainstream evangelical magazine *Christianity Today* endorsed the film. They acknowledged *Amazing Grace* for "introducing millions of moviegoers to the story of William Wilberforce and the remarkable campaign to ban the slave trade," and they went on to extrapolate four lessons that contemporary Christians might take from Wilberforce's activism.[4] Also in the pages of *Christianity Today*, regular columnist Charles Colson praised *Amazing Grace* as a film to inspire Christian activists today.[5]

Still other measures of the film's reach prove revealing. Promotion for the film included staging Amazing Grace Sunday, an event in which nearly six thousand congregations in the United States alone agreed to sing the familiar hymn during their weekly services. That effort was backed by a diverse coalition of parachurch organizations—including the National Council of Churches, the National Association of Evangelicals, Sojourners, and the Salvation Army—that find only rare occasions to collaborate.[6] As a smart marketing device, Amazing Grace Sunday gave a diverse cross section of American Christians ownership of the film that was about to be released. As a by-product, it inspired an unusual display of Christian unity, offering otherwise-divided Christians common ground through this film and its optimism for faith-based reform activism.

The film's reach also extended beyond its marginal box office success because of the ways it was explicitly tied to political causes. Just a month before *Amazing Grace* debuted, when Kansas senator Sam Brownback declared his candidacy for the 2008 Republican presidential nomination, his announcement explicitly cited William Wilberforce as inspiration. Brownback also linked Wilberforce to his own pet issues, declaring, "If Wilberforce were alive today, I believe he would passionately fight for the dignity of every human life everywhere, without regard to race, wealth, or status. . . . I think he would also feel compelled to take up the vital causes of renewing the family and the culture."[7] Then, when the film was released, the new presidential candidate attended its Hollywood premiere and participated in a panel discussion following.[8] *Amazing Grace*'s production company, Bristol Bay Films, also publicized the film's connections to the contemporary issues of global slavery. The Web site they launched, Amazing Change, detailed conditions of the twenty-seven million people who are kept in slavery globally.[9] Christian lobbying organizations, such as World Vision, Concerned Women of America, and Operation Rescue, echoed this activist impulse by issuing press releases that linked the film not only to global slavery but also to abortion.[10]

More than just being tied to these specific political issues, however, the film also asked and answered important questions about the very link between faith and politics. In a particular cultural moment, when the questions about the propriety of religious influence in politics circulated widely, *Amazing Grace* provided powerful testimony in support of the easy integration of religious commitments and political imperatives. In what follows, I argue that contemporary legal theorists and religious leaders alike are conflicted over the propriety of religious influence in politics. In the case of religious leaders, specifically, their passionate opposition closely parallels the long-standing opposition between public and private or social justice and moral reform Christianity. I argue that *Amazing Grace*, by easily reconciling faith and politics, witnesses to the possibility and the necessity of faith-based political activism. In doing so, it provides a model of Christian political activism that is characterized by a prophetic calling and genteel masculinity. Whereas this model of genteel masculinity resonates with contemporary Christians' nostalgia for leaders such as Martin Luther King Jr., Wilberforce's prophetic calling fits poorly with the conciliatory style of politics most favor in opposition to the stubborn and monolithic Christian Right.

REVISITING RELIGION AND POLITICS

Religion, Politics, and the First Amendment

On one level, the emergence of evangelical Christians as a political force has intensified ongoing disputes over the legal and constitutional standing of religious influence on politics. Although the United States famously upholds the separation between church and state, the First Amendment to the Constitution only mandates two dimensions to this separation: the federal government cannot institute a state church, nor can it interfere with individuals' free exercise of religion. The question that remains unanswered is, in Habermas' words, "How does the constitutional separation of state and church influence the role which religious traditions, communities and organizations are allowed to play in civil society and the political public sphere, above all in the political opinion and will formation of citizens themselves?"[11]

Some liberal theorists, John Rawls chief among them, would exclude religion from political argument almost altogether. Rawls introduces the notion of "public reason," which is a body of argumentative rationales that are accessible, sensible, and shared among all members of a democratic state. He contrasts public reason to what he calls "comprehensive doctrines," which are value systems (such as religions) that are unique to particular members of a democratic polity. He recognizes that those comprehensive doctrines are unavoidable in a pluralistic society, but he argues that they should not form the argumentative ground of our shared decision making. Rawls does draw a distinction between political arenas (such as courts, legislatures, and campaigns), where public reason is necessary, and "background culture" or civil society, where comprehensive doctrines are appropriate.[12] And he does allow "that reasonable comprehensive doctrines, religious or nonreligious, may be introduced in public political discussion at any time, provided that in due course proper political reasons . . . are presented that are sufficient to support whatever the comprehensive doctrines introduced are said to support."[13] In other words, religious rationales are appropriate in political debate if and only if they can ultimately be replaced by appeals to public reason. For Rawls and other advocates of this liberal approach, a political position justified by religious grounds alone is inappropriate in democratic politics.[14] Only public reason can provide justified grounds for political decision making. Such a liberal approach, if ever adopted widely, could remove faith-based rationales from political decision making entirely.

Liberal proposals like Rawls' meet significant opposition, much of which objects to the ways that these proposals make unrealistic demands of religious citizens. As Lucinda Peach has noted, because liberal proposals "fail to recognize or respect the centrality religion may have in the lives of lawmakers," they "ignore the free exercise rights of lawmakers to practice their own religious beliefs in the context of their public decision making, at least to the extent that other citizens can."[15] More than just infringing on their free exercise rights, these proposals impose "an undue *mental* and *psychological* burden [upon] citizens who follow a faith," according to Habermas.[16] For these reasons, Habermas asserts, religious citizens "should therefore be allowed to express and justify their convictions in a religious language."[17]

On a larger scale, however, Habermas also notes the role that religious institutions have historically played a role in "stabilizing and advancing a liberal political culture," and he worries that "the churches' commitment to civil society would . . . wither away . . . if they were obliged to find an equivalent in a universally accessible language for every religious statement they pronounce."[18] Thus, not only do citizens need the right to express their convictions in whatever language—moral, religious, or otherwise—they have available to them, but liberal societies need the stabilizing influence provided by religious communities.

Religion, Politics, and Christian Theology

On another level, the Christian Right's political triumph has forced theological dilemmas. Christian leaders of all political persuasions have publicly questioned the motives and tactics that engineered the Christian Right's rise to power, and they have offered alternative visions for faith-based influence in politics.[19] Some of these critiques have been written by self-described evangelicals with left-leaning politics, such as Jim Wallis, Tony Campolo, Randall Balmer, and Amy Sullivan, while others came from self-described evangelicals with right-leaning politics, such as Greg Boyd and David Kuo. Most of the other authors are known for staunch liberal political views, such as mainline Christians Robin Meyers and Bob Edgar, Jewish Rabbi Michael Lerner, and Catholic laypersons Kathleen Kennedy Townsend and E. J. Dionne. Some of these men and women are also scholars (e.g., Campolo, Balmer), party activists and elected officials (Edgar, Townsend), and journalists and cultural critics (Dionne, Sullivan). The claims staked in this debate are, for the most part, thoughtful, well reasoned, and provocative. And yet these religious leaders remain fundamentally divided over the most appropriate, faithful, and expedient role for Christians to play in politics.

They do agree almost unanimously on the character of the sins committed by the Christian Right, especially its unabashed partisanship and nationalism. These critics decry its slavish devotion to the Republican Party, which they identify in an implicit compact shared between Christian and Republican leaders. By this agreement, the GOP wins consistent support for its candidates and policies, and the leaders of the Christian Right win status, influence, and special favors for their pet issues.[20] This partisan compact, however, robs Christianity of its natural capacity to provide cultural critique or prophetic witness. The principles of the faith are distorted in order to fit the demands of politics, which diminishes the capacity of people of faith to speak out on political issues. "Whenever Christianity becomes identified with *any* political party," Campolo explains, "it tends to take on the values of that party, rather than remaining loyal to the principles of Scripture."[21] In the contemporary case, evangelical Christians' ideological kinship with the Republicans on the issues of abortion and homosexuality developed into a full-fledged entanglement between the two groups, wherein the value system of one was indistinguishable from the other. The Christian Right sold its soul to the Republican Party in exchange for promises on limited issues—primarily the appointments of "strict constructionist" judges whom they presumed would overturn *Roe v. Wade*—and, in exchange, they ended up delivering, in one election after another, voters who reliably supported Republican candidates who have pursued a war that arguably did not meet the tenets of just war theory, who have failed to be stewards of God's creation, and who have proven incapable of alleviating poverty.[22] Because leaders of the Christian Right "have shamelessly manipulated important issues—gay rights, abortion—for partisan purposes, all the while ignoring Jesus' teaching on other matters," Balmer laments, "deeply complicated subjects have become mere political cudgels in the hands of the Religious Right."[23] The Christian Right is the contemporary example that proves a larger rule for these critics: any time religion aligns itself with a political party—Democratic or Republican—the voices of faith trade away their capacity to offer Scripture-informed perspectives that might undermine party dogma.

As an extension, critics charge, this compact with the Republican Party has led to evangelical Christianity's characteristic nationalism. For Tony Campolo, this nationalism was exemplified on a South Georgia roadside, where he observed "a church that had a large, solid wooden cross on its lawn. Nailed to the top of that cross was a sign that read Support our Troops. Draped over the crossbar was an American flag."[24] Randall Balmer laments a similar expression of Christian nationalism, which he witnessed in East Texas. There, a rally hosted by evangelical pastor Rick Scarborough featured Roy Moore, the Alabama judge who fought to post the Ten Commandments in his courtroom. Rally-goers, who were there "to take back East Texas for Jesus Christ," alternated between singing "The Star-Spangled Banner" and another song about a "blood-stained Bible."[25] These two cases illustrate what critics find so detestable in the contemporary Christian Right: when the gospel of Jesus Christ becomes so closely tied to one political party, the cross and the flag, and the Bible and the national anthem, become inextricable.[26] Such extreme nationalism undermines Christians' ability to reflect critically upon the nation's policies, just as partisanship inhibits their ability to reflect critically upon the Republican Party platform.

Although these sins of the Christian Right may be fairly evident, repairing for them has proven to be a more contentious matter. Christian leaders articulate two broad visions for the ideal relationship between faith and politics, and these competing visions largely replicate the historic split Marty identified between "private Protestants" and "public Protestants." And, like Marty saw as early as the turn of the twentieth century, that split falls along political lines. In the current debate, the conservative Gregory Boyd and David Kuo, on the one side, encourage Christians to remove themselves from politics almost entirely, and the liberal Jim Wallis, Randall Balmer, Robin Meyers, and others call Christians to reassert their moral leadership in institutional politics.

Boyd's proposal may be the most radical of them all; when he introduced it through a sermon series and a book, he provoked enough controversy to cost him one-fifth of the membership at the St. Paul, Minnesota, megachurch he pastors.[27] He contends that the kingdom of God and the kingdom of the world are discrete entities that operate according to unique sets of values.[28] Because the kingdom of the world aims to control behavior, its primary instruments are laws and "the sword."[29] The kingdom of God, in contrast, aims to transform lives, so its primary instruments are self-sacrificial love and "the cross."[30] The kingdom of the world is defined by a "power over" logic, whereas the kingdom of God employs "power under."[31] The kingdom of the world operates by retributive tit-for-tat thinking.[32] It is characterized by intense tribalism that thrives on the dualism of good and evil. The kingdom of God differs because it is welcoming and inclusive. It "looks like Christ—self-sacrificial and loving. It looks like grace."[33] These two kingdoms are, by definition, incompatible. The kingdom of the world cannot become the kingdom of God. Instead, the kingdom of God can only grow like a mustard seed sown within the kingdom of the world.[34]

Recognizing that Christians must exist in both kingdoms simultaneously and that the two kingdoms may make incompatible demands on their citizens, Boyd nevertheless counsels that Christians are members of the kingdom of God primarily and the kingdom of the world only incidentally. As Christians must be only "resident aliens" in the kingdom of the world,[35] Boyd encourages civic engagement that operates by "distinctly kingdom-of-God means," such as prayer, acts of self-sacrifice, and enacting the kingdom.[36] Jesus, he explains, set the example of praying constantly, so Christians can emulate their leader by using prayer as a tool of social change. A Christian's real means of influence, Boyd tells his readers, comes from "your kingdom heart expressed on your knees in loving service to the world."[37] Christians can also mimic Jesus' ethic of self-sacrifice. When they are loyal to the kingdom of God, Boyd explains, Christians take Jesus' loving sacrifice at Calvary as their model of commitment to their civic brothers and sisters. "The distinct kingdom question," Boyd explains, "is not, How do you *vote*? The distinct kingdom question is, How do you *bleed*?"[38] Ultimately, living according to the kingdom of God calls for actions more than words. Christians need to "just *do* the kingdom." Rather than talking, voting, or arguing about distinctly kingdom-of-the-world questions, Christians can transcend the kingdom of the world by enacting the kingdom of God. "Our trust, time, energy, and resources must not be centered on improving government, but on living out the revolutionary kingdom of Jesus Christ in every way, shape, and form," Boyd contends.[39] Importantly, Boyd never suggests that Christians give up their political rights in the kingdom of this world; he does not deny that they should vote, write letters, or protest government policies. Instead, he argues fervently and repeatedly that Christians should not mistake their kingdom-of-the-world citizenship for work that advances the kingdom of God.

Whereas Boyd makes his case on theological and theoretical grounds, Kuo works from his political experience to arrive at a similar conclusion: politics does not operate by God's logic. Kuo, once the deputy director of the White House Office of Faith-Based and Community Initiatives, claims he joined George W. Bush's staff because he believed the sincerity of the new president's faith, and he trusted that Bush would use his office to promote the compassion programs that were a product of his faith. Before long, however, Bush's compassion agenda became an electoral tool, and Kuo found himself designing events to win support from Christians without the administration having to deliver on its promises to this constituency.[40] Although Kuo never doubted President Bush's faith, he did learn that even the best faith-based intentions cannot win out over the logic of partisan politics. "George W. Bush loves Jesus. He is a good man," Kuo affirms. "But he is a politician; a very smart and shrewd politician."[41] Kuo concludes, like Boyd does, that religion and politics are fundamentally irreconcilable. "The spirit of Washington is arrogance," Kuo summarizes, but "the spirit of Christ is humility."[42]

Politics, Kuo acknowledges, has done a poor job of achieving social conservatives' goals. For all the sympathetic officials they have elected into legislative and executive offices, "things are hardly better," he laments. "Divorces are rampant and more and more children are growing up in a home with just one parent. Nearly a million and a half abortions are performed every year. There are more children in poverty today than there were twenty years ago."[43] Because politics has failed to solve the problems that social conservatives care most about—abortion, divorce, poverty, et cetera—Kuo calls for a political fast among Christians. He urges his coreligionists to devote two years to other types of Christian service to the world, while they also reflect upon their religious calling to political activism. Although Kuo's two-year fast surely falls short of Boyd's call to divorce God's work from the political realm, both men agree that because faith and partisan politics are fundamentally incompatible, Christians' efforts are best spent in loving, prayerful service outside of formal politics.[44]

Other Christian leaders maintain exactly the opposite: that Christians can repair the political damage of the Christian Right by reasserting faith-based influence in politics.[45] They articulate the terms on which people of faith can introduce their religious beliefs into politics without repeating the mistakes of the Christian Right. Rather than being obsequious to one party, Christians should enter politics as a stridently nonpartisan ideological force. "The best contribution of religion is precisely not to be ideologically predictable nor loyally partisan," Wallis argues. "Both parties, and the nation, must let the prophetic voice of religion be heard."[46] Balmer makes exactly the same point when he suggests, "Religion functions best *outside* the political order, and often as a challenge to the political order."[47] Making faith a nonpartisan ideological force allows Christians to express their moral convictions on political matters even when they fail to align with one party's platform. It also ensures that no party will take people of faith for granted as a reliably supportive voting demographic.

As depicted by various critics of the Christian Right, this nonpartisan political activism takes many different forms. On the individual level, citizens may voice political opinions that are deeply informed by the teachings of their faith tradition. As they employ the standard mechanisms of legislative influence—writing public letters to the editor and private letters to representatives, donating money to candidates, arguing with friends and neighbors, speaking at civic meetings—they may express their political opinions using the language of their faith. According to Wallis, all religious people should "participate as *citizens* who have the right and the obligation to bring their deepest moral convictions to the public square for the democratic discourse on the most important values and directions that will shape our society."[48]

Also at the individual level, elected officials may bring the values of their faith to bear on the legislative decisions that they must make. Three proponents of religious influence in politics—John Danforth, Bob Edgar, and Kathleen Kennedy Townsend—are former elected officials. They all speak of the ways that their faith influenced their own public service, and Townsend recalls how, because of their Catholic faith, civil rights became a moral issue for her father and her uncle, Robert F. and John F. Kennedy.[49] Danforth also suggests that politicians' faith should influence *how* they approach politics, not simply the stances that they take. He reflects, "There is a difference between being a Christian in politics and having a Christian agenda for politics . . . The relationship of faith and politics is not about fashioning religious beliefs into political platforms. It is, instead, the way in which faithful people go about the work of politics."[50] Faithful people should approach the work of politics always mindful of the Gospels' Love Commandment, he explains.[51] Christians in politics should seek to be reconcilers and peacemakers, always modeling themselves after the image of Christ's sacrifice on the cross.[52] Furthermore, they should cultivate humility, demonstrating less certainty that their politics necessarily do God's will.[53]

Ultimately, most proponents of faith-based politics advocate more than just this legislative activism by politicians and individual citizens. These authors instead long to reinvigorate the faith-based protest tradition that they see in the historic abolition, woman suffrage, temperance, and civil rights movements. They claim that each movement was led, at least in part, by Christian ministers who used the Scriptures to support their arguments and who relied on Christian laypeople for the movements' numerical strength. Wallis, Townsend, and others praise Martin Luther King Jr. as the prototype for this faith-based social movement leadership, and Wallis adds other models—Archbishop Desmond Tutu, Nelson Mandela, and Daniel and Phillip Berrigan.[54] Meyers encourages contemporary Christians to emulate these historic leaders through "collective resistance" against the policies of the Bush administration. Reminding his fellow Christians that they are called to be "doers of the word, not merely hearers,"[55] Meyers explains that "pure cognition cannot save the world. Sometimes intelligent people need to take to the streets."[56] Meyers' proposed strategies for "collective resistance" follow directly from the American tradition of social movement protest: write a letter, join a march, begin a discussion, and boycott objectionable products and companies, he encourages his readers.[57]

Meyers' call for Christian protest in the streets stands in sharp contrast to Boyd's disavowal of any possibility for Christian political activism.

Both agree, as do most critics of the Christian Right, that its entanglement with partisan politics has undercut the values of the faith and limited Christians' capacity to reform society. When they disagree on an alternative to the Christian Right, however, Boyd and Meyers (along with Wallis, Kuo, Townsend, and others) reinvent the historic two-party split between social justice and moral reform activism. Whereas the conservatives Boyd and Kuo would agree that preachers are called to be "soul-winners" rather than politicians, liberals like Meyers, Wallis, and Townsend sound like the "social gospelers" who have always discerned an equal call to use politics to reform the unjust structures of our society.

Social Justice Activism in *Amazing Grace*

Into the midst of this public discussion over faith and politics comes the film *Amazing Grace*. Set two centuries and one continent away, in some ways, the story of *Amazing Grace* is the unlikeliest participant in a very contemporary American conversation about politics and religion. The film's heroes, after all, speak in accents foreign to an American audience and dress in stuffy antique costumes. They ride in horse-drawn carriages, sprinkle their wigs with powder, and sip tea from dainty cups. They devote their political attention entirely to subjects—the transatlantic slave trade and the French and American Revolutions—that twenty-first-century Americans know only through history books. In both subtle and significant ways, however, the film translates its historic subject matter into contemporary vernaculars. It engages in what I have elsewhere called retrospective framing, which makes a distant subject accessible and intelligible to contemporary audiences.[58] *Amazing Grace* does as much on a small level by vocabulary alone: although the characters have accents, their word choices represent a colloquial vernacular surely familiar to American audience members. On a larger level, however, the film engages in retrospective framing, first by depicting a historical figure in William Wilberforce, who carries significant cachet among American evangelicals; second, by portraying his faith according to characteristics familiar to evangelicalism; and, third, by posing as its central dilemma the reconciliation of God's work and legislative work.

William Wilberforce has long enjoyed an elevated status within evangelical and conservative Christian circles. Methodists, for instance, named the first historically black college in the United States after him; Wilberforce University in Ohio has operated almost continuously from 1856 to the present.[59] Today, Charles Colson, the Nixon administration counsel who was convicted for Watergate offenses and is now a respected Christian leader, runs a Wilberforce Forum think tank, which is sponsored by his Prison Fellowship.[60] When Wilberforce's name is invoked in contemporary political discussions, it is almost always used in service of conservative interests. Not only did Senator Brownback cite him as a hero, but David Kuo also praised Wilberforce as an ideal model of Christian reform activism.[61] Importantly, the liberals who counter Kuo's position do not cite Wilberforce; Jim Wallis, for instance, points to Martin Luther King Jr., Archbishop Desmond Tutu, and Daniel and Philip Berrigan as possible models, but he never mentions Wilberforce. Although any of these men could have been the subject of a feature film, *Amazing Grace* depicts Wilberforce, which gives the film inroads into the conservative and evangelical communities where he is commonly revered.

Amazing Grace also renders Wilberforce's faith life in terms familiar and sensible to contemporary evangelicals. Randall Balmer notes that American evangelicals define their faith in terms of a personal relationship with God in Jesus Christ, often achieved through an individual moment of conversion (also known as a born-again experience).[62] The film's Wilberforce enjoys just this type of faith: he escapes to the fields of his estate, where he inspects the blossoms, gazes at the spider webs, and then reclines in the grass to talk to God. When his butler witnesses this unconventional behavior, Wilberforce explains that although he has ten thousand engagements of state he should be attending to, he prefers to spend his day outside in God's creation. The butler goes on to ask if Wilberforce has found God, and Wilberforce discloses that God found him. Wilberforce's God is a personal God who reaches out and touches an individual's heart, and in response, Wilberforce forges an intimate relationship with that God. Because Wilberforce can meet God in his backyard, he only enters a church twice during the film. And in both of those cases, Wilberforce goes to the church to meet his former pastor, John Newton, informally. In line with American evangelicalism, and in contrast to Catholicism and mainline Protestantism, including the Church of England, Wilberforce's faith is about his personal relationship with God more than his participation in an institutional church community. The film's evangelical framing is only underscored by the language that the characters use to talk about their faith. For instance, when Wilberforce meets with Newton, the pastor advises Wilberforce using what is possibly the most familiar maxim among American evangelicals; he tells Wilberforce, "Just make sure you're in the world, not of the world."[63] Thus, in ways both small and large, *Amazing Grace* makes Wilberforce's faith sensible by translating it into terms familiar to an audience of American evangelicals or an audience familiar with Christianity through the discourse of American evangelicals.

Most importantly, *Amazing Grace* poses the relationship between faith and politics as its central dilemma. By the film's depiction, Wilberforce's abolition crusade does not come easily; he must first be convinced of the possible reconciliation of his divine calling and his political obligations. A young Wilberforce, who has clearly been groomed for the work of Parliament, initially seems inclined to give up any political ambitions in favor of following a call from God, the nature of which he cannot quite discern. At first, he wrestles with this decision alone in the garden, talking only to God about his conflict between the matters of state that beckon him and his heart's desire to revel in God's creation. When Wilberforce discloses this dilemma to his friend William Pitt, Pitt rephrases it in simple terms, demanding of Wilberforce, "Do you plan to use your beautiful voice to praise the Lord or change the world?" Pitt then arranges a dinner party of activists who might be able to persuade Wilberforce. At that dinner, the abolitionist Thomas Clarkson reiterates the fundamental dilemma. "We understand you're having problems choosing whether to do the work of God or the work of a political activist," Clarkson says, to Wilberforce's nodding agreement.

For the assembled activists, the resolution to this dilemma is clear. In response to the dichotomy outlined by Thomas Clarkson, the abolitionist Hannah More responds, "We humbly suggest that you can do both." A long silence follows More's radical suggestion, during which Wilberforce's blank expression gives little sense that he is willing to do both. After this dinner conversation, Pitt follows Wilberforce out into the garden, where the two reflect upon the subject again. Pitt urges his friend, "Surely the principles of Christianity lead to action as well as meditation." Still, it takes one more wise voice to convince Wilberforce. He visits his former pastor, John Newton, who is unimpressed by Wilberforce's inclination to join a religious order. Newton implicitly acknowledges the difficulties of combining faith and politics with his admonition, "Just make sure you're in the world, not of the world," but he goes on to remind the young man that he has work to do, and he sends Wilberforce out into the world to do that political work.

Thus, reconciling this dilemma, *Amazing Grace* depicts a political world that invites faith-based activism as well as a faith that finds institutional politics as its natural outlet. Its historic setting allows the film to depict the easy reconciliation between the two visually. At the end of the film, after Wilberforce has fretted about combining faith and politics and after he has done so successfully, the closing credits underscore the natural fit between church and state. In that visual sequence, bagpipes sound the triumphant chords of the hymn "Amazing Grace" while the credits roll over the faces of the film's main characters. After those brief credits, the song continues to play, but the image shifts to the bagpipers themselves, who are clad in full uniforms. Their kilts are dark plaid, their military jackets are red, and they wear elaborate headpieces. They march in lockstep toward the camera as it pans out to reveal the large brick structure behind the dozens of bagpipers. Soon, the bagpipes are joined by drums that beat the rhythm of the march. The camera pans further out to reveal that the drummers too wear full uniforms, with pants rather than kilts, and their headpieces display a military or police shield. Ultimately, the song swells to a full orchestral sound, and the camera pans out again to expose an entire marching band. The words on the screen intimate that the band stands in front of Westminster Abbey, where Wilberforce and Pitt are buried. Here march these dozens of men in military-style uniforms, playing a familiar Christian hymn, backed by four national flags, with Westminster Abbey in the background; this closing image fully unites church and state as the seamless whole that they were in Wilberforce's day.

Thus, with some retrospective framing, such as rendering Wilberforce's faith within the familiar logic of American evangelicalism, and subtle visual cues linking church and state, *Amazing Grace* has brought twenty-first-century American audiences into a social order within which legislative politics are a natural arena for Christian reform. As a result, political activism, on the part of both officials and activists, becomes the suitable model of Christian civic engagement. And the film celebrates a performance of civic engagement characterized by genteel masculinity and prophetic certainty.

The Genteel Masculinity of British Politics

In *Amazing Grace*'s Britain, politics happens in an almost entirely male sphere. All of the members of Parliament are men, the prime minister is a man, and even the monarch is a king. To be sure, the film's women are politically accomplished as well; Wilberforce's love interest, Barbara Spooner, for instance, matches Wilberforce's political wit from their first conversation. As they walk through the garden of his estate, she contributes her opinions on all manner of issues beyond abolition, such as the propriety of flowers in church. She also, however, knows her place. When she and Wilberforce encounter William Pitt at their wedding reception, Spooner greets the prime minister kindly and then scurries away when she recognizes that the men want to discuss politics. Excluded from formal political arenas, the film's women find alternative avenues to contribute to the abolition effort: Spooner explains that they boycott sugar, wear abolition pins, and sign petitions. None of those forms of activism is ever depicted, however, and the ultimate abolition victory is won in the masculine arena of institutional politics.

The film's men show no discomfort with their all-male sphere. Wilberforce, for example, forms his closest friendships with the other men in politics. Through most of the years of his abolition crusade, before he meets Barbara Spooner, Wilberforce's intimate relationships are with three men: Henry Thornton, John Newton, and William Pitt. Thornton is a member of Parliament and Wilberforce's cousin, in whose home Wilberforce recovers when his health deteriorates. There, the two men discuss politics while Thornton attends to Wilberforce through the night, sitting at his bedside and bringing him medicine. Newton is Wilberforce's closest spiritual confidant. In a private conversation with Newton, Wilberforce discloses his calling from God, and he follows his minister's advice to pursue social reform through politics. More than these others, Pitt is Wilberforce's closest friend. The two sit face-to-face at a small table and sip tea out of tiny cups while Pitt elaborates upon his plan to become prime minister and Wilberforce describes his own calling. Later, after the two men have increased in political power, they can still be found playing games in the garden together. With their pant legs rolled up and their feet bare, Pitt and Wilberforce conduct a foot race across a field, and when Pitt wins, they double over in laughter, sharing silly jokes with each other.

More than simply being an all-male space defined by male bonding, *Amazing Grace*'s political sphere is characterized by a particular type of masculinity that is remarkable for its gentility. This gentility comes in part from the trappings of early modern Britain so evident throughout the film: the men wear neatly combed wigs, they sit with upright posture, and they quote philosophy, for instance. But Wilberforce is a particular exemplar of genteel masculinity. Whereas many of the members of Parliament drink, gamble, and carouse, Wilberforce shows contempt for these activities. He is haunted by a nightmare featuring hundreds of his drunk colleagues packed into a theater, each with a hypersexualized woman sitting upon his lap. In the nightmare, Wilberforce interrupts their revelry by breaking the dozens of bottles of alcohol that adorn a theater box. Just a few scenes later, a lucid, awake Wilberforce finds himself in similar surroundings in a card house. When he grows disgusted by the betting at a card table, Wilberforce storms out of the salon. He glides back in only moments later and quiets the rowdy crowd by standing upon a table and singing "Amazing Grace" to them. In the juxtaposition between Wilberforce's melodic voice atop the table and the drunken, rowdy shouts below, our hero's gentility is unmistakable.

This genteel masculinity prizes intellectualism over other expressions of bravado, such as physical strength (in sharp contrast to other forms of masculinity, such as the one celebrated in *Left Behind*). In Wilberforce's case, mental and physical abilities are in perpetual contest with each other; for as smart and charismatic as Wilberforce is, his body is equally sick. Thus, all credit for Wilberforce's accomplishment is due to his intellectual skills, and he finds success in spite of his physical limitations. Wilberforce's mind-body tension is illustrated by a scene where he stands outside in the rain chopping wood. As he heaves the ax over his head, Wilberforce reflects out loud about the sufferings of African people. He cries out in pain but continues to bundle and chop wood while he says to himself, "God has set before me two great objects: the suppression of the slave trade and the reformation of society." When he picks up the ax again, Wilberforce cannot lift it over his head before he falls to the ground, clutching his abdomen. Clearly, Wilberforce's mind and passions are strong, but his body is weak. When the scene cuts immediately to Pitt chatting with a doctor who is attending to Wilberforce, Pitt jokes with the doctor that Wilberforce "doesn't believe he has a body. He's utterly careless of it. He thinks he's a disembodied spirit." Just then, Wilberforce refuses the doctor's laudanum, explaining that he would rather suffer through the pain in order to keep his mind sharp.

Wilberforce's heroic preference for intellectualism comes into sharp relief against his colleagues in Parliament, who prize a more physical form of masculinity. Some of them fought in North America against the Yankees, and their military history remains a source of pride. When Lord Tarleton rises to oppose one of Wilberforce's abolition bills, for instance, he raises his three-fingered hand and reminds the other members of Parliament that he lost those two fingers in battle with the Americans. Even an ally of the abolitionists, Prime Minister Pitt, recognizes the occasional need for violence, especially in the context of a changing global order. Always aware of the impending revolution in France and a possible war between the two nations, Pitt also worries that the abolitionists in Britain could turn to violent revolution the way the disgruntled French and Americans had done. Although he prefers Wilberforce's intellectual and genteel masculinity, Pitt also acknowledges the necessity of a military response to violent aggression from revolutionaries or foreign powers.

When Wilberforce's abolition bill finally passes Parliament, he is commended precisely for his commitment to nonviolent legislative activism. Even Lord Tarleton and the Duke of Clarence feel obliged to join the applause, and Charles Fox rises to speak. He contextualizes Wilberforce's nonviolent means with reference to the world situation when he opines,

> When people speak of great men, they think of men like Napoleon. Men of violence. Rarely do they think of peaceful men. But contrast the reception they'll receive when they return home from their battles. Napoleon will arrive in pomp and in power—a man who's achieved the very summit of earthly ambition. Yet his dreams will be haunted by the oppressions of war. William Wilberforce, however, will return to his family, lay his head on his pillow, and remember the slave trade is no more.

Fox here acknowledges that Wilberforce reformed society not by mounting an army and launching a revolution—the possibility that terrified Pitt and other members of the ruling elite—but by changing minds. Wilberforce and Pitt also celebrate their own accomplishments in very similar terms. Toward the end of the story, as Pitt lies in bed dying, they reflect joyfully upon how they "cracked crowns," but they "left the heads intact." These men of great ambition and accomplishment achieved their goals without recourse to violence, the very models of genteel masculinity.

This genteel masculinity fits precisely with one activist ideal widely celebrated within the contemporary debate over faith and politics. Many of the historical examples of religious activists that Christian leaders cite today can be characterized by similar performances of genteel masculinity. On the one hand, their historic models are typically exemplars of gentility. Martin Luther King Jr., of course, is known for his soaring rhetoric and conciliatory tone, especially in contrast to civil rights leaders who advocated violence and revolution. Daniel and Philip Berrigan were nonviolent by definition: they are remembered for their activism against the Vietnam War. Liberal Christian leaders who call for faith-based political participation consistently choose these intellectual, genteel men as praiseworthy ideals.

Importantly, within this contemporary debate, liberal Christians cite only men as models of civic participation; none of the historic leaders worthy of emulating are women. Jim Wallis and others do routinely claim the woman suffrage movement as a victory for faith-based activism, but they never name a leader of that movement or a female leader of any other movement as an exemplar.[64] Their failure to name a woman is significant, especially since they overlook leaders such as the Methodist temperance organizer Frances Willard and the Methodist minister who led the national suffrage organization, Reverend Anna Howard Shaw. Excluded from formal avenues of power, these women developed alternative forms of influence. Even beyond the tactics to which the film's Barbara Spooner alludes, women reformers have historically written letters, raised money, and given speeches (often using the "feminine style") on behalf of their causes.[65] The cost of only depicting male heroes and masculine forms of activism—for both the film and contemporary religious leaders—is the failure to see these parallel traditions of reform work. Not only do we miss the important contributions that women made, but we fail to see their strategies as productive avenues for social reform.

PROPHETIC POLITICAL ACTIVISM

The other defining feature of *Amazing Grace*'s model of faith-based political activism is its principled, even prophetic, nature. The film's Wilberforce fits precisely in the tradition of prophetic rhetoric that James Darsey sees in both the Old Testament prophets and American radical reformers. Prophets from both groups, he argues, display "a sense of mission, a desire to bring the practice of the people into accord with a sacred principle, and an uncompromising . . . stance" in the face of a reluctant or hostile audience.[66] In Wilberforce's case, his sense of mission is indisputable: he is a man called to do God's work. His early conversations with Pitt, Newton, and a dinner table full of activists reveal that Parliament is simply the venue for enacting the work that God has called Wilberforce to do. He explains his calling most clearly in the line quoted above—that God has set before him "two great objects," abolishing the slave trade and reforming society. His abolition work certainly aims to bring his countrymen "into accord with a sacred principle"—that of respecting the dignity of all human lives—even if that principle is implied more than stated.

The third characteristic of a prophet, as one who takes an "uncompromising stance" against hostile audiences, most clearly defines Wilberforce's activism. The film's opening written narrative immediately suggests the hostility that will greet Wilberforce's efforts. White letters against a solid black background explain, "Great Britain was the mightiest superpower on earth and its empire was built on the backs of slaves. The slave trade was considered acceptable by all but a few. Of these, even fewer were brave enough to speak against it." Then, early in the film, when Wilberforce and Pitt weigh the prospect of taking on the slave trade, Pitt also acknowledges the unfavorable odds. "Just think about this, Wilber," he says. "The slave trade has three hundred MPs in its pocket. It would be just you against them, but you could do it; you *would* do it." Indeed, when Wilberforce first introduces his abolition bill, his speech is met with jeers and hollering, and the bill itself garners only sixteen votes. Then, in another parliamentary debate about slavery, one of Wilberforce's foes attacks the abolition cause on the grounds of its unpopularity. "Apart from a few mendicant physicians and itinerant clergymen," Lord Tarleton charges, "the ordinary people of Britain are not at all exercised by the whole issue of slavery."

In the face of these incredible odds, Wilberforce remains the optimist among the abolitionists. At a meeting after one of their many parliamentary debates, Wilberforce had ordered enough food to serve the masses of supporters he hoped would attend. Undaunted when only two members of Parliament join the group, he proceeds on with conviction. And he and the other abolitionists continue to do so for fifteen years. In addition to introducing bills to Parliament annually, they also itinerate tirelessly through the countryside, gathering evidence about the slave trade and presenting it to the citizens, who in turn sign petitions and boycott sugar. Wilberforce's commitment is the most dramatic of all because he pursues this reform program even while suffering from deteriorating health. Against the counsel of his friends Henry Thornton and William Pitt, as well as his doctor, Wilberforce refuses to rest and regain his strength, returning to London again and again to work for abolition.

Wilberforce is so committed to his principles that he maintains them even in light of intensifying political tensions. As they monitor updates about the revolution in France, members of Parliament worry about similar havoc developing out of Wilberforce's movement. One of Wilberforce's adversaries in Parliament warns Pitt that Wilberforce is a "bloody rebel . . . because he follows no leader but the preacher in his head." Ultimately, even Pitt confronts Wilberforce about his radicalism, specifically his friendships with the suspected revolutionaries Thomas Clarkson, Olaudah Equiano, and Thomas Jefferson, and he claims that although such alliances may have been acceptable in peacetime, they prove suspicious during wartime. In the spirit of patriotism, Pitt urges Wilberforce to stifle his radical protest, but when Wilberforce refuses to bend, the two arrive at an impasse. Pitt accuses his old friend of trying "to keep your precious conscience intact and let the rest of us do the war's dirty work." Pitt's assessment is correct: in the spirit of the prophets, Wilberforce clings to his principles regardless of the political realities.

Staying true to his principles, Wilberforce does not go so far as to advocate revolution, which is an important distinction in the film's political context. Soon after his argument with Pitt, Wilberforce finds equally sharp conflict with an exuberant Clarkson, who gushes to Wilberforce about the spirit of revolution unleashed by the French and the Americans. Clarkson affirms Wilberforce's commitment to principle, noting, "You're more radical than any of us . . . you never doubt you're right." Wilberforce, however, declares his loyalty to the king and refuses to embrace the possibility of revolution. He points out the dangers inherent in revolution and expounds upon the virtues of gradual change. Ultimately, he admonishes Clarkson sternly, "You must never speak of revolution in my presence ever again." The balance Wilberforce has struck between Pitt's pragmatic patriotism and Clarkson's revolutionary radicalism is a careful one: he maintains a reform-minded devotion to the radical principles of abolition.

Performed in a twenty-first-century political context, Wilberforce's prophetic posture invites less desirable results than the ones depicted in *Amazing Grace.* Indeed, this prophetic posture almost mimics the disposition that John Danforth laments too commonly characterized the behavior he saw in the Senate. In contrast, he advocates a Christian disposition that is based on the Love Commandment: politicians should cultivate good relationships, see the merits of others' opinions, and compromise when necessary.[67] Ultimately, Christian belief should lead politicians to practice humility, according to Danforth, which is a disposition wholly incompatible with the prophetic call.[68] The prophet cannot be humble when he is so certain that his mission comes from God; doubting his mission would be, by extension, doubting God. In *Amazing Grace,* this prophetic certainty is easy and palatable because the prophet's cause is the abolition of slavery, a reform uncontroversial by today's standards. Such a prophetic disposition about one of today's controversial issues—abortion, sexuality, war, welfare—could lead to just the problems Danforth fears. Self-righteous ideologues bent on pursuing one narrow legislative reform can create a political culture of polarization and stalemate.

The only exception to Wilberforce's prophetic stance stems from the arguments he makes on behalf of his cause. In short, although Wilberforce is wholly driven by a divine call, the nature of which he discloses in private conversations, he never employs religious rationales in his public opposition to slavery. Instead, in his speeches, Wilberforce advocates abolition on political-economic or vaguely humanistic grounds. When he first introduces his abolition bill in Parliament, Wilberforce announces, "It is with a heavy heart that I bring to the attention of this house a trade which degrades men to the level of brutes and insults the highest qualities of our common nature; I am speaking of the slave trade." As other legislators shout their opposition, Wilberforce tries to continue. He acknowledges his opponents' economic interests in the slave trade, but he urges that they are all men of humanity, before his speech is entirely derailed by the rowdiness of the Commons. In another speech in Parliament, Wilberforce justifies abolition with an *ad populum* argument: he and his allies unroll a scroll that they claim includes more than 390,000 signatures, and there, in the session, Charles Fox adds his own name to the list. In yet another public speech, with jeering opponents surrounding him, Wilberforce's entire abolition argument is contained in one sentence: "In war or in peace, the buying and selling of human beings is equally abhorrent."

Much of the argument that Wilberforce and his colleagues build against the slave trade has to do with the conditions of the slave ships. Equiano takes Wilberforce on a slave ship, where the former slave shows the reformer how the slaves were locked in small spaces, and he describes how the slavers would throw the weak and dead ones overboard to lighten the load when necessary. Later, Wilberforce passes along this information to a ship full of members of Parliament and their wives. While these elites enjoy an afternoon trip around the harbor—complete with live orchestral music and finger-food appetizers—their vessel sails up next to a slave ship. Wilberforce greets them from the adjoining boat and details the prisoners' conditions as his audience members grow faint from the slave ship's stench. When Wilberforce and his allies want to develop their case further, they set to work gathering more evidence about the conditions on the ship. A voice-over describes how this renewed quest for evidence leads them to talk to slavers, ship doctors, and slaves themselves, and the images on the screen show the activists inspecting blueprints of slave ships.

For evidence, it seems, Wilberforce and the other abolitionists turn entirely to rational, empirical sources of proof. Never do they scour the Scriptures and cite them in their speeches. Never do they publicly testify to the divine call that drives their political activism. Never do they preach to other citizens, telling them that their religious obligations entail an abolition platform. *Amazing Grace*'s abolitionists, in short, follow exactly the approach to religion and politics advocated by John Rawls and other contemporary theorists who want to keep religion out of the public sphere. They choose "public reason" over "comprehensive doctrines" as they make their arguments on grounds that are accessible to all citizens, regardless of religious belief. *Amazing Grace*, then, presents this interesting paradox. On the one hand, it portrays the captivating narrative of a man driven by his faith to reform his society. On the other hand, it captures him doing so in exactly the a-religious terms dictated by Rawls and other liberal theorists. The film's Wilberforce, although he is called by God and driven by his faith, is entirely able to divorce those faith-based rationales for abolition from his public statements on behalf of abolition.

Conclusion

Amazing Grace makes an important contribution to the ongoing debate over the relationship between faith and politics: through the story of William Wilberforce, it provides witness to the positive outcome that results from reconciling the two. It presents the tension between faith and politics as its central dilemma, and it shows the resolution of that tension in the life and work of a divinely inspired politician. His characteristic disposition toward his reform work is marked by genteel masculinity and a prophetic posture, making these the film's celebrated model of civic participation.

The film's bifurcated relationship to time defines the way that it is able to intervene in this very contemporary debate. On the one hand, through its subtle retrospective framing of its historical subject matter, *Amazing Grace* is able to translate Wilberforce, the British parliament, and the abolition crusade into terms that make it familiar and accessible to contemporary audiences. Its Wilberforce shares the evangelical Christian faith so common today, and he understands the difficulties associated with fulfilling God's call in the arena of politics. On the other hand, however, the film's historical positioning allows it to sidestep many of the issues that confront today's Christians who try to integrate faith and politics. Wilberforce and his colleagues never replicate the partisanship and nationalism that critics find so objectionable in today's Christian Right.

Partisanship never becomes an issue simply because Wilberforce and his allies unify around a single cause rather than a broader party platform. Their single cause is so morally unambiguous that they never have to make the pragmatic compromises so problematic for the Christian Right. That is, critics accuse the Christian Right of giving their support to such Republican Party planks as war and tax cuts in exchange for party support on issues including gay marriage and abortion. But because *Amazing Grace*'s Wilberforce and his colleagues are so narrowly focused on abolition and so unanimous in their moral certainty, they cannot make the trades and compromises characteristic of the Christian Right's partisanship. The film's characters do succumb to nationalism, but their nationalism is easy and uncontroversial. In *Amazing Grace*'s Britain, because church and state are so neatly fused, Christians can declare allegiance to God and king together. As the film's closing scene intimates, when church and state are reconciled as a peaceful whole, a military band flying national flags can pay tribute to God and king with its performance of the world's most famous Christian hymn on the plaza in front of the state cathedral. The symbolism here is as mixed as the roadside image that horrified Tony Campolo, a cross decorated with an American flag and a sign insisting, "Support our troops." Unlike Campolo, the film's Wilberforce shows no hesitation to demonstrate the patriotism expected of him and his fellow Christians. Especially in the context of revolution and war in Europe, Pitt challenges Wilberforce to prove that his loyalty to the king is as strong as his loyalty to God, and Wilberforce is able to make this commitment because God and country are so thoroughly united.

Through its dual use of time, *Amazing Grace* is able to introduce this historic narrative into contemporary concerns, and in doing so, the story of a conservative Christian hero comes to support what are usually liberal Christian ends. Thus, simply because it depicts Wilberforce (rather than King or the Berrigans, for instance), *Amazing Grace* has the unique potential to make political organizing palatable among conservative Christians. This use of Wilberforce's legacy is all the more notable because it differs from the other ways his story has been mobilized. Indeed, whereas Jim Wallis celebrates King and the Berrigans as the paragons of Christian political reform leadership, the conservative David Kuo exalts Wilberforce on almost opposite terms. Acknowledging the good that Wilberforce accomplished through Parliament, Kuo also explains,

> He worked with friends inside and outside parliament. He worked with bishops and influential people throughout British society. He worked with the poor; he worked to establish educational reform, prison reform, health care reform, and to limit the number of hours children were required to work in factories. But it was much more than a legislative effort. Wilberforce believed that he and his supporters should attempt to cure every social ill in the country, and not by governmental decree. They established organizations that would work to improve or rectify

each injustice. While the effort wasn't devoid of politics, politics wasn't its driving force.[69]

Kuo's Wilberforce stands in sharp contrast to *Amazing Grace*'s; in the film, the reformer focuses his efforts almost exclusively on legislative measures to end slavery, whereas Kuo remembers Wilberforce's work to establish organizations that would cure social ills. Neither Wilberforce is necessarily truer or more faithful to the historical record. Given that his legacy can be mobilized to support either a moral reform or a social justice agenda, however, *Amazing Grace* does important work by depicting Wilberforce as a political hero.

Even if Wilberforce embodies the film's most celebrated form of faith-based activism, *Amazing Grace* does not entirely neglect the alternative avenues to social change pursued by its minor characters. These men and women, who share Wilberforce's faith, demonstrate how the call to activism can also be fulfilled through grassroots reform work. They engage in many types of organizing—arranging a boycott, circulating a petition, gathering evidence, lecturing in small towns, et cetera—all oriented around one legislative goal. Within *Amazing Grace*'s plot, as in the history of American reform movements, these activist avenues were available to women who were otherwise excluded from formal politics.

Amazing Grace, however, does not give equal treatment to this extralegislative organizing. These forms of activism are commonly described rather than shown, and many of them figure into one visual montage where the voice-over explains activists' grassroots work. Ultimately, abolition is won by parliamentary fiat, and Wilberforce alone is celebrated in Parliament. The film concludes with a narrative reflecting on Wilberforce's continuing activism, as well as his and Pitt's burial in Westminster Abbey. Because the film never deviates from its primary focus on Wilberforce, alternative forms of activism are never more than supplementary. As hard as Equiano (the former slave) and the women may have worked to demonstrate the horrors of the slave ships and gather signatures on petitions, the credit for ending slavery ultimately goes to the white men who worked through the channels of institutional politics to bring the practice to a legislative end.

This total preference for legislative politics stands in sharp opposition to the present-day Christian Right. That movement has certainly earned a reputation for its legislative and electoral efforts on such issues as abortion and same-sex marriage. With the help of Democrats, they won the Defense of Marriage Act as well as a series of similar state laws, and they have tried to legislate a marriage amendment to the U.S. Constitution. Political activism on both of these marquee social issues, however, has been accompanied by social and cultural activism, the types of efforts that Boyd celebrates because they enact the kingdom of God. So he relates the story of a woman who stopped one girl's potential abortion, not by protesting abortion laws or advocating certain judicial appointments, but by showing that one girl love and helping her raise the child. Similarly, on a larger scale, Christians committed to ending abortion have opened Crisis Pregnancy Centers that counsel women away from abortion, and Christians concerned with homosexuality have developed programs like Exodus International that claim to reform people out of gay lifestyles. *Amazing Grace*, in contrast, focuses narrowly on legislative activism rather than social/cultural efforts such as helping individual slaves escape, teaching them to read, or preaching the gospel to them.

Finally, in addition to depicting these dispositions for Christian political activism, *Amazing Grace* and its marketing also contribute to the contemporary debate over the *content* of a Christian political platform. Many critics of the Christian Right, in addition to questioning the movement's motives and tactics, have also challenged its political positions. They note the Christian Right's fixation on the issues of abortion and homosexuality, and Tony Campolo concludes, "To say that Evangelicals are hung up on these two subjects is an understatement."[70] Objecting to this narrow focus, they propose expanding the faith-based moral purview to a broader range of issues, which, for Wallis, includes "poverty, the environment, war, truth-telling, human rights, our response to terrorism, and a 'consistent ethic of human life' that included abortion, but also capital punishment, euthanasia, weapons of mass destruction, HIV/AIDS and other pandemics, and genocide around the world."[71] Balmer also adds environmental policies, government use of torture, poverty, and the separation of church and state as contemporary political issues that merit Christian attention.

Although the film itself focuses on the antiquated and now-illegal transatlantic trade in African slaves, publicity around the film tied it to present-day issues of slavery and human trafficking, in addition to linking it to abortion and family values in more minor ways. The Amazing Change Web site, set up by the film's production company, raised awareness of the twenty-seven million people globally who still endure slavery, thousands of whom are trafficked into the United States.[72] Christian political organizations issued press releases to make the same point. World Vision cited U.S. State Department figures that suggest that 800,000 people are trafficked every year, and Concerned Women of America called human trafficking "a modern version of slavery."[73] Popular press coverage of *Amazing Grace* picked up on the connections between the slavery practiced by the British Empire and the slavery that continues today. In the *Washington Times*, for instance, an article about the film links its crusade to "combating sex trafficking, the caste system in India, the global AIDS epidemic, and domestic poverty issues," citing in particular the sex trafficking that it predicted would take place around the 2008 Beijing Olympics.[74] Only Senator Brownback and a press release from Operation Rescue tried to link William Wilberforce's legacy to the issue of abortion. Instead, the publicity around *Amazing Grace* largely buttressed a larger trend to broaden the agenda of a faith-based politics. And it showed the promise of legislative politics to realize that agenda.

3

VIOLENCE, SUFFERING, AND FEMININE SUBMISSION

The Passion of the Christ

Let every person be subject to the governing authorities; for there is no authority except from God, and those authorities that exist have been instituted by God. Therefore whoever resists authority resists what God has appointed, and those who resist will incur judgment.

Romans 13:1-2

He was oppressed, and he was afflicted, yet he did not open his mouth; like a lamb that is led to the slaughter, and like a sheep that before its shearers is silent, so he did not open his mouth.

Isaiah 53:7

We also boast in our sufferings, knowing that suffering produces endurance, and endurance produces character, and character produces hope, and hope does not disappoint us . . .

Romans 5:3-5

He delivers the afflicted by their affliction, and opens their ear by adversity.

Job 36:15

In April 2004, *Time* magazine's Holy Week cover story posed the question that Christians have disputed for centuries: "Why did Jesus die?" Ever an appropriate question in the days approaching Easter, it was especially salient that spring amidst *The Passion of the Christ*'s blockbuster cinematic run. Even if Jesus' death and its atoning power have not always been at the top of the theological agenda among American Christians, David Van Biema's *Time* article confirmed that *The Passion* had made these topics interesting anew. Christians, he described, hold competing interpretations of the significance

57

of Jesus' death, some following Anselm's impulse to read it as the substi-tutionary atonement for human sins and others following Peter Abelard's teaching that Jesus' suffering was exemplary for humans. Van Biema's article also made the important observation that these varying interpretations are not matters of theology only: they grow out of political dynamics, and they have political implications.

At the very least, theologies of Jesus' suffering and death influence how individual Christians make sense of the suffering in their own lives. Conflict over precisely this issue animates the debate between liberation theologians and other contextual theologians that follows centuries after Anselm and Abelard. Whereas many liberation theologians see relating to Jesus' suffering as a way for the poor and marginalized to escape their own oppression, other feminist and womanist theologians worry that such empathy only leads Christians to accept the suffering in their own lives. The implications for relating to Jesus' suffering are not only private and individual; when Jesus' suffering death is framed as a state-sponsored act of violence, how Christians understand their role in the passion drama influ-ences how they conceptualize their relationship to the state and the possi-bilities for civic participation.

By all conventional wisdom, *The Passion of the Christ* should not have been a tremendous box office success. No major studios had expressed interest in the film, forcing Mel Gibson to finance it with $25 million of his own money. Six months prior to the film's release, in August 2003, *New York Times* arts columnist Frank Rich stated what seemed to be obvious: "It's hard to imagine the movie being anything other than a flop in America, given that it has no major Hollywood stars and that its dialogue is in Aramaic and Latin."[1] Spurred in part by significant controversies over its graphic violence, its purported anti-Semitism, and its unconventional artistic qualities, such as casting unknown actors and conducting all the dialogue in ancient lan-guages, *The Passion* proved all skeptics wrong when it earned $370 million dollars in box office receipts.[2] Premiering on Ash Wednesday in February 2004, the film remained on the big screens through the Christian season of Lent, ultimately reaching the top ten of all-time grossing movies in the U.S. and becoming the top all-time foreign language film and the top all-time grossing R-rated film.[3] By winter 2005, 44 percent of respondents to the Baylor Religion Survey reported having seen the film.[4]

For all the qualities that earned the film notoriety, it is the unrelent-ing graphic violence that drives the story line. There is little disputing just how violent the film is. In the *New Republic*, Leon Wieseltier declared that the film "breaks new ground in the verisimilitude of filmed violence,"[5] and Richard Corliss claimed, in *Time,* that Gibson invented "a new genre—the religious splatter-art film."[6] David Van Biema described the film's "relentless, near pornographic feast of flayed flesh."[7] According to AP entertainment writer Christy Lemire, "The beating and whipping and ripping of skin become so repetitive they'll leave the audience emotionally drained and stunned."[8] And in the *New York Times,* reviewer A. O. Scott explained, "The final hour of 'The Passion of the Christ' essentially consists of a man being beaten, tortured and killed in graphic and lingering detail."[9]

Not only is *The Passion* violent, and not only does this violence drive the film's plot, but this violence gives the Christian passion story relevance for contemporary models of civic participation. *The Passion*'s violence is a public act of discipline performed by vengeful Jewish leaders and unruly Roman authorities before an audience of angry and frightened citizens. The story opens in a public garden, where Jesus prays and his disciples sleep until they are interrupted by temple guards, who arrest Jesus and bind his hands and torso with rope and chains. As they drag Jesus out of the garden and through the city streets, the spectacle starts to attract a crowd. Along this walk, just fourteen minutes into the film, the violence officially begins when the guards push Jesus over the edge of a wall and he descends quickly, until the ropes and chains that bind him reach their end, and he jerks to a stop. The next ninety-six minutes depict all manner of violence: beating, binding, dragging, flesh-tearing, spitting, taunting, piercing, and crucifying.

As the plot progresses, public attention swells around Jesus, and the masses around him all participate in the escalating violence. The Jewish leaders and temple guards initiate the arrest, the Roman guards eagerly take up their charge to torture and kill him, and even the townspeople who line the walk as he carries his cross contribute to the beating. When Jesus is in the custody of the Jewish leaders who question and taunt him, a Jewish mob surrounds him as the high priest, Caiaphas, tears his own robe, spits in Jesus' face, and commences hitting him before the other priests follow suit. Then, when the Jewish leaders turn over Jesus to Pilate, and Pilate is reluctant to have Jesus crucified, his lieutenants spare no expense in destroying Jesus' flesh. The soldiers chain Jesus to a stump and beat him with an assortment of lashes, including one with a metal claw that vividly tears Jesus' flesh from his body. The scourging only pauses—after nearly eight minutes of screen time—when a Roman official comes out to protest the soldiers' excessive beating, given that their orders were to torture the man, not kill him. When Pilate returns Jesus to the crowd, the angry masses shout, "Crucify him," and the reluctant Pilate consents. The soldiers begin the arduous process of forcing Jesus to carry his cross and then nailing him to it and watching him die.

Because this graphic violence distinguishes *The Passion* from previous Jesus films and from the Hollywood establishment more generally, it inspired significant controversy in the pages of the mainstream press.[10] In particular, it led journalists and reviewers alike to wrestle with two central questions: Does it need to be so violent? And why? Some reviewers ultimately concluded that there is no explanation for all this violence, at least not a sensible one, from Gibson or the film itself. A. O. Scott called it Gibson's "most serious artistic failure" that the film "never provides a clear sense of what all this bloodshed was for."[11] Most reviewers, however, at least offered speculations. Negative critiques of the film were likely to explain the utility of the violence in terms of the filmmaker's motivations and psychoses. Favorable reviews more often understood the violence's redeeming qualities in theological terms.

Given the controversy surrounding the film's anti-Semitism, one option was to read the violence as a vehicle for that anti-Semitism—that this excessive violence is the filmmaker's mechanism for depicting just how evil the Jewish priests were. Mel Gibson had provoked this controversy about *The Passion*'s anti-Semitism as early as thirteen months before the film's theatrical release. In January 2003, during an interview with Fox News' Bill O'Reilly, Gibson was asked if the film would upset Jewish audiences. He explained, "It may. It's not meant to. I think it's meant to tell the truth. . . ."[12] Religious leaders, especially Jewish leaders, had reason to be concerned that Gibson might produce an unorthodox or inflammatory depiction of the Passion Narrative: Gibson belongs to a traditionalist Catholic sect that rejects Vatican II teachings (and affirms the Jews' collective guilt for Jesus' death).[13] Out of concern over Gibson's anti-Semitism, religious leaders carefully studied a "leaked" version of the screenplay, and an ad hoc group of Catholic and Jewish leaders, including officials from the Anti-Defamation League, sent Gibson an eighteen-page report documenting their concerns. Then, ostensibly to assuage such concerns, Gibson invited religious leaders to prescreenings of the film beginning in the summer of 2003.[14] Whether these efforts at dialogue genuinely aimed to facilitate interfaith understanding or whether they covertly aimed to generate interest in the film, by the time *The Passion* was released, controversy still raged over its treatment of Jewish characters.[15] Of course, in the summer of 2006, when a drunken

Mel Gibson verbally assaulted a police officer with his rant against Jews, his personal anti-Semitic opinions were confirmed.[16]

With or without the anti-Semitism, Mel Gibson's colorful public life gave reviewers plenty of ways to tie the film's excessive violence to his psychoses. David Denby analyzed the director in his *New Yorker* review: "At that point, I said to myself, 'Mel Gibson has lost it,' and I was reminded of what many other writers have pointed out—that Gibson, as an actor, has been beaten, mashed, and disemboweled in many of his movies. His obsession with pain, disguised by religious feelings, has now reached a frightening apotheosis."[17] Eric Harrison, writing for the *Houston Chronicle*, concurred. He explained Mel Gibson's martyr complex where, "in film after film, he's subjected himself—or, rather, his characters—to gruesome tortures that stretched past the point of entertainment. He threw himself into these pummelings, disembowelings, and symbolic crucifixions with such fervor we saw a deep-seated need we dared not question."[18] Other skeptical reviewers explained the extensive violence in terms of Hollywood's financial imperatives. In *USA Today*, reviewer Claudia Puig speculated, "Director Mel Gibson has tackled the brutality not for the sake of titillation or even entertainment but to enlighten as well as to shock and awe audiences." And according to the *New York Times*, Mel Gibson "has exploited the popular appetite for terror and gore for what he and his allies see as a higher end."[19] These skeptical reviews of the film and its violence consistently implicate the filmmaker himself in the violence, most often attributing it to his anti-Semitism, his inexplicable love of violence, or even just his desire to make money. They suggest that the violence is extraneous to the point of the film, and that rather than a necessary plot device, it is the expression of the director's madness.

The film's more sympathetic reviewers have been more inclined to read the violence as integral to the film's message. By making real the pain of Jesus' death, they suggest, this violence forces Christians and non-Christians alike to appreciate Jesus' sacrifice as well as their culpability in his death. One such sympathetic reviewer, S. T. Karnick, explains, "This film is meant to be like the spikes that are so vividly and horrifyingly driven into the Christ's hands and feet as he is fastened to the cross. . . . *The Passion of the Christ* is as pointed as those spikes. It does one thing. It implicates the viewer in the suffering and death of Jesus Christ nearly 2,000 years ago, and it does so with undeniable power."[20] David Neff, editor of the evangelical Christian magazine *Christianity Today*, echoes this explanation for the violence. "The film's bruising bloodiness," he argues, is necessary to convey "the sense of one's own sins being responsible for the Crucifixion, the sense of the enormous weight of the world's sins on the Savior's shoulders, the horror of the suffering that Christ endured. . . ."[21] Without the violence, these reviewers suggest, the film would not have been able to so convincingly portray the eternal significance of Jesus' sacrifice for human sins, and it would not have been able to make that sacrifice personal for viewers.

Regardless of the filmmaker's intentions, or the Hollywood imperatives that may have driven it, this violence is integral to the ways the film disciplines the possibilities for Christian civic participation. The two questions that drove these reviews of the film's violence—does it need to be so violent? And why?—apply equally well to the Christian gospel, and they are questions that have interested theologians for centuries. Just as those questions have led Christians to the theological and political implications of earlier Christian celebrations of suffering, interrogating *The Passion*'s graphic violence illuminates the film's theological and political implications. Specifically, it forces the question, in a world run by a tyrannical state and a crazed religious structure, where torture is divine-willed, state-sponsored, cleric-approved, and crowd-cheered, how do faithful Christians perform civic participation?

The Passion, I argue, animates the basic conflict between liberation theologians and other feminists and womanists who contest the implications of Christ's suffering death for contemporary Christians. On the one hand, *The Passion* allows viewers to do just what liberation theologians celebrate— to relate to Jesus through his suffering and death. In the film's narrative, however, that empathy does not lead Christians to a sense of agency that allows them to work for social change, as liberation theologians promise it will. Instead, the film disciplines the possibilities for civic participation by presenting its villains as assertive, barbaric, masculine men and its model citizens as the feminine characters who demonstrate submission to the earthly injustices they meet in the public sphere.

Playing the Victim

For the wide variety of contexts that have produced liberation theologies, and the diverse set of beliefs masquerading under this general heading, liberation theologians generally share a common commitment to finding hope for liberation through empathy with the suffering Christ. Liberation theology is commonly associated with its Latin American origins, at least in part because Roman Catholic priest Gustavo Gutiérrez was working in Peru when he published his groundbreaking 1969 essay, "Toward a Theology of Liberation," which was later developed into his book *Teología de la Liberacion: Perspectivas.*[22] In the same era, North American theologian Frederick Herzog, whose work was based in rural African American sharecropping communities in North Carolina, published his own 1970 essay, "Theology of Liberation," followed by his 1972 book *Liberation Theology: Liberation in the Light of the Fourth Gospel.* Also in 1972, the North American feminist theologian Rosemary Radford Ruether published her own book called *Liberation Theology: Human Hope Confronts Christian History and American Power.* Liberation theology grew out of oppressed and marginalized communities, and its fundamental goal was always relief from oppression.

Since its origins, liberation theology has proliferated globally, but it never coalesced into a unified movement or dogmatic theology. Mary Potter Engel and Susan Brooks Thistlethwaite explain that "it is not wholly correct to say that the theologies of liberation share a perspective, for each liberation theology, whether African, Latin American, African American, Native American, Hispanic, *mujerista*, womanist, feminist, gay, lesbian, bisexual, or transgendered (as well as the varied specific contexts within each of these contexts), is characterized by its distinctive viewpoint."[23] Engel and Thistlethwaite's statement makes two clear points about liberation theologies: (1) they are multiple, and (2) they are contextual and positional. For all their diversity, however, liberation theologies share a common commitment to pursing liberation for the poor, oppressed, and marginalized victims of the world. They suggest that theology's goal should not only be to understand the divine better, but to follow Jesus' path, "to bring good news to the poor . . . to proclaim release to the captives and recovery of sight to the blind, to let the oppressed go free."[24]

Liberation theologies also commonly proclaim the value of understanding Jesus as a suffering victim. James Cone, for instance, reads "the Jesus story" as "the poor person's story, because God in Christ becomes poor and weak in order that the oppressed might become liberated from poverty and powerlessness. God becomes the victim in their place . . . This is what Christ's resurrection means."[25] Cone, a prominent scholar of black theology, suggests that Jesus is best read as black. As a victim in his own social world, his situation is most analogous to African Americans in our contemporary society, and as such, Jesus is indeed black. Helen Orchard, affirming the value of reading Jesus as a victim, interprets the Gospel of John in such a light, claiming that through the lens of victimhood, the Fourth Gospel is much less troublesome for progressive theology. "An effective and credible liberator," she argues, "must be closely identified with the oppressed and seen to share their experiences"—which she sees the Johannine Jesus as capable of doing.[26]

Not only do liberation theologies see Jesus as a victim, but they celebrate the strategy of meeting Jesus from the perspective of victimhood. This epistemology is firmly experiential, and it acknowledges that theologies take their shape from their adherents' sociohistorical location. According to James Cone, "What people think about God, Jesus Christ, and the church cannot be separated from their own social and political status in a given society."[27] In Jon Sobrino's terms, "All thought comes from somewhere and derives from some concern; it has a viewpoint, a 'from where' and a 'to where,' a 'why' and a 'for whom.'"[28] Given that thinking must necessarily be so grounded, Sobrino, like other liberation theologians, chooses a particular grounding, "a *partial, definite, and concerned* viewpoint: the victims of the world."[29] Rosemary Radford Ruether expands on these sentiments as a theological methodology specifically. She explains that her experience has led her to a method that affirms "the need to put oneself in the context of the oppressed in order to have some understanding, not only of their experience, but of the total system of society."[30] Never one to shy away from provocative language, Cone goes so far as to suggest that Christians can *only* encounter Jesus from the position of oppression. He explains, "The God of the Christian gospel can be known only in the communities of the oppressed who are struggling for justice in a world that has no place for them. . . . We can know God only in an oppressed community in struggle for justice and wholeness."[31] By this argument, not only is theology necessarily experiential, and not only can Christians encounter Jesus through the experience of oppression, but it is from this position that he is *best* understood.

Liberation theology is fundamentally a political system of thought, as Cone has said all theologies are, because liberation itself is an explicitly this-worldly concern, even if it may be tied to spiritual, other-worldly liberation.[32] Within liberation theology, the function of meeting Jesus-the-victim from the perspective of victimhood is not only to know the divine better, but also to work for liberation from oppression. Jacqueline Grant ties black women's experience of Jesus' suffering directly to their work for liberation. "As Jesus was persecuted and made to suffer, so were they," Grant explains. Jesus' experience of suffering "inspires active hope in the struggle for resurrected, liberated experience."[33] James Cone focuses on Jesus' suffering on the cross, explaining that "because he was one with divinity and humanity, the pain of the cross was God suffering for and with us so that our humanity can be liberated for freedom in the divine struggle against oppression."[34] By his formulation, through Jesus' suffering on the cross, God came among the suffering, giving hope for their liberation. Understanding Jesus as suffering victim allows the poor and the oppressed to relate to him through their own experiences of victimhood, liberation theologies suggest, which opens up fruitful possibilities for liberation.

This basic assumption common to many liberation theologies—that empathy with the suffering Christ opens up avenues for civic agency—is partially realized, at least in mediated form, through *The Passion of the Christ*. The film, I maintain, invites viewers into an experience of empathetic suffering like the one so privileged by liberation theologians. The indisputably extensive violence allows viewers to experience Jesus as a victim. By their overzealous aggression, the Roman and temple guards become obvious oppressors, situating Jesus as the victim. Moreover, Jesus' victim status is made even more evident by his intimately depicted enactment of the victim role. Finally, amidst this violence, Jesus' followers too become victims of the oppressive tendencies of religious and state powers.

State-Sponsored, Cleric-Approved Oppression

The film's extensive violence comes largely at the hands of the temple and Roman guards, who, by their very aggression, set up a relationship of oppressors and oppressed between themselves and Jesus. Jesus and his followers simultaneously become the victims of power-crazed Jewish leaders, an incompetent Roman authority, and their unruly fellow citizens.

From the film's opening, the Jewish leaders are depicted as unceasing in their quest to punish Jesus. They convince Judas to turn over Jesus in exchange for thirty pieces of silver and, upon making this deal, follow Judas immediately to the garden, where he exposes Jesus, and they take him into captivity. After they drag him through town, Jewish leaders interrogate Jesus in the temple in front of a standing-room-only crowd of onlookers. The interrogation is short, as the priests need little confirmation of the conclusions they have already drawn—that Jesus is a dangerous blasphemer developing a following of rebels. Although the temple guards and Jewish leaders inaugurate the violence against Jesus, ultimately they must turn him over to Pilate because only the Roman governor has the power to sentence a criminal to death.

From the moment the Jewish leaders approach him, Pilate appears annoyed by their demands on him. Looking at the bloody and battered

Jesus, Pilate's first question to the Jewish leaders is, "Do you always punish your prisoners before they're judged?" When Pilate presents Jesus before the crowd in the basilica, the shouts of the citizens gathered there demonstrate that they share their priests' anger toward Jesus. Skeptical of the priests' demands for Jesus' death, but also fearful of mass uprisings that could result by freeing Jesus, Pilate seeks every possible alternative to crucifying this man that he assumes is a common criminal. He takes him to Herod, claiming that the Galilean should fall under Herod's jurisdiction. When Herod refuses to take the case, Pilate asks his guards to beat Jesus, hoping that a beating will satisfy the priests and the Jewish citizens. After the beating, when the Jews are still demanding that Jesus be crucified, Pilate allows them to choose whether to free Jesus or Barabbas. When Pilate presents them with Jesus and the rowdy mob shouts, "Crucify him," Pilate has little choice but to sentence Jesus to death.

Jesus' tortured, suffering death thus comes simultaneously at the hands of the Jewish priests, the Roman leaders, and the unruly mob. Together, they are his oppressors, and they make his death the most public of affairs: arrested in a public place and interrogated before the mob, Jesus is hung to die on the hill above town, all in plain view of his most loyal followers. Jesus' death is depicted, in part, as the expression of power dynamics—the Jews' desire to retain religious hegemony and the Romans' need to maintain order among the citizenry. The Christian Passion Narrative always has implications for agency based in the way that believers understand Jesus' suffering death. But the film makes this dilemma about public agency, or civic participation, precisely because it makes Jesus' death the product of a political conflict between state officials, religious leaders, and conflicted groups of citizens. When Jesus and his followers become victims of crazed religious and political leaders, they provide models for contemporary Christians who understand themselves as victims of religious or political authorities.

Jesus Christ as Victim

More than simply showing the Roman and Jewish officials as obvious oppressors, *The Passion* also makes Jesus' victimhood readily apparent. *The Passion* conveys a low Christology; that is, it depicts the Jesus of history rather than the Christ of theology. Focusing only on the last twelve hours of Jesus' life, plus occasional flashbacks to his earlier ministry, the film pays no attention to the later Christian tradition, articulated by Peter, Paul, and the other church fathers who tried to make theological sense of Jesus' death, or even to Anselm's soteriological explanation or Abelard's exemplary one. *The Passion's* fleeting moments that hint at theological explanations for Jesus' death come mainly in the form of predictions. For instance, the film opens with the abridged text of Isaiah 53 in white lettering on a black background. "He was wounded for our transgressions, crushed for our iniquities; by His wounds we are healed," the screen reads, dating this passage 700 B.C.E. Moments later, in the garden, as Jesus wrestles with his impending capture, his disciples try to make sense of their leader's agony by reading it in terms of his previous explanations of the divine plan. Predictions like these, however, are the only clues given about the theological significance of Jesus' suffering death; rather than a heavy-handed interpretation of the salvific function of Jesus Christ's death, the film depicts Jesus the human being who died this miserable death.

Jesus' humanness is made evident also by the damage that the violence inflicts on his body. By the time he is given his cross to begin the walk of the via dolorosa, Jesus wears only a loincloth, his head bleeds from the crown of thorns, one of his eyes is swollen shut, and his body is wholly covered by red slash marks. The weight of the cross is too heavy for him to bear in this dilapidated condition, and Jesus falls repeatedly, especially as the guards continue to beat him as he walks. This twenty-minute walk, defined by the rhythm of the soldiers' lashes and Jesus' falls, finally ends when the crowd reaches Golgotha and Jesus is tied to the cross. His arms are stretched out (and one arm must be stretched so far that it seems to pop out of its socket), his hands and feet are nailed to the cross, and he is erected on the cross to die. When the Roman officials ultimately want to test whether or not Jesus is actually dead, they pierce his side one more time with a sword. Again they draw blood, and his blood spurts out over the onlookers gathered nearest to the cross.

Beyond his physical dilapidation, Jesus' intimately depicted reactions to the torture also demonstrate his victimhood. As violence is inflicted upon Jesus, he displays his suffering both verbally and nonverbally. Verbally, Jesus' prayers to God from the very beginning of the film suggest just how desperate he is to be saved from the impending violence. On his knees in the garden, Jesus cries out, "Hear me, father . . . rise up. Defend me. Save me from the traps they set for me . . . Father, you can do all things. If it is possible, let this chalice pass from me . . . but let your will be done, not mine." In this moment, Jesus-the-victim pleads with God for deliverance, but his desperation also shows through vocally: his prayer is marked by panting and gasping for breath as the trembling Jesus can barely form his words, eking out each as if it could be his last.

Later, when Jesus is brought before the Jewish priests for questioning, his facial and bodily expressions convey the pain of a victim. His evident pain here is, importantly, contrasted with the flashback shortly preceding it. In that scene, a young, handsome, muscular Jesus has just finished constructing a table and proudly shows it to his mother. Not only is the Jesus of that scene bright and innovative (he has, after all, designed the modern table), but he is jovial and playful, laughing with his mother and splashing water on her as she pours it out to wash his hands, before kissing her on the cheek. Just moments of cinematic time later, though, when Jesus is questioned by the Jewish priests, the camera's repeated close-ups of his face show the many lacerations he has already received. He delays in answering the priests' questions, his pauses suggesting how painful it is to respond. When he does respond, he does so with very little facial expression: he can barely open his eyes or move his swollen cheeks. When, unsatisfied with his answers, the temple guards hit him, knocking him to the ground, Jesus recovers slowly, returning to his feet. In the beating scenes, Jesus plays the victim role even more explicitly, as his facial expressions especially betray his evident misery. While the Roman guards prepare for the extensive flagellation they will pursue, Jesus too prepares himself, praying to God that his "heart is ready." As the guards pick up their lashes, the close-up shot of Jesus shows him tensing up, holding his torso steady for the beating he anticipates. The beating begins with three successive lashes by different guards; as each one hits Jesus' back, his spine rolls forward, lunging his chest into the air, his face wincing. As the lashing continues from all sides, Jesus gasps with each strike, his body falling and correcting itself each time, until he finally falls to the ground entirely, almost hugging the stump that binds him.

The scenic framing of Jesus and his oppressors only intensifies this sense of victimage. When Jesus is brought before the Jewish priests, he stands, plainly dressed, at the center of a crowded room, surrounded immediately by formally garbed priests and guards, who are flanked by dozens of citizens skeptical of Jesus. The abused Jesus stands all alone amidst a crowd of people who wish death upon him. The scene is framed similarly when, moments later, the priests and guards bring Jesus before Pilate in the basilica. Entering the large space, Jesus is guided by the guards on all sides of him, who carry the chains binding him, and those guards are flanked by priests all around them. The growing crowd follows behind. From the moment they enter the basilica, a close-up of Jesus shows him looking down at the floor, his lacerated eyelids barely open. As Caiaphas makes his case to Pilate, Jesus maintains this stance, only glancing up once, opening his functioning eye to look at a bird in the sky. His face largely remains expressionless, as he is the willing victim in the sentencing drama unfolding around him.

Jesus' Followers as Victims

Jesus is not the only victim of the drama depicted by *The Passion of the Christ*; the film also affords Jesus' followers—both ancient and contemporary—the role of victim. In the film, the only of Jesus' followers depicted are Mary his mother, Mary Magdalene, John, James, Peter, and Judas. This small band is usually scattered throughout the crowd; though Mary, Magdalene, and John remain together throughout the film, James disappears shortly into the film, and Peter and Judas are both depicted alone, haunted by their own acts of betrayal. That very few of Jesus' followers are developed as characters underscores Jesus' aloneness, and it also makes his followers seem small amidst the powerful crowd. They too become victims of the loud, angry, violent Jewish mob.

In addition to making Jesus and his original followers into victims, the film also offers the role of victim to its contemporary viewers. Indeed, the ninety-six minutes of extensive, graphic violence serve to abuse the film's audience members, submitting viewers to forms and extremes of violence unknown to many moviegoers. Sitting in a darkened theater for two hours, there is little release from this violence, and audience members endure the pain of watching inescapable violence. Short of walking out of the theater, this violence cannot be avoided; even looking away from the screen for the full eight minutes of the flagellation scene, an audience member would still be subjected to the sounds of the lashes hitting flesh, the guards grunting, and Jesus gasping for breath. Even if the experience is only mediated, audience members also become victims of this violence, watching abuse piled onto the hero of this film. Yet millions of audience members have knowingly subjected themselves to this violence, seeking out the experience of victimhood.

In short, *The Passion* offers mediated access to just what liberation theology celebrates: the experience of empathetic victimhood with Jesus. The film depicts a power-hungry religious authority, plus a brutal state authority, which, by their aggression, make Jesus and his followers victims. Viewers are thus allowed to see Jesus as victim as they also share in his oppression. Whereas liberation theology suggests that the empathetic experience of suffering engenders activism, I argue next that *The Passion*'s celebration of violence constrains the possibilities for agency to a model of civic participation I identify as "feminine submission." In doing so, the film demonstrates the limitations of victimhood as a starting point for liberation.

The Gospel of Submission

As clearly as *The Passion* constructs Jesus and his followers as victims of an oppressive religious and state hierarchy, it also does so within a divinely ordained world. Thus, when Jesus becomes the victim of these overzealous Jewish leaders and Roman guards, it is according to his own Father-God's will. Because this violence is God-sanctioned, and because they trust God's providence, Jesus and his followers willingly accept their suffering. In accepting this violence, Jesus and his followers model civic participation as feminine submission, a disposition brought into sharp relief by contrast to the masculine aggression performed by the film's antagonists. By modeling feminine submission, the protagonists fulfill the fears of contextual theologians who have maintained that the privileging of suffering so common in the Christian tradition ultimately minimizes resources for civic agency and limits believers to the obedient acceptance of public injustice.

Just as some contextual theologians—Latin American, feminist, black, and others—have developed liberation theologies that rely on identifying with Jesus through the experience of oppression, other contextual theologians—primarily feminists and womanists—have detailed the dangers of such identification. According to these theologians, the Christian celebration of Jesus' suffering death leads contemporary Christians to accept the suffering in their own lives. If Jesus is the perfect role model, and if his suffering ultimately served a divine purpose, this thinking suggests, then so too might our suffering fulfill a divine plan. In Brown and Parker's rendering, this is "the deep and painful secret that sustains us in oppression: We have been convinced that our suffering is justified."[35] Christian celebrations of suffering, in combination with the straitjacket of divine will, ensure the perpetuation of suffering in faithful Christians' lives.

Christians have been so willing to accept suffering because they have put their full faith in the God who wills suffering. Feminist and womanist critics, however, take issue with the conceptualization of a paternal God figure who visits violence and pain upon his followers. This Father-God was so angry with humanity that he had to kill his own son in order to save humans.[36] Rita Brock argues,

> When the Christian tradition represents Jesus' death as foreordained by God, as necessary to the divine plan for salvation, and as obediently accepted by Jesus the Son out of love for God the Father, God is made into a child abuser or bystander to violence against his own child.[37]

Not only is the crucifixion itself divine child abuse, but this theology more generally relies on an angry, paternal God figure, for whom these feminist theologians cannot profess affection.

Moreover, in constructing a world controlled by a Father-God who wills violence, this theology creates a model of discipleship wherein faithful Christians acquiesce to the suffering in their lives. If Christians only have enough faith, they should be able to trust that God has a plan for their pain. Brock and Parker note that when "power is structured as benevolent paternalism in Christianity," then "adults are asked to surrender their lives passively and obediently in exchange for salvation."[38] Jesus' experience at the cross, specifically, encourages Christians to accept their suffering. Marie Fortune takes issue with theologies that celebrate suffering, arguing, "Sometimes Jesus' crucifixion is misinterpreted as being the model for suffering: since Jesus went to the cross, persons should bear their own crosses of irrational violence (for example, rape) without complaint."[39]

As Fortune's comment suggests, many of these feminist theologians are concerned with theologies that condone the human acts of violence that they have encountered in their lives and work as Christians, pastors, and counselors. All acts of violence, Carole Bohn suggests, are "the products of a theology that enables and encourages them."[40] According to Brown and Parker, "Christianity has been a primary—in many women's lives *the* primary—force in shaping our acceptance of abuse."[41] Carole Bohn lists the myriad responses that women have described hearing from ministers upon reporting abuse to them, and one among them is a direct entailment of empathy with the suffering Jesus: "All of us must suffer: it makes us more Christ-like. Offer up your suffering to Jesus and he will give you strength to endure."[42] This theology, then, leads women

> to keep silent for years about experiences of sexual abuse, to not report rape, to stay in marriages in which we are battered, to give up creative efforts, to expend all our energy in the support of other lives and never in support of our own, to accept it when a man interrupts us, to

punish ourselves if we are successful, to deny so habitually our right to self-determination that we do not feel we have an identity unless it is given to us by someone else.[43]

Theologies that justify suffering, in combination with willing acceptance of a vengeful patriarchal God, these feminists contend, have concrete manifestations in the lived experience of faithful Christian women the world over. Bohn and Fortune draw upon examples of suffering in the private sphere, such as domestic violence and rape, but *The Passion of the Christ* introduces these theologies of suffering into the public sphere and, in so doing, demonstrates that they can similarly be used to justify all manner of public oppression, including state-sponsored violence.

This body of feminist thought about theologies of suffering works at cross-purposes with the work that other contextual theologians are doing in developing liberation theologies. Liberation theologians would suggest that identifying with Christ's experience of oppression helps the victims of the world understand that God cares for even the lowliest, and, equipped with that knowledge, even the most oppressed find agency to work for social change. But these feminist theologians would suggest exactly the opposite: that identifying with the suffering Christ leads to willing submission in the worldly public sphere, as Christians see suffering as part of God's plan for them or for humanity. *The Passion of the Christ* fulfills these feminist fears about celebrations of suffering: it situates faithful Christians as obedient onlookers to divine-willed, state-sanctioned violence. Even though it starts with the experience of victimhood that liberation theology so privileges, *The Passion*'s strong demarcation between human and divine capacities leaves humans with only one limited model of civic participation: feminine submission to earthly powers in the face of God-willed violence.

The Omnipotent Divine and Impotent Humans

In the film's world, the divine is an all-powerful God who, from a position on high, orchestrates the worldly events below. The human sphere is sharply demarcated from the divine, and humans are at God's mercy for intervention in their lives. Only occasionally do elements of the divine order make their way into earthly reality—such as Satan and the demons that appear among the crowd—and the distinction between human and divine is otherwise sharply maintained, with even Jesus firmly situated in the human realm. Jesus only moves into that divine space upon his death, but before that moment, he, just like all the other humans, must submit to God's will in the unfolding human drama.

Through the film's visual framing alone, a clear divide between human and divine emerges, as the human on Earth is always set in opposition to the divine above. The opening image of the film is an expansive camera shot across the cloudy sky, which is lit only by the full moon, with the sound of wind in the background. As the camera moves slowly down from the moon to the earth, a male voice singing becomes audible, which is then replaced by the breathy Aramaic emanating from a body just coming into focus on the earth. The Aramaic is not subtitled, and the first widely familiar words come when the camera has zoomed in on the back of the body, which is looking upward and pleading, "Adonai, adonai." The camera follows this body—slowly revealed to be Jesus—as he wanders through the garden, praying. Jesus wakes the disciples, and the camera stays with them as they watch Jesus, who walks on ahead and, in the sliver of light from the moon, looks up to the sky and then falls down on his knees. From his knees, he looks up and his words suggest the nature of his human relationship to the divine. As he prays, "Hear me, Father. Rise up. Defend me. Save me from the traps they set for me," it becomes clear that Jesus, like all humans, is impotent in the face of divine will. He can only fall down on his knees and ask God above for mercy. Later, he does the same, looking up to God, asking "Father, you can do all things. If it is possible, let this chalice pass from me . . . but let your will be done, not mine." One last time, as he is on the cross, Jesus must supplicate himself, seeking God's intervention. As Caiaphas and one of the criminals hung with Jesus taunt him, asking why he cannot save himself, Jesus prays for them. Slowly and painfully, he raises his head to look skyward, and he asks God, "Father forgive them. They know not what they do." In all of these cases, Jesus is visually situated as the human on the earth, looking up to the divine figure in the sky.[44] As the earthly human, he is powerless to do anything except make requests from God above.

Throughout the film, Jesus' disciples demonstrate a similar relationship with this all-powerful deity always represented by skyward glances. In the opening scene in the garden, for instance, as Peter and the other disciples struggle to understand Jesus' agony, Peter casts a long, questioning gaze at the moon. Here, the visual relationship between humans and God is again recreated, and the nature of the relationship is also made clear: humans must look to the all-powerful God for help and for answers.

Through its sharp distinction between the human and divine, the film portrays the power relationship between the two realms—that power comes from above, and humans must request God's favor. In constructing this authoritarian God figure, the film suggests a divine desire to bring about Jesus' death. Plead though Jesus and his disciples might, ultimately God's will must be done, and God's will is to bring about the death of his son. The film's temporal framing only enhances this narrative: because the film focuses on the last twelve hours of Jesus' life, his ministry is framed from within the lens of his impending death, as if his violent death was the inevitable conclusion to his life. By the time we, as the audience members, join the story, Jesus is already in the garden, about to be arrested—by which point in the Gospel narrative, all signs point to his death. Unlike other films that focus on Jesus' life more holistically, including his parables and miracles, this film treats those earlier moments through the prism of Jesus' impending death. Jesus' violent death becomes the fulfillment of God's plan, the primary achievement of his years on Earth.

In an earthly social order defined by an all-powerful God who uses state agents to bring violence upon his son and his followers, the suitable response for faithful Christians is to demonstrate obedience to that God and his agents. More than simply obedience, however, I argue that *The Passion*'s models of faithful Christian civic participation are defined by their submissive femininity, whereas the anti-models of Christian civic participation display a barbaric masculinity. The film's graphic violence facilitates these characterizations, as the guards who beat Jesus are dangerously masculine, while the faithful followers of Christ demonstrate their femininity and their willingness to accept this extreme violence.

The Anti-Models of Faithful Citizenship

The temple guards, in their very brief role, and the Roman guards, who receive considerably more screen time, all display particularly barbaric forms of hypermasculinity as they perform their public duties.[45] In actions, the Roman guards are loud and aggressive. In appearance, they are coarse and ill-groomed, with the armor of the Roman authority clothing their overweight frames. They are so out of shape that during pauses in the beating, they fold forward with their hands on their knees, trying to catch their breath. Most sweat profusely and have crooked, uneven, and discolored teeth. Their most common form of communication seems to be grunting (presumably in Latin). Their idiocy is demonstrated throughout the film, especially as typified by their repeated failure to comprehend or follow orders.

Although the Roman guards figure prominently throughout the film, they receive their most intimate treatment in the extended flagellation scene, where, for more than eight minutes of film time, they are responsible for beating Jesus. In those eight minutes, there are nearly eighty camera shots of the guards and approximately sixty of Jesus, plus another handful of long shots that depict Jesus and the guards together. In that space of time, there are less than forty shots of other characters.[46] The action in this scene moves quickly, especially for the first few minutes. When the beating begins, there is a consistent rhythm to the visual images: a guard takes a big step back and, with all his weight, thrusts a lash forward into Jesus' flesh; then Jesus lurches forward in a compensatory fashion; then another guard, in a manner similar to the first, propels his whip at Jesus; again, this whip is followed by Jesus' reactionary lurch. When the beating begins, this pattern is repeated six times in succession before the camera work diversifies. Just moments later, though, after a pause in the action while the guards switch weapons, these two coordinate shots—the guard whipping and Jesus recoiling—define the visual pattern again.

As the guards perform this extreme violence, they carry themselves with a masculine swagger. When they are initially preparing for the flagellation, the guards carefully contemplate the numerous whips and lashes laid out on a table. Each having chosen the lash that best suits his needs, the men strut and stretch out with their instruments. Each holds his wooden lash with one hand at each end and raises it above his head, circling his shoulders back and arching his spine, as if to ensure that he is properly limber for the task at hand. One guard then stretches in the opposite direction, holding the lash in front of his abdomen, arching his spine forward. Also as they prepare, two guards engage in a jovial dogfight: bringing their faces close together, they make biting motions while they growl and grunt.

In addition to their masculine swagger, these guards' collective persona is defined by their glee in performing this beating. They are a rowdy, jovial bunch throughout the scene, a tone striking in contrast to the stoic Jewish priests and the sympathetic Mary, Mary Magdalene, and John around the edges of the room. Even as they enter the room with Jesus, the guards are already giddy: the first close-up of Roman guards in this scene is of them laughing. While they prepare to beat Jesus, a full one-third of the camera shots are of guards laughing or playing around. Even once they begin the flagellation, the guards continue to laugh, while Jesus' followers look on in tears and even the Jewish priests become so disgusted that they turn away. At the climax of the flagellation scene, one guard lashes Jesus with a tool that tears his flesh away from his body, and then the guard is propelled backward by the thrust of his own swinging motion. As he moves backward, he laughs heartily before the camera pans to other guards sharing in the laugh. Even the Roman official supervising the beating, who generally appears stern, cannot fight back a smile as the violence gets particularly gruesome.

The Roman guards, who are agents of the state, gleefully perform their civil service duties in a mode defined by excessive, barbarous, unintelligent, unattractive hypermasculinity. Though it should come as no surprise that the film vilifies these men who beat Jesus, their characterization in terms of barbaric masculinity is important for its contrast with the more favored characters. Moreover, their enactment of violence and their extreme pleasure in inflicting it further solidify the relationship between the state and Jesus as oppressors and oppressed.

Models of Christian Charity

In clear opposition to the oppressive guards, the characters of Mary, Mary Magdalene, and John, who are typically depicted together, offer the film's model of faithful Christian participation in the public sphere.[47] Because these three receive the most visual attention throughout the film, and because the narrative operates from their perspective more than any of the other characters', Mary, Magdalene, and John become the most familiar, accessible, and sympathetic of the film's characters. These three, with whom the film encourages audience members to identify, uniformly model feminine submission. Even if they occasionally try to intervene in the unfolding narrative, their interventions consistently prove fruitless, demonstrating the futility of trying to stop divine will. Like Mary, Magdalene, and John, other feminine characters—Pilate's wife Claudia and the women who line the walk up the hill—also try to resist the violence, but all are refused, and they too resort to feminine submission. Ultimately, in a world with such a sharp divide between divine and human, where the divine power orchestrates human events and the worldly government is rendered impotent in the face of unruly citizens, submission is the most fitting mode of civic participation for the faithful believer.

While Jesus-the-victim and his oppressors perform most of the film's action, the submissive feminine followers provide audience members their vantage point. Mary, Magdalene, and John's story begins when Mary awakes with a start, announcing that this night is "different than any other" "because once we were slaves and now we are no longer." Mary and Magdalene cling to each other, and John bursts into their home, shouting, "They've seized him!" Immediately, these three recognize what has begun. Mary recognized it by her own premonition even before John's arrival, a sharp contrast to the disciples in the garden, who could not make sense of Jesus' agony. John's encounter with Mary and Magdalene here, just moments into the film, marks his own transition: previously, he was in the garden with the men, and now he has come to the home of the women, with whom he will remain for the rest the film. Indeed, these three are inseparable throughout the passion drama; together they follow Jesus through his presentations before Pilate and the crowd, his flagellation, his walk, and his crucifixion. In each of these scenes, Mary, Magdalene, and John receive consistent camera attention, and their visual prominence makes them available as models for audience members. For instance, in the repeated scenes where Pilate brings Jesus before the crowd in the basilica, the masses always consist of the Jewish high priests up front with the Jewish crowds surrounding them. In the midst of this rowdy mob, the film captures Mary, Mary Magdalene, and John—seemingly Jesus' only loyalists—in repeated close-up shots. In these scenes in the basilica, the camera alternates among a limited number of shots: it shows Pilate and Jesus up above the crowd; Claudia in an interior window off to the side; the mass of Jewish citizens and religious leaders down below, including the Jewish leaders; and Mary, Magdalene, and John together. Whereas Jesus, Pilate, and the masses are frequently (though not exclusively) captured in long shots, Mary, Magdalene, and John are consistently the subjects of close-up shots that encourage identification on the part of audience members.

Just as the basilica scenes alternate visually among these four images, the violence toward Jesus is portrayed in a similar fashion. As noted above, when Jesus is scourged by the Roman guards, Mary, Magdalene, and John watch from the side, and the camera alternates between shots of the beating of Jesus and shots of them. Even though there are numerically more shots of the Roman guards during this scene, the images of Mary, especially, linger much longer. One cutaway of Mary, for instance, lasts thirty-four seconds, as she prayerfully meanders out of the open space where they are beating Jesus and into a corridor. As we visually follow Mary as she walks, we still hear the sound of the whips, the laughter of the guards, and the moans and cries from Jesus. While we move with Mary, we still hear what she hears. In this moment, we experience the beating of Jesus through the ear of Mary.

As the film progresses, after Pilate has decided to have Jesus killed and the Roman guards begin his public procession, Mary, Magdalene, and John follow along with the crowd, and the film depicts their experience with Jesus' death. In the twenty minutes of the procession, the camera cuts to Mary, Magdalene, and John no fewer than fifteen times, in addition to depicting many other women along the way. In the last half hour of the film, once the crowd has reached the hill where the three men will be crucified, the camera focuses in on the three sympathetic characters no fewer than thirty-nine times, and many of these are lingering shots. In a very slow and detailed scene, Jesus is nailed to the cross, cut against shots of Mary Magdalene and the others watching the nailing. In the three minutes and thirty seconds of film time that begins with a close-up of a hammer hitting a nail, the camera develops a rhythm of rotating back and forth between shots of Jesus, shots of the instruments of violence, and shots of the women. The camera initially focuses on that hammer hitting the nail as it hits it three times. The hammer keeps hitting the nail, though, as the camera moves to focus in on a still Mary and then a close-up shot of an also-still Magdalene before a distanced shot of a chaotic band of Romans, and then a shot of a still John. All the while, the hammer continues to hit the nail, blood spurts, Jesus moans in agony, and the dramatic music increases its intensity. The scene flashes back to the Last Supper, and when it returns to the crucifixion, the camera zooms in on Mary weeping, and then Jesus laying on the cross, his arm being stretched by a Roman guard. Here, some distant visual attention is paid to the Roman guards who cannot figure out how to hang Jesus, and one guard yells, "Idiots! Let me show you how to do it. Like this." With all his strength, he stretches Jesus' arm, trying to get his hand to line up with the marked nail hold on the cross. When Jesus' arm snaps, Mary gasps, and then the Roman yells, "No, get it in there. Hold the hand open." There is a close-up shot of Jesus' hand as the nail starts to touch it, and then on Jesus' face as he says, "Father, forgive them."

The camera follows with a series of close-up shots: first John, then the hammer striking the nail, then Jesus' face, then Mary, then Jesus' arm, then Jesus' face, then Magdalene on her knees as her face falls to the ground, then the blood spilling below the cross, and then John. The camera pans out to show the Romans manipulating Jesus' legs; then it zooms back in on Jesus' face and then Mary, then back out to a Roman on a horse, and then back in to dwell on Jesus' face. The shot zooms back out to the Romans at Jesus' feet laughing, then back in on the hammer hitting the nail and on the Roman hammering that nail. The camera displays Jesus' body as he cries out, "My father, my father . . . my God," but the camera has moved to a kneeling Mary before Jesus finishes his utterance, and as a result, the English subtitles for these words frame the shot of Mary. She closes her eyes, and the camera moves down to her hands as they dig in the soil. We see Caiaphas, and then the Romans in the background across a shot of Jesus' body, as Jesus calls out, "They don't know . . . they don't know."

The visual exchange between Magdalene and Jesus' body becomes especially intense as the Romans decide to turn the cross over. Up until this point, the cross had been resting on the ground, with Jesus laying on it as they nailed him down. Now, the guards decide to turn the cross over so that Jesus will be facing the ground. As the Romans very slowly pick up the cross from one side, so as to be able to flip it over, Jesus' body is slowly lifted perpendicular to the ground, and all the while, the camera focuses on Jesus' body. As the cross falls to the ground, however, the camera focuses in on Mary Magdalene, who is kneeling in the background, with the descending cross and face of Jesus obscured in the foreground by dust and shadows. As the cross falls, Magdalene covers her face, and the cross stops just short of Jesus hitting the ground. While the Romans are laughing, Magdalene looks up, and the camera zooms in on her, then on Jesus, then back to Magdalene, then back to Jesus, then to Magdalene again, and then back to the hammering in the foreground, with Magdalene in the background. Throughout this scene, Mary, Magdalene, John, and Jesus receive almost the only close-up shots. Indeed, these characters become more visually accessible than anyone else at Calvary.

These three sympathetic characters, who become most accessible to audience members, are all very similarly feminine. Even though two are female characters played by female actresses and one is a male character played by a male actor, all three perform submissive femininity. All three actors are feminine in appearance: they are small in stature with fine features. Even John has the small stature and fine features, plus short, soft, curly hair, with only slight evidence of facial hair. Moreover, they behave in very submissive ways. In the scenes described above, where camera shots of Mary, Magdalene, and John are juxtaposed against camera shots of the Roman guards, the three are defined by their silence in contrast to the loud buffoonery of the guards. Mary, Magdalene, and John speak rarely, and when they do, it is in hushed tones, often reverential in prayer. The characteristic slow, lingering camera shots of them only underscore their stillness. In the longest scene focused exclusively on Mary and Magdalene (with John nearby), the women accept cloths from Claudia so that they can mop up Jesus' blood after the scourging. As they wander the corridor next to the courtyard where the guards beat Jesus, Mary and Magdalene are met by Claudia. Dressed entirely in white, Claudia brings white cloths to the women. As she extends her arms offering the cloths, Claudia keeps her eyes low, and Mary and Magdalene do the same as they accept the cloths. The camera alternates back and forth ten times, capturing a prolonged, silent exchange between these three. Not a single word is spoken, and as soon as Mary and Magdalene have accepted the cloths, Claudia scurries away. After the guards have untied Jesus and taken him out of the courtyard, the women, on their knees, prayerfully wipe up Jesus' blood. Because the camera depicts this scene from above, we see the expanse of Jesus' splattered blood as the women work methodically. Off to the side, John stands silently, shedding a discreet tear, which he wipes away with the back of his hand.

These feminine characters, who are largely submissive, show sparks of resistance throughout the film, but their resistance always proves futile, only underscoring the virtue of accepting, rather than challenging, the divinely controlled state government. Shortly after Mary and Magdalene learn that Jesus has been seized, they venture out into the crowds, where a distraught Mary looks up to a Roman guard on a horse and appeals to him for help, crying out, "In there! Stop them! They've arrested him! In secret!" Even though one guard looks compelled by her cries, they collectively decide that she is crazy and that the Jewish leaders have simply arrested another criminal. In this scene, she explicitly accepts her incapacity to stop the unfolding of the divine drama when she acknowledges, "It has now begun, Lord. So be it."

Even more than Mary, Magdalene, and John, the film's other feminine characters also try to intervene to stop Jesus' death, foremost among them Pilate's wife, Claudia. With Pilate when he receives the news from a Roman official that the Jewish high priest Caiaphas has had some prophet arrested, Claudia becomes interested when she hears it was a Galilean. She establishes a watchful presence over the proceedings in the basilica, occasionally making eye contact with Mary, Magdalene, and John. In private conversations, as Pilate carefully weighs his options about whether or how to punish the Galilean, Claudia consistently urges him not to punish Jesus. She begs, "Don't condemn this Galilean. He's holy. You will only bring trouble on yourself." Even though she cannot convince him at this point, Claudia does not give up but pleads again with Pilate in subsequent scenes, never finding success, of course. As Jesus carries his cross, other female characters along the way also try to help him, if not to stop the procession toward crucifixion. For instance, one woman, who is first shown with a pitcher of water, is disturbed by the noise of the crowd and immediately falls to her knees and looks upward as if asking something of God. The woman will later approach Jesus with a towel and water. She will have time to give him the towel, with which he wipes his face, but her attempt to offer him water is thwarted by the Roman who shoves her away, demanding, "Who do you think you are? Get away." Just moments later, another unidentified woman cries out, to no avail, "Someone stop this!" As the guards and men in the crowd push Jesus on, alternately beating him and instructing him to keep going, the camera pans past a series of women in the crowd, all of whom hold their shawls tight or cling to each other, looking distraught but unable to do anything.

These sympathetic characters, as much as they might want to stop Jesus' crucifixion or lessen his pain, find themselves unable to do either. Even still, they are the celebrated characters of the film, lauded visually for their unceasing devotion to Jesus. They are, remarkably, the most feminine characters in the film, and their femininity is especially obvious in contrast to the barbarous masculinity of the film's villains. The film's implicit suggestion is that Christian discipleship is performed as submissive femininity, especially as juxtaposed with barbarous masculinity. Indeed, in a social order defined by a power struggle between religion and the state, where God uses that power struggle as the productive space to bring violence upon a religious leader, faithful Christians have little choice but to accede to state oppression, trusting that God has a plan for all this suffering.

CONCLUSIONS AND IMPLICATIONS

Making Jesus' brutal, tortured death vivid for audience members, *The Passion of the Christ* has reintroduced the questions that have challenged Christians for centuries: Why did Jesus have to die? Why did he have to suffer? What did Jesus' suffering death do for humanity? As pertinent as the film's graphic violence makes these questions, however, *The Passion* does not answer them explicitly. It does not take sides in the age-old debate over the reasons for Jesus' death and argue, with Anselm, that Jesus' death atones for human sins (even if the opening passage from Isaiah intimates as much), or, with Abelard, that Jesus' suffering death provides an example for faithful Christians to follow. Instead of entertaining these questions of soteriology and Christology, the film's clear focus on the excruciating death of the Jesus of history invites speculation about the related questions: What does Jesus' suffering death mean for Christians today? How should Christians respond to the suffering in their own lives?

The Passion invites Christians into the experience so valued by liberation theologians: encountering the suffering Jesus. The film's Jesus is unquestionably a powerless victim, brutalized by the earthly authorities and abandoned by the God he trusts. Moreover, *The Passion* allows today's believers to encounter the suffering Jesus from our own position of suffering, in part because we witness the passion drama from the vantage point of the film's faithful disciples who suffer with Jesus, but also because the hyperreal violence makes us mediated participants in the passion drama.

The film deviates from liberation theology's commitment to suffering, however, because it allows *all* audience members to understand themselves as oppressed. Whereas liberation theologians concern themselves with "the poor" and "the oppressed," especially in Latin American and other developing-nation contexts, *The Passion* allows white, middle-class, North American audiences to see themselves as victims. As followers of Christ, even economically secure, well-educated audience members become victims of the persecution of Christians so evident in the film. *The Passion* demonstrates, then, that oppression is a fundamentally discursive category. Even if liberation theologians often want to consider economic discrepancies when they talk about "the poor" and "the oppressed," the experience of victimhood provided by *The Passion* ignores such discrepancies, portraying oppression instead based on religious discrimination. By allowing contemporary Christians to understand themselves as victims, *The Passion* feeds the persecution complex common to American Christian discourses, which set themselves at odds to the hostile world inhospitable to Christian value systems.

The Passion further breaks from liberation theology in its failure to transform empathetic suffering with Jesus into a sense of earthly agency Christians might use to realize liberation from their own oppression. The film's failure to make this transformation suggests the problems more generally with empathetic suffering as the starting point for a model of activist civic participation. While the film clearly depicts Jesus as a victim, it bifurcates the blame for his suffering and death. On the one hand, the film's use of prophecy, in combination with the way that it demarcates human and divine powers, makes Jesus' death the product of divine desire. Although it never justifies this divine will to inflict a tortured death upon God's incarnate Son—either by spelling out atonement theology or by some other explanatory system—*The Passion* encourages Christians to trust that the omnipotent, omniscient God controlled this drama. At the same time, however, the film also blames the Jews for Jesus' death; shortly before his crucifixion, Jesus explicitly tells Pilate that it is the Jews who have sinned. Thus, Jesus is simultaneously the tragic victim of the bloodthirsty Jews and the chosen victim within the divine plan. By both explanations, he is a reluctant subject of larger social and cosmic forces. Because Jesus' death is simultaneously the result of unjust actions by a crazed power structure and the fulfillment of divine will, this bifurcated blame intimates that political injustices can be the manifestations of God's plan.

The Passion's narrative thus implies the unfortunate outcomes that feminist and womanist theologians commonly see in atonement theology: by sanctioning violence as God-willed, The Passion encourages audience members to suffer injustices, trusting that they have a purpose. Even though we may not always understand God's plan for our pain, just as The Passion does not explain God's plan for the suffering inflicted upon Jesus, we can trust that this suffering is necessary and may be redemptive. Moreover, by the film's example, it is clear that human institutions—such as political and religious authorities—may be working on God's behalf even when they cause great injustices. To resist such authorities might be to resist God's plan in its unfolding. The Passion, thus, demonstrates that whenever suffering is construed as God-willed, citizen agency is always limited to prayerful submission. The transformation that liberation theologians envision—from empathetic suffering to civic activism—is impossible as long as faithful Christians must trust the God who doles out the oppression they know in their lives.

The possibilities for activist civic participation are undercut further when the heroes of the Christian tradition—men and women such as Mary the mother of Jesus, Mary Magdalene, and John—are depicted as willing subjects acquiescing obediently to horrendous suffering. Although Christianity has long venerated femininity, and has given women the role of sacrificial martyr since its earliest days,[48] such submissive femininity has not traditionally been the outgrowth of these three characters' role in the passion drama. Even if Catholics the world over have celebrated Mary's role in the gospel drama for centuries, their attention has been to the Lukan Mary—the Mary of the Magnificat, the virgin birth, and Simeon's blessing. This is the Mary who, by saying yes to God, became "the sole human agent in the generation of Jesus" and thus ushered into humanity God's promise for a new creation.[49] She is "the pre-eminent human agent in those events which led to the birth of Jesus and the coming into being of that new humanity of which he is both the first member and the source."[50] This Marianism focuses less on the Mary at the cross, the Johannine Mary who is only known as Jesus' mother.[51] Even the subset of Catholics who celebrate Mary as a co-redemptrix do so for her affirmative response to God's call in her life, not for her willing accession to her son's violent death. This Mary of Catholic Marianism does share some of The Passion's Mary's submissiveness: she, too, accepts God's will. She does so, however, in the hopeful promise of bringing about the Messiah and a new humanity. In the prayer that concludes Pope Benedict XVI's first encyclical, he praises Mary because, by abandoning herself to God's will, she has "given the world its true light" and become "a wellspring of the goodness which flows forth from him."[52] Whereas traditional Marianism sees her as the willing and hopeful participant in the new birth of humanity, *The Passion* portrays her as the reluctant participant in her son's violent death.

Similarly, *The Passion* alters conventional depictions of Mary Magdalene and John. In their analysis of "Christ films," Babington and Evans note a persistent emphasis on Mary Magdalene's sexuality. The two Marys are typically depicted as opposites, with "the reduced, idealized sexuality of the Virgin contrast[ing] markedly with Mary Magdalene's traditionally heightened eroticism."[53] *The Passion* desexualizes Magdalene entirely, redeeming her for history. As it does so, however, it robs her of whatever agency that sexuality has customarily brought her. In books and films such as *The Last Temptation of Christ* and *The Da Vinci Code*, for instance, Magdalene's sexuality wins her a role in Christ's inner circle, as well as leadership of his church. John is stripped of his typical agency most obviously; whereas he is usually depicted as one of the disciples whom Jesus trusts to carry on his church, *The Passion*'s John becomes a submissive victim with no greater power than a woman.

Surely, Mary, Magdalene, and John do not transform their victimhood into the civic activism that liberation theologians hope the passion story will inspire for oppressed and marginalized people, but theirs is still a viable model of civic participation. Just as they participate in their cinematic public sphere by obediently submitting to the Roman and Jewish powers, so too can contemporary Christians demonstrate civic participation by prayerfully submitting to the inexplicable political injustices in their lives.

Contemporary Christians have actively cultivated this disposition of civic participation, including its primary mode of activism: prayer. For instance, the National Prayer Center, located in Washington, D.C., mobilizes Christians specifically to pray for United States political leaders.[54] It maintains a building near the Capitol, where citizens and leaders alike can pray for the nation's well-being. The World Prayer Center, operated out of Colorado Springs' New Life Church, has a larger mission. Its massive physical facility invites Christians the world over to pilgrimage to its sacred space, but its related Web site allows Christians to join global prayers virtually at their convenience. The Web site asks its visitors to pray for concerns in three categories: the Worldwide Prayer Focus, which lists individual countries; the Billion Soul Prayer Focus, which collects the names of unbelievers submitted by other visitors to the site; and Personal Prayer Requests, which detail the individual concerns of other visitors. The screen displays one request in each of these categories for thirty seconds at a time, and cycles through them constantly for as long as the visitor wishes to pray. The countries presented as the Worldwide Prayer Focus cycle through in alphabetical order, and the Web site provides a brief description of each country. The Worldwide Prayer Focus, in particular, implies a model of civic participation consistent with the feminine submission exemplified in *The Passion*: Christians can impact national and international politics collectively by submitting themselves in prayer.

4

Brutish Masculinity and the War on Evil

Left Behind

"Do not think that I have come to bring peace to the earth; I have not come to bring peace, but a sword."

Matthew 10:34

For the Lord himself, with a cry of command, with the archangel's call and with the sound of God's trumpet, will descend from heaven, and the dead in Christ will rise first. Then we who are alive, who are left, will be caught up in the clouds together with them to meet the Lord in the air; and so we will be with the Lord forever.

1 Thessalonians 4:16-17

Then I saw a new heaven and a new earth; for the first heaven and the first earth had passed away, and the sea was no more. . . . Then he said to me, "It is done! I am the Alpha and the Omega, the beginning and the end. To the thirsty I will give water as a gift from the spring of the water of life. Those who conquer will inherit these things, and I will be their God and they will be my children."

Revelation 21:1, 6-7

As the year 2000 approached, Americans succumbed to millennial fever. Whether the new millennium would technically dawn at the advent of 2000 or 2001, Americans could not deny that they were possibly facing the end of civilization or the beginning of a new era in human history. The Y2K computer glitch was just one popular framework for making sense of this potentially cataclysmic change; Americans also drew on the theological frameworks developed and popularized by their parents and grandparents.[1] Indeed, Christian visions of apocalypse and millennium, Armageddon and the New Jerusalem, have resonated with American cultural identities through the generations as the colonists, like their descendants, were eager to envision themselves playing a central role in God's unfolding plan for humanity.

These apocalyptic and millennial narratives have also, however, found themselves fundamentally at odds with the American ethos that otherwise privileges individualism and self-determination. Many of these millennial and apocalyptic belief systems place faith in a God who has preordained human history and who continues to control its progression. These belief systems, then, share a fundamental dilemma: what capacity for agency can human actors have in a world where events are entirely controlled by God? In other words, why should Christians work to create better schools, safer streets, and a cleaner environment if they know that God will soon bring the present world order to a careening halt, only to reward believers with a new heaven and a new earth? These questions have certainly been apt in the most recent generation of millennial enthusiasm. Some of the most outspoken heralds of the apocalypse—public preachers such as Jerry Falwell and Pat Robertson—were also the political leaders of the Christian Right. If their example suggests that an apocalyptic or millennial worldview is not fundamentally incompatible with earthly activism, they prompt another question: how can the two be reconciled?

The *Left Behind* books fit this millennial hysteria perfectly. Spanning twelve volumes and nearly five thousand pages, the novels offer a fictional account of apocalypse and millennium, based on the Christian Scriptures and the theological tradition of dispensational premillennialism. The brainchild of influential evangelical Christians Tim LaHaye and Jerry Jenkins,[2] the novels have now sold more than sixty-two million copies. From just one novel in 1996, published with only tentative plans for a few more, the series has grown beyond the twelve volumes for adults to include another forty-book series for children, graphic novels, feature films, shorter video adaptations of the stories, prequels to the original series for adults, and, ultimately, a final thirteenth sequel to that original series. Originally distributed only through the niche Christian bookstores, the *Left Behind* series ultimately benefited from extensive promotions by the national chain booksellers (Walmart, Sam's Club, Costco, and Barnes & Noble).[3] By winter of 2005, exactly 19 percent of respondents to the Baylor Religion Survey reported having read at least one of the novels.[4] The first of the three feature films, starring Kirk Cameron, was also released widely, premiering in 867 theaters in February 2001.[5]

Surely, the *Left Behind* books became a cultural phenomenon in part because they coincided so perfectly with the millennial fervor awaiting the year 2000. They captivated readers with a combination of apocalyptic theology espoused by likable characters set within thrilling action-adventure sequences. The first novel opens with the Rapture almost immediately: commercial airline pilot Rayford Steele is working a transatlantic flight and lusting after his flight attendant when he hears reports of disappearances on the plane. Passengers have simply vanished, leaving all their earthly possessions behind. Reports from the ground below only magnify the chaos on the plane: millions of humans have instantaneously disappeared, causing car accidents, fires, electrical outages, and widespread panic. After Rayford reroutes his flight back to Chicago and begins searching for his family, his findings confirm his suspicions about the disappearances. His wife and son, faithful Christians who warned him about the impending Rapture, have disappeared, while he and his daughter Chloe, for their stubborn rationality, have missed this heavenly reunion.

Rayford immediately makes his way to his wife's church, where he discovers that only one of its pastors and a few of its members were left behind. Together with Bruce, the remaining pastor, Rayford repents of his sins and accepts Christ, and he soon persuades Chloe to do the same. These three form the "Tribulation Force," with the explicit purpose of studying Scripture's warnings about the end time, so that they can identify the antichrist, speak out against him, and oppose his domination. They are soon joined by Buck, the rising star journalist of one of the nation's newsweeklies, whom Rayford had met on his flight the night of the disappearances. Through the series, the ranks of the Tribulation Force swell, due to its members' evangelism efforts and their good fortune in encountering other hidden cells of believers around the globe. Important additions include Rabbi Tsion Ben-Judah, an Israeli Jew who becomes the group's spiritual leader because his study of the Scriptures has led him to the conclusion that Jesus Christ was the Messiah, and Dr. Chaim Rosenzweig, a chemist who received global acclaim for developing a formula that made Israel's deserts arable. By the time of Christ's second coming in the final book, dozens of men and women have passed through the Tribulation Force or worked as allies of the group. Of the original four, only Rayford lives to the end of the Tribulation, but all are reunited upon Christ's second coming.

Almost immediately upon its inception, the Tribulation Force watches the political ascent of Nicolae Carpathia, a young Romanian legislator who, within days of the disappearances, wins the post of president of Romania and then secretary-general of the United Nations, before remaking the United Nations into the Global Community and installing himself as global potentate. Promising peace and security in an uncertain time, Carpathia convinces the United Nations to eradicate all national borders (dividing the world into ten regions instead), to put the world on one monetary system, and to dispose of 90 percent of the world's weapons systems, leaving the remaining 10 percent in the control of the Global Community. While his ambitious plans for peace endear Carpathia to the rest of the world, Tribulation Force members immediately recognize him as the antichrist. They watch him shore up power by weakening or eliminating other global leaders and by developing Global Community troops. Over the seven years of the Tribulation, Carpathia follows God's preordained script for the antichrist: he ascends to power with the signing of a peace treaty, he is assassinated exactly halfway through the Tribulation and rises three days later, and he seals his followers with the mark of the beast. Finally, upon Christ's second coming, the antichrist is sentenced to one thousand years in the lake of fire.

Recognizing Carpathia as the antichrist and anticipating each of these developments foretold by Scripture, Tribulation Force members devote themselves to resisting and countering his dominance. Some of them fight Carpathia from within his Global Community (GC) administrative structure. While Rayford works as his personal pilot, Buck as the editor of his global magazine, and others as his helicopter pilot and computer technology experts, they use their inside positions to gather information useful to Tribulation Force missions and to undermine Carpathia's own work. The majority of Tribulation Force members, who never make their way into Carpathia's employ, conduct external, oppositional missions. Oftentimes, they travel around the world rescuing believers endangered by Carpathia's soldiers. At one point they organize and execute the world's largest global gathering of Christians, foiling Carpathia's efforts to disrupt the event.

All the while, as the books' heroes and heroines fight the antichrist, they also endure the plagues that define the Tribulation. In the first major calamity after the Rapture, one-fourth of the world's population dies in a global earthquake that is accompanied by a worldwide blackout, a meteor shower, and the moon turning blood red. At other points in the series, the world's rivers turn to blood, the sun grows so hot that it scorches people to death, and a global horde of scorpion-like locusts attacks all nonbelievers. These locusts cause six months of pain so intense that sufferers wish for death but find themselves unable to die. And, of course, the four horses of the apocalypse bring their own devastations.

Finally, in the twelfth book, all the believers' efforts, their steadfast faith, and their endurance through these tribulations are rewarded when Jesus Christ rides triumphantly back into Jerusalem. The believers who survived the final battle at Armageddon witness Jesus returning, accompanied by all the deceased and raptured believers the Christian community has ever known. All of Christendom is united as Jesus divides the sheep from the goats, and while he sentences the goats to hell, he demonstrates nothing but love for his own sheep, calling each of his children by name and welcoming them into his kingdom.

This Rapture and apocalypse narrative captured the imaginations of American Christians at a historical moment rich with millennial speculations. The *Left Behind* novels, as they build upon the rich tradition of American apocalypticism, also make a significant contribution to this discourse: by depicting a tenable performance of human agency within a preordained worldview, they offer one solution to the basic dilemma of individual agency that haunts premillennial apocalypticism especially. The *Left Behind* novels make space for their image of human agency by disrupting the dualisms that have typically characterized American millennialisms: they are either premillennial or postmillennial, tragic or comic, literal or analogical, telic or cyclical, and imminent or immanent. Although the *Left Behind* story is unquestionably premillennial, its apocalypse is simultaneously tragic and comic, imminent and immanent, telic and cyclical, and literal and analogical. It becomes comic, immanent, cyclical, and analogical for its readers, in part, by its very form as serialized fiction novels. Additionally, it constructs a world order characterized by the familiar binaries of good and evil, reality and appearance, and truth and persuasion, which by their easy analogy to readers' lives make the apocalypse and millennium immanent and cyclical. Those familiar binaries also give shape to *Left Behind*'s celebrated model of civic participation: brutish masculinity. Demonstrating anti-intellectualism and physical strength, *Left Behind*'s heroes become valiant warriors for Christ.

RECASTING THE APOCALYPTIC WORLDVIEW

Apocalyptic fears and millennial visions run deep in both Jewish and Christian theologies. Believers through the centuries have turned to the books of Daniel, Ezekiel, and Revelation, as well as passages in the Gospels and Epistles, for clues to God's plan for the future of humanity. The early

Christians, including the author of Revelation, eagerly awaited what they assumed was Christ's impending return. So, too, have later generations of Christians assigned their own eras a central role in the promised end time. The great thinkers of the Reformation, such as Martin Luther, John Calvin, and Ulrich Zwingli, used eschatological frameworks to make sense of their own period of religious turmoil, and Martin Luther argued publicly that the pope might be the antichrist.[6] Soon, influential Christians from John Milton to George Fox to Isaac Newton could all fit the pope-as-antichrist into their eschatological schemes.[7]

Apocalyptic and millennial theologies have fared especially well in the American context, where they have resounded with prevailing attitudes of American exceptionalism and thrived with religious freedom. Early Puritan visions for the new world, as expounded by men such as Increase and Cotton Mather and Jonathan Edwards, assigned the colonies a central role in the coming millennium, recognizing the possibility that their new home was God's New Jerusalem.[8] Early Christian sects and utopian communities throughout the Northeast developed around their novel eschatologies, and many of these sects, such as the Mormons, Jehovah's Witnesses, and Christian Scientists, would mature into lasting religions.[9] In the mid-nineteenth century, William Miller preached the impending apocalypse far and wide. Even when his prediction that Christ would return between March 21, 1843, and March 21, 1844, was disproved, a realization his followers called the "Great Disappointment," the legions of Millerites remained faithful to their apocalyptic doctrine and institutionalized themselves as the Seventh-Day Adventist Church. Apocalyptic thought grew even more mainstream with the preaching of John Nelson Darby, who itinerated through the United States and Canada between 1862 and 1877. Darby promoted the already-popular idea of dispensationalism, which posited that Christian history could be divided chronologically into seven dispensations, among which Christians were currently living in the penultimate, the church age. He added the idea of the Rapture, a concept that had been tentatively formulated within the previous two centuries.[10] Darby's teachings were systematized and preserved with the publication of the *Scofield Reference Bible*. Written by a Darbyite, Cyrus Scofield, the book remains in print and in circulation among conservative Christians who still rely on the apocalyptic interpretations contained in its footnotes.[11]

In recent years, it has been easy to identify apocalyptic theologies in fringe sects—the Branch Davidians, Heaven's Gate, and other groups that clearly anticipate cataclysmic global transformation[12]—but fervent belief in an end-time narrative is hardly confined to these extreme groups known for their dramatic self-destruction. Discourses of apocalypse and millennium continue to manifest themselves in mainstream religious and secular settings. The bestselling nonfiction book of the 1970s was Hal Lindsey's *The Late Great Planet Earth*, and the film *A Thief in the Night* and its sequels also fared well in that era.[13] In 1980s U.S. politics, President Reagan's secretary of the interior, James Watt, famously speculated in congressional testimony about the imminence of Christ's return; Secretary of Defense Casper Weinberger acknowledged his fascination with Revelation; and President Reagan himself drew upon apocalyptic language, albeit more vaguely and allegorically, in his Cold War discourse.[14] This American fixation with all things eschatological only intensified as the year 2000 approached, and the *Left Behind* books provided just one outlet for apocalyptic and millennial speculation.

Through all these centuries of development, Christian eschatology has been riddled by a central dilemma over the possibility of earthly human agency. According to Boyer, prophecy preachers have had to negotiate answers to these fundamental questions: "How ought the believer whose hope lies in a future age relate to the present-day world and its concerns? Should one plunge into secular politics and social activism, or passively withdraw and await the unfolding of God's plan?"[15] Each eschatology's answers to these fundamental questions have been shaped in large part by its location within a series of disjunctions: whether it is premillennial or postmillennial, tragic or comic, literal or analogical, imminent or immanent, and telic or cyclical. Identifying with each pole of each of these binaries has radical implications for the way that an apocalyptic or millennial theology conceptualizes the possibilities for human agency.

The most basic and abiding distinction within apocalyptic thought is between premillennialism and postmillennialism, two largely incompatible eschatologies that not only tell distinct stories about the end time, but also imply distinct models of divine and human agency.[16] In a premillennialist worldview, God will bring the present world order to an abrupt halt when Christ's second coming ushers in a millennium of peace and prosperity.[17] Some premillennialists trust that faithful Christians will be raptured prior to the end of the present world order, while others acknowledge that even Christians will have to endure the tribulations accompanying that revolution. In both cases, a premillennialist worldview believes in an apocalypse in the truest sense of the word: an unveiling of God's hidden plan. God controls this sequence of events, and although we may not know the day nor hour,[18] we can trust that God's plan is unfolding. Postmillennialism, conversely, asserts that Christ will only return *after* a millennium of peace and prosperity on Earth.[19] The responsibility for achieving that millennium rests with humans, who must reform their societies, ameliorate injustices, and create the conditions for peace.

Although premillennialism and postmillennialism have recurred across American history, they have waxed and waned independently of each other.[20] Early colonists articulated a largely postmillennial worldview, trusting that "Christ's return would crown a long period of growing Christian influence and diminishing tyranny—a process in which America would figure prominently."[21] But the great nineteenth-century prophecy preachers William Miller and John Nelson Darby espoused clearly premillennialist doctrines, as did Hal Lindsey more recently.[22] The Social Gospel movement prominent at the turn of the twentieth century was driven by postmillennial sentiments, and a markedly different postmillennialism has since been popularized by the proponents of Christian Reconstruction, such as Rousas John Rushdoony and Gary North.[23] Premillennialist and postmillennialist scripts have not always been distinct, and innovative prophets have woven themes from the two together.[24]

The two worldviews, although they share a common anticipation of Christ's millennial kingdom, imply radically different expectations for the role Christians play in achieving that kingdom.[25] Because premillennialism assumes that history is foreordained, that the passing days simply unfold God's plan, it leaves minimal space or need for human agency. Often popular among oppressed or dispossessed groups, premillennialist theologies trust God to mete out ultimate justice and reparations.[26] Unlike postmillennialism, which trusts humans to create the conditions favorable to a peaceful millennium and Christ's return, premillennialism rests ultimate power for human transformation with the divine authority.[27] Boyer explains,

> The premillennial outlook seemed to imply passivity, since society's evils and injustices merely bore out the prophesied degeneracy and wickedness of the present age. And, indeed, from John Darby's day on, a vast body of premillennialist writing warned against the lure of social activism. . . . Through the Depression and World War II, prophecy writers emphasized the uselessness of human efforts at social betterment: regardless of what governments and uplift organizations might do, war, suffering, and conflict were bound to grow worse. . . . Belief in the rapture . . . further diluted the impetus to political activism. The redeemed would watch history's climax from the skies.[28]

Premillennialism can lead to a bleak worldview: because God exercises all control, humans have little cause to expend any effort in their worldly lives.

Most premillennialists, however, do not give up earthly work entirely.[29] At the very least, premillennialist believers must take whatever action is necessary to get themselves on the right side of history. If good and evil are locked in a battle for humanity, and believers trust that good will ultimately overcome evil, they must secure themselves a place within the ranks of the good, whether that means committing their lives to Christ or securing God's favor otherwise. Within this premillennialist scheme, believers also might recognize an imperative to evangelize, to help the lost find their way to Christ before the ultimate judgment day.[30] Stephen O'Leary frames this imperative to evangelize as the need to "argue the apocalypse"—to pronounce, explain, and predict all that they know about God's plan for history.[31] Boyer even notes that throughout American history, many premillennialists have maintained active reform programs even while they patiently await the apocalypse. He cites, for example, the Millerite movement, whose leaders "were veterans of a variety of reforms, including antislavery, temperance, and other causes . . . . To be sure, earthbound concerns faded as the predicted date approached. But many Millerites saw no contradiction in working for reform while awaiting the end."[32]

Premillennialism and postmillennialism's contrasting worldviews mimic the oppositions inherent in the tragic and comic frames, frames that O'Leary argues have been useful resources for apocalyptic rhetors. He explains, "The interpretative traditions that surround the Apocalypse have tended to emphasize elements of either tragedy or comedy in the eschatological narrative, and thereby to adopt the perspectives of the tragic and comic frames in their constructions of historical time."[33] Those elements include, according to O'Leary, their "depiction of time, human action, and agency."[34] In tragedy, time is closed and predetermined, and in comedy it is open and episodic. Tragedy moves toward an unhappy ending and comedy a happy one. Because tragedy depicts evil as inherent and unchanging, it restores moral order only by sacrifice and victimage. Comedy, conversely, sees evil as human error, so it restores moral order "by exposing the foolishness of pretension and vanity."[35] In comedy, humans are capable of repairing for error and thus affecting the course of history, but in tragedy they are consigned to accept their fate.

According to O'Leary, the book of Revelation, the primary apocalyptic text for most Christians, can be read in either tragic or comic terms. It is tragic when it is read to predict a structured sequence of historical events that necessarily end in catastrophe and rebirth. Revelation can be read in comic terms, however, when its aesthetic and hortatory qualities are emphasized. When apocalyptic theologies take a tragic frame, the narrative catharsis must come through the ultimate moment of redemption when the world is transformed. When they take a comic frame, however, "the experience of time through the text takes on the episodic structure of comedy; the drama of the end is continually re-enacted and experienced in the present while the End itself is delayed."[36] Like the book of Revelation, other apocalyptic texts can be read along both comic and tragic lines. In every case, the choice of frame implies certain commitments; in particular, a tragic frame curtails human agency, whereas a comic frame encourages it.

Whether Revelation, or any apocalyptic text, is framed as tragic or comic depends in part on whether it is read literally or analogically. The narrative of Revelation describes a sequence of events revealed to the author, John of Patmos. He sees a heavenly throne, next to which are the seven seals, each of which reveals a further vision to John—from the figures we commonly know as the Four Horsemen of the Apocalypse to earthquakes and other seeming natural disasters. Finally, the seventh seal promises heavenly bliss, as the faithful are presented before the Lord upon the throne. The book is filled with details of catastrophic destruction, angelic and beastly creatures, and all the numbers that have transfixed generations of prophecy believers: forty-two months, 1,260 days, a beast with seven heads and six horns, the twenty-four elders, the 144,000 faithful, and, of course, 666, the mark of the beast.

John's visions can certainly be read as literal predictions of the future, and many believers trust that they are. They assert that one day, possibly soon, a trumpet will sound and the Lord will return. He will be either preceded or accompanied by all these fantastical things that John saw on the island of Patmos: signs and wonders, disasters and plagues, and angels and demons. These literal readings of Revelation are particularly common among Protestants because, at least since Saint Augustine, Catholic and Eastern Orthodox doctrines have been persuaded by the great theologian's tendency to read John's apocalypse allegorically or analogically.[37] By his reading, John's images should speak to the issues that Christians and the church face in the present age, if only metaphorically. Not only do Christians face plagues, beasts, demons, and all the other things John saw, but we have faced them repeatedly throughout the generations of church history. An analogical reading of Revelation encourages us to see these trials and tribulations as persistent and ongoing rather than cataclysmic, but also to see God's redemption as persistent and ongoing rather than millennial. According to O'Leary, Augustine's allegorical reading of Revelation makes it also comic. "In Augustine's provisionally comic view of history," O'Leary argues, "calamities become episodes, recurrent events that all human communities must face without recourse to an apocalyptic understanding, while the millennial kingdom becomes an obscure allegory of the church in the present age."[38] Whereas Augustine's reading of Revelation leaned toward the comic and the allegorical, American premillennialisms lean to the tragic and the literal. Occasionally, apocalyptic discourses find solid ground between these poles.

In a related vein, apocalyptic narratives range from the rectilinear to the cyclical. The literal reading of Revelation makes human history rectilinear, or telic. History is marching forward and onward to a certain destination, the exact nature of which only God has foreknowledge. In an allegorical reading, however, human history might be cyclical, moving through the same narratives repetitively. Most Protestant premillennial systems, the popular apocalyptic doctrines, have tended toward the rectilinear, which follows naturally from their literal reading of Revelation and fits with their tragic frame. Kermode explains, "Broadly speaking, apocalyptic thought belongs to rectilinear rather than cyclical views of the world . . . But basically one has to think of an ordered series of events which ends, not in a great New Year, but in a final Sabbath. The events derive their significance from a unitary system, not from their correspondence with events in other cycles."[39] By this formulation, an apocalyptic system is made meaningful only because it invests faith in the coherent narrative progressing toward a foreordained end.

Kermode has, however, also identified the growing tendency to perceive the apocalypse as immanent, rather than imminent, which seems to underscore a cyclical orientation rather than a rectilinear one. Within an imminent framework, the apocalypse is a definite set of impending events that Christians anticipate and await. An immanent framework, conversely, leads Christians to recognize God's apocalypse as ongoing within human history. Ideas of an immanent apocalypse may not be entirely new; Maxine Montgomery notes, for instance, how African Americans have traditionally clung to narratives of an immanent apocalypse even when whites preferred to imagine an imminent one. Given the disparity in the two groups' socioeconomic and political situations, African Americans were necessarily more invested in an immanent apocalypse that could give them immediate relief in their earthly lives. Montgomery explains, "While white Americans espoused a theological perspective which entailed a belief in a futuristic heaven divorced from the present, blacks looked forward to a reversal of their sociopolitical situation in this world and the release that comes from defining the self through terms drawn from within the culture."[40]

Joshua Gunn and David E. Beard take Kermode's passing comments about the possibility of an immanent apocalypse as a starting point to hypothesize that narratives of immanent apocalypse are particularly engendered by the conditions of postmodernity. Postmodernity, and specifically new media technology, has facilitated "the emergence (or perhaps reappearance) of circular or 'spherical' temporalities, hastened by technologies of representation that collapse the symbolic distance between the sign and its referent."[41] These circular or spherical temporalities allow for immanent apocalyptics in which, rather than awaiting the ultimate ending, "one realizes she is (already) dwelling in the 'end period.'"[42] Dwelling in this end period, however, is a profoundly destabilizing experience, and Gunn and Beard postulate the subject of the immanent apocalypse to be the destabilized subject of postmodernity more generally. They explain, "Within traditional, imminent apocalyptics, Western individualism is assumed: a stable self moves in concert with others toward some particular religious or secular end."[43] The immanent apocalypse leaves the subject scrambling for foundations, without a grounded role in the telic narrative. Although Gunn and Beard do not assert as much, the locally stable subject of the immanent apocalypse may have access to greater resources of agency than the overly determined subject of the telic imminent apocalypse. At the very least, the immanent postmodern apocalypse seems to allow more flexibility for invention in creating the individual subject position within the larger apocalyptic narrative.

The most traditional premillennialist theologies, like those espoused by William Miller, John Nelson Darby, and Hal Lindsey, tend to understand the apocalypse in tragic, literal, telic, and imminent terms. Theirs is a world coming to a careening halt by God's design, where humans can do nothing to change its course. Yet this theological system is also espoused by some of the most outspoken religious-political leaders of the Christian Right, who encourage their followers to join their political activism. This fundamental contradiction can cause cognitive dissonance for politically active premillennialists, who develop a number of rationalizations in order to make their worldviews coherent, as Clyde Wilcox, Sharon Linzey, and Ted Jelen have demonstrated.[44] I maintain that the *Left Behind* narrative offers a discursive resource for reducing that cognitive dissonance. *Left Behind* puts an immanent, cyclical, and analogical cast on the tragic premillennialist narrative, and in doing so, it carves out a space for human agency unparalleled in traditional literal, telic, imminent, tragic premillennialist narratives.

In some ways, the *Left Behind* narrative adheres closely to the tradition of telic, tragic, premillennial theologies that predict a literal and imminent apocalypse. It depicts characters who endure a series of tribulations that the group's spiritual leader, Rabbi Tsion Ben-Judah, finds embedded in the Scriptures. According to his reading of the Scriptures, the seven years of the Tribulation will be inaugurated with the signing of a peace treaty between Israel and the world, as well as the rise of the antichrist to power, which the characters witness immediately following the Rapture. Once those seven years have begun, Rabbi Ben-Judah can use the Scriptures to predict an even more precise timeline: the first twenty-one months will bring the seven Seal Judgments, the second twenty-one months will bring the seven Trumpet Judgments, and the last forty-two months, known as the Great Tribulation, will bring the most devastation of all, the seven Vial Judgments.[45] Rabbi Ben-Judah also uses the Scriptures to predict the antichrist's assassination and resurrection at the Tribulation Era's half-way point. The timing for other events, such as the implementation of the mark of the beast, is predicted less precisely, but those events remain imminent and unavoidable. Ultimately, the Tribulation Era must end with the battle at Armageddon. Jesus Christ will return, a scene depicted in the twelfth book, when he triumphs over evil, consigns the antichrist to one thousand years in the lake of fire, and reunites faithful Christians from across centuries.

To the extent that the *Left Behind* novels depict a series of events, purportedly foretold in Scripture, that lead up to Christ's millennial kingdom, the novels convey a literal, telic, imminent, premillennial apocalypse. At the same time, however, the novels complicate that tradition in part by their form alone: as a series of fiction novels. They map a non-literal story line on top of the biblical predictions they claim to reveal, and that fictional story line demands an analogical or allegorical reading. Because the books' characters—Rayford, Buck, Chloe, and the rest—are not real people, they must be understood as fictional analogues whose lives contain lessons for the Christians who encounter them through the pages of a novel. The serial form of these novels also makes the apocalyptic narrative immanent, especially for serious fans, who read the first novel when it was published in 1996 and awaited each subsequent one until the twelfth was published in 2004 and the surprise thirteenth in 2007; they followed along as this apocalypse unfolded slowly. When consumed in serialized fiction, the apocalypse is not an imminent event to be anticipated; it is, instead, an ongoing drama, in which the reader can participate in the present time.

The *Left Behind* novels also make the apocalypse and millennium immanent and cyclical because they depict a social order sensible and accessible in present-day terms. That is, on top of all their fantastical imagery of flying locusts and blood-flowing rivers, the novels superimpose sociopolitical characteristics analogical to readers' own worlds outside the books. When the books' world resonates with the external world, the apocalypse so evident within the books becomes an immanent apocalypse in readers' lives. Specifically, *Left Behind*'s world order is defined by three binary pairs—good and evil, reality and appearance, and truth and persuasion—just as easily immanent in readers' lives as they are imminent in some future apocalypse.

Good and Evil

The *Left Behind* narrative is set within the "great supernatural war between good and evil," and this very basic divide gives shape to all of the characters' actions.[46] Christ and antichrist exemplify good and evil, but the sharp distinction between good and evil runs much deeper than these two supernatural figures. The antichrist commands an empire of henchmen who also embody evil, and citizens the world over who accept the mark of the beast join the ranks of the evil as well. Profession of faith in Christ secures sanctuary from evil for believers, and it also marks them among the good. From *Left Behind*'s opening scene, this disjunction between good and evil is obvious: in the Rapture, only the good, faithful Christians are taken up into heaven, leaving behind on Earth all those who had been tempted away from Christ by Satan's wickedness.

The disjunction between good and evil only grows stronger as the novels progress. As Nicolae Carpathia rises to power (in books one and two), his evil becomes more apparent. His early talk of global peace and harmony gives way to his penchant for violence and his willingness to kill those who oppose him. Soon, the lines between good and evil are drawn even more sharply as Christians are marked with the sign of the believer (in books three and four), a cross on their foreheads visible only to other believers. The division between the two groups is complete when the antichrist imposes his own mark upon his loyal citizens (beginning in book eight). By the end of the Tribulation, all humans bear either the mark of the believer or the mark of the beast, designating that all of humanity has been divided into good and evil. Jesus then validates these allegiances upon his return when he welcomes the faithful into his family and assigns the unfaithful to hell.[47]

Beyond simply dividing good from evil, the *Left Behind* books show these forces in perpetual contest. The two never enjoy a fair fight because evil is always a goliath force oppressing the slingshot-wielding soldiers of Christ. This disparity reaches its apex at the final battle of Armageddon. There, George Sebastian, the commander of the Christian army, stands at the edge of Petra, and, scanning the forces they face, he acknowledges that "it was just he and his ragtag bunch of earnest, impassioned believers, ringing part of the Petra perimeter with a handful of fairly sophisticated armaments . . . against the largest fighting force in the history of mankind."[48] Lest there be any doubt, Sebastian's observation here makes it clear that Nicolae Carpathia's Global Community forces, which have run the world for seven years, have far more military might than necessary to overtake the last band of opposition they face.

Even while they make Christians the oppressed victims of personified evil, the *Left Behind* books also constantly depict the growing strength of the global Christian community. Indeed, the books nearly fixate on numbers, repeatedly defining the Christian community in terms of its size. Once Tsion Ben-Judah takes over as spiritual leader of the movement, the books note in more than one place that his following quickly grows to more than one billion.[49] In the penultimate minutes before Christ's second coming, Chang, the group's technology expert, monitors people's conversions over the computer, as "tens of thousands every few minutes were totaling in the millions now," and ultimately there are "more than two hundred million martyrs."[50] Throughout the Tribulation, Tsion posts daily messages on what becomes "the most popular Web site in history,"[51] and his subversive television messages are equally popular. He holds all of the television broadcast records, as "nothing Carpathia ever broadcast had come close; in fact, the previous three records had all been held by Tsion Ben-Judah."[52] Even when evil seems an overwhelming foe, Christians can rest assured that they do not fight it alone. In *Left Behind*'s starkly polarized world, Christians can further rest assured that theirs is the God who will protect them from evil.

Reality and Appearance

The polarity between good and evil is buttressed by related disjunctions between reality and appearance and truth and persuasion, which make good and evil easily identifiable. Not only are good and evil clearly distinct, but good can be trusted for its association with the real, whereas evil always operates in the realm of appearances. This dissociation between reality and appearance operates on two levels within the narrative: first, *real* Christians can be distinguished from merely *apparent* ones, and second, those *real* Christians can be further distinguished from Carpathians, who are defined by their *appearances.*

Dissociating real from apparent Christians begins early in the first novel: when the humans left behind on Earth after Christ's Rapture grapple with the nature of the disappearances, they discover that real Christians were raptured and apparent ones were not. The difference becomes apparent in the case of the Steele family, where the mother, Irene, and son, Raymie, are raptured, while the father, Rayford, and the daughter, Chloe, are left behind. Prior to the Rapture, Irene had warned Rayford about Christ's impending return, and Rayford had professed to share her faith, but the Rapture exposes all of them for their true beliefs. Rayford's story matches the experience of the many other apparent Christians who missed the Rapture:

> For years he had tolerated church. They had gone to one that demanded little and offered a lot. They made many friends and had found their doctor, dentist, insurance man, and even country club entrée in that church . . . Rayford . . . even served on the church board for several years. When Irene discovered the Christian radio station and what she called "real preaching and teaching," she grew disenchanted with their church and began searching for a new one . . . Irene's new church was interested in the salvation of souls, something he'd never heard in the previous church.[53]

The Rapture teaches Rayford that the outward signs of faith, such as attending church, were insufficient; Rayford needed the inward spiritual reality of a commitment to Christ. Many others made the same mistake. After the Rapture, the church pastor, Bruce, admits he even "knew that true Christians were known by what their lives produced and that I was producing nothing,"[54] but he continued to live a "phony life of pietism and churchianity for years."[55] As Bruce and Rayford meet more people who were left behind, one after another, they admit to some time before the Rapture spent as apparent Christians. And they all quickly rectify their situations; confessing their sins and professing their faith in Christ, they become real Christians.

The divide between real and apparent Christians endures even after the Rapture, however, as a few people persist with their Christian appearances.

Cardinal Peter Mathews of Cincinnati, for instance, refuses to recognize the Rapture for what it was. An influential religious leader who is widely rumored to be the most popular candidate to succeed the raptured pope, Cardinal Mathews believes that the disappearances were a great spiritual cleansing, leaving behind people possessing the "basic goodness of human-kind."[56] The cardinal also does not object to the global efforts to form one world religion, and he even becomes the leader of the unified religion. Cardinal Mathews never trades in his apparent Christianity for a real pro-fession of faith in Jesus Christ. His apparent Christianity thus serves as a foil for the protagonists' real Christianity—a reminder that, even after the Rapture, true Christianity demands more than appearances.

This reality/appearance divide further distinguishes Christians from Carpathians.[57] Whereas Christians operate in the realm of the real, Carpathia and his followers can never be more than appearances. Their study of Scripture teaches Tribulation Force members that the antichrist necessarily "will appear to be their friend and protector, but in the end he will be their conqueror and destroyer."[58] Indeed, Carpathia offers a compel-ling appearance, so much so that even Christians wish he could be reality: "Every time Buck looked at Carpathia's strong, angular features and quick, seemingly genuine disarming smile, he wished with everything in him that the man was who he appeared to be and not who Buck knew him to be."[59] Like Buck, however, all Christians can see through Carpathia's appearances; indeed, Christians are almost the only ones who can. Another time, when the antichrist tries to prove his own divinity, or at least essential goodness, by referencing his ability to raise the dead, Rayford too recognizes him as appearance.[60] He claims, "The enemy has been known to imitate miracles."[61] But that is all the antichrist ever is—an imitation, an appearance, a surface—never the reality that Christians can trust Christ is and will be.

Truth and Persuasion

Good and evil are further distinguished by their commitments to truth and persuasion, respectively. Whereas Christians have access to the truth, which is pure, holy, and unshakable, the antichrist and his followers rely instead on deceptive persuasion. Carpathia's persuasive capabilities become evident early in his rise to power. He "is young and dashing and all that, charming and persuasive," and his capacity for public speaking enables his rise from a lowly member of the Romanian senate to the president of Romania to the secretary-general of the United Nations to the potentate of the Global

Community within weeks. He wins leadership of the United Nations immediately following the widely acclaimed speech he gives to that body as the newly elected Romanian president. That speech wins admiration, for

> not only did he not use notes, but he also never hesitated, misspoke, or took his eyes off his audience. He spoke earnestly, with passion, with a frequent smile, and with occasional, appropriate humor . . . Carpathia spoke primarily in perfect English with only a hint of a Romanian accent. He used no contractions and enunciated every syllable of every word. . . . He employed all nine languages with which he was fluent, each time translating himself into English.[62]

As he finishes his speech by listing all the United Nations member states by name, Carpathia's delivery was so moving that the representatives of the various nations begin standing in turn, the rest of the assembly applauding each nation, until the whole assembly has risen. When Carpathia displays similar persuasive skills in interpersonal exchanges, well-accomplished men like the brilliant Israeli chemist Dr. Chaim Rosenzweig and the respected journalist Steve Plank fall prey to his persuasion. As Buck explains it: "Steve is a hard-nosed journalist from the old school. That he could be talked into leaving legitimate news coverage to be a spokesman for a world politician shows Carpathia's power of persuasion."[63]

Carpathia is not simply persuasive; he is also deceptive. The *Left Behind* novels consistently couple persuasion and deception, setting them both at odds with the truth. Bruce explains to Buck what the Scripture teaches about the antichrist: "The antichrist is a deceiver. And he has the power to control men's minds. He can make people see lies as truth."[64] Tsion Ben-Judah explains similarly that Satan, who dwells within the antichrist, is "deceiving, persuasive, controlling, beguiling, possessive, oppressive."[65] Christian leaders, by contrast, can be trusted for their truthfulness. The difference between the two is obvious to Buck, who characterizes Carpathia as "choreographed, manipulated," whereas "Bruce wasn't trying to impress anyone with anything but the truth of the Word of God."[66]

The comparison is even starker between Carpathia and the Christian leaders who can transcend communication—the prophets Eli and Moishe, the spiritual leader Tsion Ben-Judah, and Christ himself. These prophets predicted in Scripture, preach day and night without rest or nourishment; they smite any challenger with a ball of fire, and they possess the gift of speaking to every auditor in his or her own tongue. Buck and Tsion Ben-

Judah are amazed to discover that they hear the two witnesses in their own languages—English for Buck and Hebrew for Tsion—and the people standing around them hear the witnesses in Spanish, Norwegian, and other global languages.[67] Even Tsion Ben-Judah is blessed with this power when he speaks to a mass meeting of the faithful at a stadium in Israel; the dozens of translators are suddenly rendered unnecessary when the whole crowd can understand the rabbi in their own languages.[68] And in the final book, when Jesus reappears, he calls to each of his children by name in their own languages. As one of the faithful realizes, "We're hearing Him in our hearts instead of with our ears."[69] Upon Jesus' reappearance, even believers come to understand each other without a shared or spoken language. As Rayford walks through masses of people, a woman comments to him about how full and healthy the trees and bushes look. He understands her even though he only knows English and she claims to be speaking Russian.[70] Such is the virtue of Christian truth: it can be conveyed without language or any form of representation. Evil dwells in the messy realm of representation, where one thing must stand in for another and language becomes an appearance for reality, but Jesus offers Christians the opportunity to escape this slipperiness of representation and the possibility of appearances. Christians' ability to communicate directly to one another's hearts, transcending the realms of communication, persuasion, and appearances, is one more characteristic that distinguishes good from evil.

These three polarities—good and evil, reality and appearance, truth and persuasion—give shape to the world order portrayed in the *Left Behind* series. These polarities, however, are certainly not limited to the world contained within the books; they provide readers with resources for reading the conflicts in their own lives. Armed with *Left Behind*'s framework, readers can understand their theological differences with other Christians, for instance, as a matter of real Christianity versus apparent Christianity. Or they can interpret violence as the product of the cosmic struggle between good and evil. Thus, to the extent that these polarities resonate with readers' lives outside the books, they make the depicted apocalypse analogous to events readers know from their own lives. The apocalypse becomes immanent and cyclical because readers can believe that they live in a world where good battles with evil, truth with persuasion, and reality with appearances. Any time good fights against evil, truth against persuasion, and reality against appearances, Christians can trust that they are living amidst God's unfolding plan for this world.

Muscular Christian Activism

As they make the unfolding apocalypse immanent and cyclical, these binaries also create spaces where humans can exercise agency even in a predetermined world. *Left Behind*'s approach to human agency, or disposition for civic participation, follows directly from these three polarities. The good/evil binary draws such sharp demarcations between social groups that *Left Behind*'s protagonists have little trouble distinguishing enemies from allies. Such clear battle lines give Christians the certainty necessary to emerge as public citizens fully capable of navigating the public sphere as they do God's work on Earth. The reality/appearance binary allows that civic participation to adopt a particularly anti-intellectual disposition because individuals must exchange rational thinking for faith in order to become *real* Christians. Moreover, the truth/persuasion binary, by assuming a transcendent truth that is knowable through faith alone, renders communication useless and thus makes civic participation a non-discursive practice. These three binaries in combination facilitate exactly the disposition of civic participation that *Left Behind*'s characters model: brutish masculinity.

Here I Stand, for I Can Do No Other

Whereas premillennialist discourse generally situates Christians in a tenuous position between their earthly realities and their future roles in a new world order, *Left Behind*'s primary characters are unambiguous about their devotion to doing God's work on Earth. As sad as they are to have missed the Rapture, and as much as they long for the loved ones taken away, the books' protagonists consistently express their dedication to their lives and work in this world. Although these faithful Christians can safely trust that a heavenly reward awaits them in another world, they share a fierce devotion to survive the deadliest earthly battles so that they can continue their work. Chloe and Buck, for instance, make an agreement at the halfway point of the Tribulation; Buck suggests, "Let's watch out for each other, keep each other alive. We've only got three and a half years to go, but I want to make it."[71]

More than just a will to live, time and again these characters express their desire to be involved in the action that defines public life during the Tribulation Era. Not content to spend their days waiting for Christ's return, the protagonists seek out action-oriented ways to realize their faith, starting with the founding of the Tribulation Force. In the first novel, soon after

Pastor Bruce Barnes, Rayford, and Chloe have accepted Christ and started meeting together as a study and support group, they decide to enlarge their collective mission. Bruce explains,

> "I've been praying about sort of an inner circle of people who want to do more than just survive."
>
> "What are you getting at?" Rayford asked. "Going on the offensive?"
>
> "Something like that. It's one thing to hide in here, studying, figuring out what's going on so we can keep from being deceived. . . . But doesn't part of you want to jump into the battle?"
>
> "A cause," [Chloe] said. "Something not just to die for but to live for."
>
> "Tribulation Force," Bruce said . . . "Make no mistake, it won't be fun. It would be the most dangerous cause a person could ever join. We would study, prepare, and speak out. When it becomes obvious who the Antichrist is, the false prophet, the evil, counterfeit religion, we'll have to oppose them, speak out against them."[72]

And just as Bruce describes, from its inception, the Tribulation Force takes on this ambitious mission of fighting back against the antichrist. Buck joins the group soon after its formation, and its ranks continue to swell throughout the Tribulation Era, but its mission remains the same. When the Tribulation Force commits itself to battle-oriented activism, it distinguishes itself from the types of private sphere activism that have typically characterized premillennialist believers, such as prayer, Bible study, and evangelism to loved ones. Although its members continue to do those things, they also make clear that hiding and studying are insufficient forms of activism, especially when their other option is to "jump into the battle."

Throughout the following eleven books, *Left Behind*'s growing ranks of Tribulation Force operatives repeatedly echo the sentiment that drove Bruce and the others to form the group in the first place—they seek escape from their safe houses so that they can wage battle against the antichrist and the forces of evil. The narrator explains of the characters sequestered in hiding, "Each wanted an assignment, something away from the safe house. They wanted to be proactive, not waiting for Nicolae and the GC to be the only ones on the offensive."[73] Chloe and Buck acknowledge together, "We've already declared ourselves. We're enemies of the world order, and we're not going to just sit by and protest in our minds."[74] And when a group of believers tries to dissuade two Tribulation Force members from conducting a jailbreak, the response is clear: "'We are people of faith,' Hannah said . . . 'And we know you are too. We must also be people of action. We know the odds and we accept them.'"[75] These characters certainly get their wish. They are sent all over the globe on missions to transport goods (especially once Christians are excluded from global commerce), sabotage GC plans, conduct jailbreaks, and rescue exposed believers.

Left Behind's protagonists devote their lives to this activism even after it is entirely clear that God ultimately controls all of human history. They watch knowingly as one biblical prediction after another is realized, and yet they still work to bring those events about, rather than sitting idly by and waiting for them to take their course. For instance, based on their Bible study, the characters know that the antichrist will be assassinated halfway through the Tribulation. Book six of the series, *Assassins*, follows three characters—group leader Rayford Steele and two unconverted skeptics, Hattie Durham and Chaim Rosenzweig—as they race around the world trying to be with Carpathia at the moment that he is to be assassinated, so that they might be the one to make it happen. Conceivably, as Hattie and Chaim have not yet converted, they may not fully believe that God's prediction will come true at the appointed hour. But Rayford was the first of the characters to convert, and as he has been consistently faithful, he knows that God's plan will be fulfilled. Yet he has "prayed for the permission, the honor, of being the one assigned to assassinate Carpathia at the halfway point of the Tribulation. Now, truth be told, he found himself to be angling to be in position at that time."[76] Rayford always trusts God's will to run its course, but he wants to play a role in its unfolding. Ultimately, although it is Chaim, a former Carpathia loyalist, who turns against his hero and murders him, Rayford's efforts still set a powerful example of the Christian imperative to work as God's agents in earthly affairs.

Seeking Salvation

Left Behind's possibility for individual agency grows directly out of its theology of salvation, or soteriology. In the *Left Behind* world, salvation is simple, instant, and irreversible. The only requirement for salvation, the only criterion by which humans are judged, is the acceptance of Christ as savior. Rabbi Tsion Ben-Judah teaches his followers that they need only pray:

> Dear God, I know I am a sinner. Forgive me and pardon me for waiting so long. I receive your love and salvation and ask that you live your life

through me. I accept you as my Savior and resolve to live for you until you come again.[77]

This prayer initiates a transaction, in which the believer exchanges faith for salvation. Believers need not prove any special merit or good deeds, nor must they be granted any special favor by God.[78] Following the rabbi's guidance, one character after another intones this simple prayer and receives salvation instantly. Even during the final battle at Armageddon, in the moments before Christ's return, individuals ask for God's salvation. When the mark of the cross appears instantaneously on their foreheads, they have been sealed by Christ. This decision for Christ, like the decision to take the mark of the beast, is everlasting and unchangeable. Rabbi Ben-Judah puts it simply: "The Bible tells us that once one is either sealed by God as a believer or accepts the mark of loyalty to Antichrist, this is a once-and-for-all choice."[79]

Having made that choice, and having been sealed by the mark of Christ, the *Left Behind* Christians might rest easily, assured of their salvation, until Christ's return. But none of them do. Instead, they actively work on God's behalf because their activism is not an effort toward their salvation but the result of that salvation. The group's first pastor, Bruce, explains that many people have been taken by the misconception that being saved "has something to do with doing good and living right. We're going to do that, of course," he assures Rayford, "but not so we can earn our salvation. We're to do that in *response* to our salvation."[80] By this soteriology, the requirements for salvation are simple—confess your sins and profess faith in Jesus Christ—but the demands for faithful discipleship are higher. Blessed by their salvific relationship with God-in-Christ, *Left Behind*'s Christians are called to work as God's agents on Earth.

Soldiers for Christ

As God's agents on Earth, Tribulation Force members are called to perform remarkably battle-oriented activism, framed within the ongoing contest between good and evil. They use the language of war and battle to talk about their work, and they think of themselves as soldiers. When Rayford socializes a new Christian to their shared way of life, he explains that opposing evil (the antichrist) necessarily entails battle. "When you got the mark you became his archenemy," Rayford says, "so now you're on the front lines."[81] After he and the group's doctor rush Hattie to the hospital to deliver her stillborn baby, Rayford refers to their work as "the heat of battle."[82] And when he and Ken fly to Israel to evacuate three trapped Tribulation Force members, Rayford exclaims, "Hoo, boy, back in the battle!"[83] This battle-oriented language is hardly unique to Rayford; even the group's spiritual leader, Tsion Ben-Judah, calls out to a mass rally of the faithful, "We shall be here in Israel two more full days and nights, preparing for battle. Put aside fear!"[84] Given this war-oriented framework, the civic activism that *Left Behind's* characters perform is almost exclusively masculine in nature. This masculinity is particularly brutish, prizing strength, instinct, and courage over rationality and intellect. A persistent anti-intellectualism runs through the books, deriding and disciplining characters who demonstrate any book learning and transforming them into valiant warriors for battle.

The series' anti-intellectualism develops early in the first book and persists throughout the narrative. The characters who miss out on the Rapture were typically well educated and intellectual, and it was always their rationality that precluded them from hearing the truth of God's word. The dichotomy is made clear in the Steele family: whereas Irene was thoughtful and emotional, Rayford was rational. She was "a more emotional, more feelings-oriented person" and "he was brighter—yes, more intelligent," "a technically minded person," "an organized, analytical airline pilot."[85] Even of the two kids, whereas the raptured twelve-year-old Raymie had faith like a child, the left-behind Chloe was a hardened, scholastic Stanford student. Raymie never had "the killer instinct"; he was "too compassionate, too sensitive, too caring."[86] When Rayford tries to persuade Chloe to accept Christ, he has to admit that she gets her rationality from him. Before the Rapture, "he had run everything through that maddening intellectual grid—until recently, when the supernatural came crashing through his academic pretense."[87] Buck, too, was an Ivy League–educated investigative reporter. As he struggles to accept that the disappearances were the product of a supernatural force, he too has to run it past his "cognitive reasoning skills."[88] After missing the Rapture, these characters learn that they have to strip away their "academic pretense" in order to see Christ's essential truth.

The practice of Christian discipleship throughout the Tribulation Era is marked by this absence of intellectualism. Faithfulness demands very little in the way of study, including Bible study, especially for believers who are mature in their faith. In the first two books, as the protagonists are new to the faith, in their "'first love' of Christ,"[89] they devote extensive attention to learning the Scriptures and especially the end-time prophecies. Soon, however, these heroic characters leave all the Bible study to their spiritual leader, Rabbi Ben-Judah, and they remain biblically illiterate themselves. Telling her story of devouring the Bible when she first became a Christian, for instance, Hannah explains that she "started in at the beginning and I loved all those stories in Genesis, but when I got into Exodus, and then— what's the next one?" Someone answers "Leviticus," and Hannah continues, unembarrassed at her ignorance. Later, when Rayford and Chaim encounter a new believer in former news reporter Bernadette Rice, she explains to them that there is one verse that really explains her conversion. It "is the verse that both Dr. Rosenzweig and Dr. Ben-Judah have often quoted—how does it go, Doctor? Something about not wrestling with flesh?"[90] Failing to remember the scripture that explains her conversion, this new Christian is glad to have one of the group's spiritual mentors recite it for her, also exposing no remorse over her biblical illiteracy. These spiritual mentors, in turn, have very low intellectual expectations for their followers. When Tsion preaches to a large group of believers at Petra, he instructs them, "Turn in your Bibles to Zechariah 13. That is the second-to-last book in your Old Testament."[91] Even though he is speaking to people who will fight and die for Christ's cause, Tsion has no expectation that they will know the order of the writings of the minor prophets in the Hebrew Scriptures.

These heroes instead devote themselves to the public work of God's kingdom—going to war against evil—an effort that requires more brawn than brain. Rayford's character sets the standard for that brawn, as he is "a man's man. Six-four and thickly muscled, he had played sports through pain of all sorts."[92] Buck is similarly masculine, and he gets his name because he "bucks" "the traditions and the trends and the conventions."[93] Both Buck and Rayford establish their masculinity at the beginning of the second book when, in back-to-back scenes, they are depicted demonstrating insubordination in their workplaces: Rayford refuses to stand down when he is chastised by his boss for evangelizing to his first officer on the job, and Buck refuses to take the orders of his (female) direct supervisor until she ultimately calls her supervisor, who supports Buck's insubordination. By the most basic character descriptions, these men both show the makings for brutish masculinity.

This brutish masculinity serves them well in the violent, action-oriented missions that drive the plot of the *Left Behind* books. The characters' typical adventures include flying helicopters and fighter jets, running from legal authorities, chasing operatives who have uncovered too much information, and shooting high-powered rifles, grenades, and directed energy weapons; as such, the venerated heroes of these books are the ones who can run, fight, shoot, fly, rewire computer systems, and do other similarly masculine things. On these missions, the heroes consistently commandeer the most sophisticated technology, which they revere for its own brand of masculinity. The story opens with Rayford, while his "fully loaded 747" is "on autopilot above the Atlantic."[94] Later, he flies a 757, which is "different from the huge, bulky feel of the 747, but Rayford managed. When he received clearance, he throttled up and felt the unusually responsive thrust from the aerodynamic wonder."[95] Rayford also gets a refresher on flying a helicopter, which he and Mac McCullum then fly throughout the Middle East. Ken Ritz flies a Learjet, and Albie gets them access to a fighter jet. Buck, although he does not fly planes or helicopters, does buy the most expensive and best-equipped Land Rover ever designed, and he drives assorted Hummers and stolen GC army vehicles on missions. Just like the planes do for Rayford and the other men, these tank-like vehicles become an extension of Buck's masculinity. When he steals a Hummer and drives it for the first time, he celebrates the power it gives him:

> Buck pulled away slowly, the gigantic Hummer propelling itself easily over the jagged terrain. He wanted to get used to the vehicle, the largest he had ever driven. It was surprisingly comfortable, predictably powerful, and—to his delight—amazingly quiet. . . . He couldn't wait to compete with whatever toy the GC was using.[96]

In addition to planes, helicopters, and tanks, Tribulation Force members gain access to equally sophisticated computer equipment. For instance, the group's technology mole secures "handheld electronic organizers" that are "solar powered, satellite connected, and contain geographic positioning chips. You can access the Internet, send and receive, use them as phones, you name it."[97] All of this technology—planes, tanks, computers—is instrumental to the characters' battle missions, through which it becomes an extension of their already-unimpeachable masculinity.

Upon his second coming, even Jesus marches into battle displaying this masculine strength. The books make clear that Christ's ultimate purpose in coming to Earth is to bring peace, but they depict Christ-the-demon-slayer who rules the earth with a "rod of iron,"[98] killing the enemy in droves by his words alone, which are described as "that sword from his mouth," which can "slice through the air, reaping the wrath of God's final judgment."[99] Upon Christ's first words spoken on Earth, tens of thousands of Unity Army soldiers fell dead, simply dropping where they stood, their bodies ripped open, blood pooling in great masses . . . with every word, more and more enemies of God dropped dead, torn to pieces. Horses panicked and bolted. The living screamed in terror and ran about like madmen—some escaping for a time, others falling at the words of the Lord Christ.[100]

Beyond killing the masses simply with his words, this living Christ has come to Earth with a mission to enact vengeance upon all those who have made his followers suffer, especially the antichrist. When he finally comes face-to-face with the five most evil men—the antichrist, his false prophet, and three other "froglike demonic creatures"—Jesus Christ forces them all to bow and proclaim his lordship before sentencing each one. He contends with the trio of demons first, and as he sentences them to death, "their reptilian bodies burst from their clothes and exploded, leaving a mess of blood and scales and skin that soon burst into flames."[101] With regard to the antichrist and the false prophet, Jesus excoriates them for their transgressions, makes them bow down, and sentences them to one thousand years consigned to the lake of fire.[102] Through his ultimate triumph over Nicolae Carpathia, the man who has spent seven years as the most powerful and destructive force the world has ever known, Jesus Christ establishes his total dominion over the earth.

As battle scenes dominate the books' plots, this masculinity becomes the necessary civic activism performed by faithful Christians, which means female characters share in the men's bravado. The women who work for the Tribulation Force, although they sometimes fulfill traditionally feminine roles in the private sphere—nursing and childcare especially—also participate in missions alongside the men. Annie Christopher, for instance, works with David Hassid as a mole inside the GC palace, where they steal equipment and information from Carpathia's operation. Ming Toy Wong works as a prison guard at the GC's women's prison in Belgium until her Christian identity is compromised and she must escape the antichrist's employ. The starring female character—Chloe Steele Williams, the only woman in the core group of Tribulation Force members—takes on one battle-oriented mission after another, her masculine swagger marching in step with the men's. Spirited though Chloe may be in joining Tribulation Force missions, however, her skills always fall short of what is needed to complete a mission successfully. She never performs the masculine tasks quite as well as her male counterparts.

If Chloe had failed to anticipate the Rapture because she inherited too much of her father's rationality, she becomes a valiant soldier for the Tribulation Force because she also inherited his courage. Chloe is "as brave and as strong as the men," so self-assured that, upon meeting Buck, "she looked directly at him and gave a firm handshake," unlike the women who Buck usually meets, who "felt it was feminine to offer a limp hand."[103] She is outspokenly independent, occasionally defiant, and always bent on demonstrating her strength. At the outset of one mission, as she and Buck begin to choose among the cars abandoned in a parking garage, Buck refers to a car with a female pronoun, and Chloe immediately protests his gendering cars female. After a long discussion about cars and other inanimate objects and their genders, Chloe and Buck settle on a Hummer, which Buck notes is a "muscle car," and he suggests they call it Chloe. As is typical, Chloe has spoken her mind, gone head-to-head with one of the men, and ultimately demonstrated her strength.

The spirited Chloe seeks opportunities to participate in the group's missions because, like the other members, "she wanted to be where the action was."[104] Occasionally she persuades the group leader—her father, Rayford—to send her on official Tribulation Force missions, but more often, Chloe invents, engineers, and executes her own missions. On her biggest officially commissioned mission, Chloe travels with Hannah Palemoon and George Sebastian to Greece to rescue two believers whom Buck and Tsion had helped sneak out of prison.[105] Her first individual mission takes her from the group's suburban safe house into downtown Chicago, where she follows a tip about a high-rise that could potentially be used as a safe house.[106] Later, when the group is living in that downtown Chicago office building, Chloe detects a light elsewhere in the desolate core of office buildings, and she sneaks out to investigate it.[107] There, she discovers another group of believers in hiding, whom the Tribulation Force is able to incorporate into their community. Finally, when she and the others are living in yet another safe house in San Diego, during one of Chloe's night watch shifts, she detects movement outside and follows her instincts to discover that GC police are patrolling the surrounding area.[108] Each of these smaller missions parallels the types of missions that the group's men perform on a routine basis. Chloe cannot fly planes or helicopters, and she does not commandeer the large ground vehicles, but she still undertakes missions that require her to run, fight, evade, outsmart, and embarrass GC police.

Lest there be any doubt, however, Chloe's missions always find her wanting as a Tribulation Force operative. During the mission to Greece that she undertakes with Hannah and George, the three are fooled by GC police, who manage to catch and torture George (who ultimately overpowers the GC guards and wins his way out of captivity). Thus, that mission is unsuccessful, and only George's military training saves him. None of Chloe's three solo missions brings unqualified success. In her first mission, Chloe performs a helpful service to the group by scouting and securing a new safe house. Because she foolishly ventures out in the daylight and makes a series of other costly errors, however, Chloe finds herself trapped in downtown Chicago, and her father must come rescue her. Her second mission is equally successful: not only does she locate the source of the light that she has seen, but she finds another group of believers to add to the community. That mission's success is tempered when it turns out that Chloe has endangered her safe house's secrecy. And her third mission's success is even more mixed. Her early discovery of a GC patrol outside the safe house allows the others to escape, but Chloe herself is captured. She faces days of torture in a GC prison and demonstrates her valor by resisting nearly all of the GC's torture devices and refusing to divulge any information about her fellow believers. With an angel's protection, she even resists a truth serum. Living in an all-metal jail cell, with no pure water, Chloe endures full days with less than 250 calories, her cell lights glowing around the clock, the television at full volume blasting lie-filled news stories about her, her family, and her capture, and the incessant playing of the international anthem, "Hail Carpathia." Finally, when she proves totally useless as a prisoner, displaying absolute resilience against her captors, Chloe is sent to the guillotine.

Upon her death, when Chloe is celebrated by Christians the world over as a martyr, she is praised for the same sort of femininity that defined her raptured mother. Unlike the muscular military hero George Sebastian, who endured GC prison tortures and then overcame the prison guards to win his escape, Chloe assumes the martyr's role. Her GC captors subjected her to the most extreme tortures they could devise, knowing that as a leader of the international Christian movement, Chloe had access to all the information they needed to be able to eliminate this band of opposition. Even as the GC officials tried to bargain with Chloe—offering to commute her execution in exchange for information about her family—Chloe protected her father, husband, and son by guarding the secret of their whereabouts, even when it meant sacrificing her own life. She tried to escape by overpowering the guards, but such a display of physical strength was just beyond Chloe's capabilities. Ultimately, for *Left Behind*'s lead female character, performing masculinity—the venerated expression of faithful citizenship—is untenable, and her only recourse is to the femininity that served her mother and other pre-Rapture Christians so well.

Conclusions and Implications

To the persistent question that haunts apocalyptic and millennial theologies—can Christians exercise agency in their predetermined earthly world?—*Left Behind* answers with an unequivocal yes. Because *Left Behind* recasts the traditional literal, linear, imminent premillennialist narrative, so that it is analogical, cyclical, and immanent, individuals exchange their tragic fates for comic possibility. The novels immerse readers in an ongoing, unfolding apocalypse, and they render it in terms analogous to our contemporary sociopolitical reality: good versus evil, reality versus appearance, and truth versus persuasion. Thus, when *Left Behind* depicts faithful Christians doing God's work within this polarized world, the work those characters do is analogous to the work that readers can do within their own immanent apocalyptic world. And the work they do expands beyond securing one's personal future and evangelizing to others—obligations that premillennialism has typically recognized—to include working as God's agents to bring about the events foretold in Scripture. Christians do this work, *Left Behind*'s soteriology implies, not in order to earn salvation, but in response to their salvation. Committing their lives to God in Christ does not allow a resignation to do nothing but trust God; it obligates the believer to work on God's behalf in his or her worldly life. *Left Behind* puts contemporary Christians into a hybrid tragicomic frame, where they must accept the foreordained unfolding of events while they also pursue active participation in those same events.

Left Behind's unique model of civic participation, which I have called brutish masculinity, grows directly out of the three polarities that define its worldview. The good/evil binary organizes the world into discrete factions: the global government that has come to take over the world is "evil" and the citizens who band together to resist that government are necessarily "good." This fundamental binary divides the world into two distinct camps, and its dividing line facilitates the most suitable mode of engagement between the two groups. That is, if there are only two groups of people in the world—good and evil—and if evil is the tragic, irreversible, and essential nature of some people's souls, then the only possible mode of engagement with evil is aggression. If evil cannot be changed into good, and there is no possible middle ground between the two positions, then there is no reason for good citizens to engage the other with any means beyond violence. Unlike other modes of civic participation that might encourage "people to step out from familiar and comfortable situations to encounters in which our beliefs and values will be tested," this polarized worldview leaves no space for "genuinely engaging difference."[109] When the other side's difference is rooted in inescapable, irreversible evil, reform becomes impossible and violence necessary.

The binary opposition does not only lead to brutish masculinity within the confines of the *Left Behind* novels. Instead, this worldview colored U.S. foreign policy at the beginning of the twenty-first century. When the world can be divided into good and evil, and when the unredeemable evildoers threaten the freedom and the existence of "good" people everywhere, then the only possible solution is to eradicate evil from the earth. President George W. Bush proclaimed this approach to foreign policy in the fall of 2001, beginning almost immediately after the attacks on the World Trade Center and the Pentagon. In his September 20, 2001, address to a joint session of Congress, the president famously put the world on notice: "Either you are with us, or you are with the terrorists," he declared.[110] With that simple phrase, Bush divided the world into two clear camps, where "us" signified the defenders of freedom and democracy, who were at war against the "enemies of freedom," those who "hate our freedoms—our freedom of religion, our freedom of speech, our freedom to vote and assemble and disagree with each other."[111] These enemies of freedom bore the face of evil— they were "evildoers"—and enemy nations became the "axis of evil."[112] These clearly drawn battle lines between good and evil produced in our foreign policy a mode of global citizenship that mimics the mode of civic participation produced by that same binary in the *Left Behind* world. Just like the Tribulation Force operatives who model brutish masculinity as the suitable way to engage evil, United States foreign policy has taken on this same swagger. As a manner of global citizenship, brutish masculinity produced wars as its defining acts—conventional wars in both Afghanistan and Iraq, as well as the overarching "War on Terror"—rather than diplomacy, a deed that might have followed naturally from a different manner of global citizenship. The parallelism between U.S. foreign policy and the *Left Behind* novels does not rest on a simplistic view of media effects for its significance; after all, surely the Bush administration does not take its foreign policy cues from fiction novels. Instead, the parallel cases demonstrate how naturally a polarized worldview produces brutish masculinity as a mode of citizenship.

The other binaries that give shape to *Left Behind*'s polarized world also influence its model of civic participation. The disjunctions between truth and persuasion and reality and appearance naturally facilitate a model of citizenship that is both anti-intellectual and non-discursive. The reality/appearance binary develops its salience because of the lurking dangers of intellectualism. That is, prior to the Rapture, intellectualism, or Rayford's "academic pretense," separated real from apparent Christians. Thus, becoming a real Christian requires stripping away that intellectualism in favor of faith. The beauty of the reality/appearance dissociation for believers is that it eliminates the need for thinking, assessing, or judging—especially with regard to the character of other citizens. The moment that citizens become real Christians, they are marked with the seal of the believer on their foreheads, which means that they can and should be trusted, while anyone who lacks that symbol can be assumed to be loyal to evil.

The truth/persuasion binary underscores this anti-intellectualism, while also paving the way for a markedly non-discursive performance of civic participation. This binary renders communication both useless and dangerous. Evil dwells in the realm of persuasion, which is indistinguishable from deception, both of which rely on communication for their powers. Truth, in contrast, is so pure, so clear, so transparent that it does not need the tools of communication or representation in order to be shared among good, faithful Christians. The echoes of Plato ring through here—there is a universal Truth, and it stands opposed to public rhetoric, which is only capable of trickery. There is no possibility for persuasion that is any more virtuous than deception. Unlike Plato, however, the books' proponents of Truth believe that it is simple and self-evident, which renders intellectualism as useless as communication. If ultimately the only truth that matters is Jesus Christ's saving grace, and believers acquire that grace through a one-step transaction, then even the matters of faith require no intellectual work. Thus, this truth/persuasion binary, in association with the reality/appearance binary, is directly responsible for producing the anti-intellectual and non-discursive performance of citizenship that defines *Left Behind*'s characters' actions.

The implications of the truth/persuasion and reality/appearance binaries, plus their attendant unintellectual and non-discursive citizenship, are particularly troubling. Within this worldview, evaluating public discourse rests on discerning the nature of the rhetor—good or evil, reality or appearance—instead of the discourse itself. That is, if *real* Christians have ownership of universal truth, and if they are incapable of producing deceptive persuasion, then their discourse can always be trusted and need not be evaluated on its merits. This type of thinking has certainly already influenced presidential politics, as the authenticity of candidates' faith is tested again and again. During presidential campaigns, when journalists question candidates about their religious beliefs, and when candidates share their personal conversion testimonies or their church attendance records, these exchanges imply that the candidates' character as *real* Christians makes them suitable for office. Their rhetoric becomes more trustworthy because of their character. When the world can be divided into truth and persuasion, and the authentically Christian candidate necessarily operates within the realm of truth, then faithful Christian political participation need only entail discerning the authentic Christian among the candidates. Once the authentic candidate is identified, civic participation need not involve critical listening or judging that person's discourse. Furthermore, if the authentic Christian is elected, then his or her authenticity certifies his or her actions while in office. When George W. Bush claimed to act in God's interest or as God's messenger, the *Left Behind* model of Christian civic participation would entail trusting the president only because he is an authentic Christian; regardless of the merits of his policies, this logic assumes they are trustworthy because the president himself is trustworthy.[113]

The analogies between *Left Behind* and contemporary politics make the novels' model of civic participation troublesome. They show the dangers of an immanent apocalyptic worldview that so easily envisions the world's dark forces irreparably controlled by the antichrist. The dangers of this particular model of civic participation, however, should not take away from the radical contribution that *Left Behind* makes in providing such expansive possibilities for human agency. Breaking with the presiding premillennialist tendency to encourage Christians to surrender obediently to the omnipotent God, and reducing the cognitive dissonance that so often accompanies premillennialist political activism, these books do important work by making the apocalypse immanent, analogical, cyclical, and tragicomic, and by giving humans an active role to play in God's unfolding apocalypse.

5

FEMININE CHARITY, SECULAR SALVATION, AND SOCIAL REFORM

7th Heaven

For you always have the poor with you . . .

Matthew 26:11

For I was hungry and you gave me food, I was thirsty and you gave me something to drink, I was a stranger and you welcomed me, I was naked and you gave me clothing, I was sick and you took care of me, I was in prison and you visited me . . . Just as you did it to one of the least of these who are members of my family, you did it to me.

Matthew 25:35-36, 40

It is surely no more than coincidence that the television family drama *7th Heaven* premiered in 1996, the same year that the U.S. Congress passed the Personal Responsibility and Work Opportunity Reconciliation Act. Yet this coincidence is remarkable. Dismantling the federal welfare bureaucracy and making it harder for families to acquire welfare benefits over an extended period of time, this signature legislation promised to revolutionize the role that private charities and public/private partnerships would play in poverty relief. Welfare reform denied government its prior role as the central arbiter of wealth redistribution and instead called individuals to work through their schools, churches, and other civic organizations to care for the needy in their communities and to foster social reform. A bipartisan effort, this welfare revolution realized President Bill Clinton's vision to "end welfare as we know it," fulfilled components of the Republican Congress' Contract with America, and called citizens to be President George H. W. Bush's "thousand points of light."

Increasing the burden placed on private charities, the welfare reform bill opened the avenues available for religious organizations to participate in poverty relief and social reform. Its Charitable Choice provision enabled state governments to use federal money to fund religious charities on equal terms with nonsectarian ones. Although this provision generated little controversy as part of the welfare reform bill, it attracted public attention during the 2000 presidential election. That year, both major party candidates, Al Gore and George W. Bush, made government funding of faith-based charities planks in their campaign platforms. Then, as president, Bush established the White House Office of Faith-Based Initiatives, which would target private religious charities to receive government resources. Soon after taking office, President Barack Obama announced his intention to continue President Bush's faith-based initiatives.

When 7th Heaven premiered in 1996, it may have received even less public attention than congressional debates over welfare. Its initial low ratings gave little indication that the show would stay on the air for eleven seasons, becoming the longest-running family drama in television history.[1] Indeed, they would have brought certain cancellation on any other network, but 7th Heaven was the property of the fledgling WB network. Desperate to turn its investment into a profit, the new network gave this Aaron Spelling production the time to develop a following and improve its ratings. At the end of the series, 7th Heaven's longevity could again be attributed to network economics. Even after its series finale at the end of the tenth season, 7th Heaven was brought back to life by the newly merged CW network, which needed to anchor its lineup with a few assuredly profitable shows. Over the course of its run, the show reached 41 percent of Americans, as reported by the Baylor Religion Survey.[2] Among religious-themed dramatic television, only Touched by an Angel reached more viewers (57 percent), and that show was broadcast on a big-three network (CBS).

The story of the Camden family—a minister, his wife, and their five (later seven) children—7th Heaven defied the conventions common among the television shows of its era. Whereas other family shows portrayed dysfunctional families (e.g., Roseanne, Married with Children), other religious shows depicted the supernatural (e.g., Touched by an Angel), and other Aaron Spelling productions dramatized hypersexualized teenagers in racy story lines (e.g., Beverly Hills 90210, Melrose Place), 7th Heaven features an agreeable, loving family, whose minister-father espouses nondescript mainline Protestant Christianity, and whose teenage children's occasionally destructive behavior brings sure punishment. From its start, 7th Heaven earned a reputation for family-oriented content and its feel-good aesthetic. The Atlanta Journal-Constitution lauded, "Television has finally fashioned a bona fide modern-day family drama with sit-down meals and Sunday-go-to-church excursions in a watchable hour focusing on the simple problems of every day life."[3] The *New York Daily News* called "inspiration and affirmation . . . the very qualities that characterize this weekly drama."[4] The *New York Times* noted that "family values . . . are bursting out all over the place in this series."[5] Even negative reviews acknowledged these same characteristics. The *Boston Globe*, for instance, complained, "Wholesomeness has its place, but the Camdens are so clean they squeak, achieving an unnerving hyper-normalcy."[6] There is little room to quarrel with these reviews; *7th Heaven* is a touchy-feely family drama featuring predictable story lines consistently resolved to everyone's satisfaction.

The characters themselves are accessible, friendly people who, even if shallow and underdeveloped at some points, are likable nonetheless. The show's patriarch, Reverend Eric Camden (Stephen Collins), is the minister of the Glen Oak Community Church and a fixture in their suburban community. He is an engaged parent who, from the show's pilot, takes his middle daughter's first period as seriously as any of his professional obligations. The show's matriarch, Annie Camden (Catherine Hicks), is a college-educated stay-at-home mom, whose skills extend beyond cooking, cleaning, and advice-giving to include car repair, plumbing, and electrical wiring. At the show's premiere, the Camden kids are high school junior Matt (Barry Watson), high school freshman Mary (Jessica Biel), eighth grader Lucy (Beverly Mitchell), sixth grader Simon (David Gallagher), and pre-kindergarten Ruthie (MacKenzie Rosman).[7] Season three brings the arrival of two new Camdens—twin baby boys, Sam and David (Lorenzo and Nikolas Brino).[8] The Camden kids deal with all of the fixtures of American adolescence, including parties, dances, grades, and maturing bodies. Their emotions run the adolescent gamut: they are giddy and giggly, jealous and jaded, angsty and angry, moody and melodramatic, sad and sentimental. Through it all, the kids maintain a fundamental equilibrium that leaves them balanced as healthy, stable people, whose extreme adolescent emotions are only deviations from that norm.

The show's warm and sunny disposition begins with its setting in Glen Oak, California, where even the weather is consistently warm and sunny. After commercial breaks, the show tends to open with orienting exterior camera shots, which, when daytime, always, without exception, reveal a clear, sunlit sky.[9] These exterior images of Glen Oak also depict it to be a place characterized by tranquility and abundance. The common image of the Camden family home is often preceded by a visual pan of their wide, tree-lined street, where cars drive slowly and neighbors jog and bike along the sidewalk. The deciduous trees are always leafy and green, and the Camdens' lawn, like those of their neighbors, is perfectly manicured. Other exterior images orient viewers to the church, the kids' schools, and other local community establishments such as "the promenade," the cluster of shops and restaurants where the teenagers and their parents socialize. Shots of the church often begin with the spire of the steeple and work their way down, revealing a modest, traditional brick structure. Interior visual images underscore the tranquility and abundance evident in the community. After the show's opening sequence and credits, it often reopens with an exterior shot of the Camden home and then an interior image montage in the family kitchen. These image montages frequently pan counters full of food, where one member of the Camden family—often Annie, the mother, but occasionally one of the others—prepares a meal. If the meal is breakfast, the counter will be filled with fresh fruit, bagels, and orange juice. If the meal is dinner, the kitchen counters might be a staging area for a luscious salad, filled with lettuce, cucumbers, tomatoes, onions, avocados, and other vegetables. The lighting in the Camden kitchen is bright, the ceilings high, and the décor warm, making it a friendly and inviting space.

Glen Oak itself is a welcoming place for a minister's family. The kids never find their religion an object of scorn or derision. They are never discriminated against because of their faith, nor do they ever find their religious tradition under siege by secularism or other religious groups. Their church is the center of community life, and their father's community standing is derived largely from his status as a minister. Because many of the kids' peers participate in the church, being a minister's kids does not even hurt their social lives. Simon and his friend Luke, for instance, encounter the hottest girls in their class, the Murphy twins (played by Mary-Kate and Ashley Olsen), during the cookies-and-punch time after a Sunday service.[10] In another episode, two cute guys pursue Lucy in the halls of the church on a Sunday morning.[11] The Camdens' closest friends, the Hamilton kids, are also the children of a minister, who pastors another church in town.[12] Only occasionally does the kids' religious standing inhibit their social lives. For instance, Matt and Simon both get teased as "preacher boy" upon occasion.[13] And Lucy and Mary lament that, as long as their dad's a minister, they will never have call waiting or call forwarding or a fax machine—minor inconveniences for their family's very public declaration of faith.[14]

Within sunny and friendly Glen Oak, where the Camden family is loved and respected, many of the show's story lines revolve around the most mundane of family issues. For instance, Matt, upon being named class valedictorian, must decide whether to leave early for his summer internship or stay to deliver his speech at graduation.[15] Mary, a talented high school basketball player, asks the family not to attend her games, only to relent later.[16] Lucy must learn geometry well enough to navigate the school halls efficiently before her geometry teacher steals her lunch.[17] Simon negotiates peace between the bullies and the geeks on his school bus by convincing the geeks to help the bullies with their homework.[18] Ruthie competes with her friend and classmate Lynn for the affections of their substitute teacher.[19] Beyond intervening in these dilemmas of their kids' lives, Eric and Annie occasionally have their own concerns. Annie deals with the death of her mother, her father's remarriage, and his ultimate diagnosis with Alzheimer's disease.[20] Eric struggles to write a sermon under the pressure of his church service being televised to the local community.[21] These story lines are mundane but not trivial, and their sheer familiarity surely makes the show accessible to a broad audience.

On top of these very typical teenage and family issues, what sets *7th Heaven* apart from standard television fare are its religious themes and its sustained commitment to address difficult and sensitive social issues. The show consistently portrays controversial topics that other programs largely avoid, and it depicts its characters actively involved in efforts to solve these social issues. In the first six seasons alone, *7th Heaven* devotes episodes to the topics of teenage pregnancy, racism, mental illness, drug addiction, domestic abuse, learning disabilities, alcoholism, divorce, poverty, old age infirmities, foster care, homelessness, epilepsy, suicide, criminal rehabilitation, murder, gang violence, childhood terminal illness, the Holocaust, autism, the war on terror, fraternity hazing, self-mutilation, organ transplants, veterans' benefits, gun violence, kidnapping, anti-Muslim discrimination, sexual harassment, pet death, gender roles, Japanese-American internment reparations, rape and molestation, and Tourette's syndrome. Some of these issues recur more than others, with domestic violence, poverty, alcoholism, divorce, and teenage sex and pregnancy being the most common. In every case, members of the Camden family alleviate the suffering of a person struggling with one of these social issues. Eric does so out of his professional obligation as a minister, but his social reform ethic carries over into his and Annie's parenting, and the Camden family works together as a mobile social reform unit. Sometimes they alleviate poverty by reconciling families, other times they help drug addicts find rehabilitation resources, and still other times they rescue children from their abusive parents. In every case, the social issue in question enters the Camdens' universe only momentarily, and the fundamental equilibrium of the family and the community is easily righted again by the issue's resolution.

Through its abiding attention to these social ills and their ameliora-tion, *7th Heaven* embodies the discursive and ideological shifts characteris-tic of the post-welfare era. The show articulates the fundamental skepticism toward government bureaucracy that facilitated welfare reform. Moreover, it models the type of charitable civic participation necessary to ensure service provision and social reform in a post-welfare world. It depicts citizens as car-ing, thoughtful community members who provide for the needy people in their communities. In doing so, *7th Heaven* provides counterevidence to the pronounced skepticism over private charities' capacity to fulfill the service provision role once performed by government and their ability to do so without threatening religious freedom.

7th Heaven further models post-welfare ideology because its ideal of civic participation bridges the public and private spheres. The show's pri-mary model of social service provision, Rev. Camden, performs his civic duties as an extension of his professional obligations, which are grounded in the domestic sphere and characterized by the feminine norms typical of that sphere. Through his and Annie's frank discussions of parenting, the show also models the most domestic activity of childrearing as a form of civic participation. Bridging the public and the private, *7th Heaven* inti-mates that the solution to public social problems, such as poverty, lies in the private sphere.

SOCIAL REFORM IN THE POST-WELFARE ERA

Welfare reform accompanied a number of discursive and ideological trans-formations in American politics, as Robert Asen has documented. He claims that during the early-1990s welfare debates, the popular image of the welfare recipient shifted from the contract signee to the ward of the state.[22] In the popular imagination, welfare recipients became needy children, for whom the government was asked to provide care. Legislators also inspired antipa-thy toward the old welfare system by describing welfare recipients' abuses of the system, invoking the costs imposed by immigrants, and praising the potential of American voluntarism to solve the social ills welfare had been unable to solve. Asen describes how Robert Sirico's congressional testimony during the welfare debate articulated this last justification in specifically religious terms. He promoted the merits of faith-based organizations provid-ing poverty relief on the grounds that they could, unlike the government, develop personal relationships with recipients and could serve as moral teachers. If the welfare state had discouraged this sort of religious charity, he argued, scaling back the federal welfare bureaucracy would renew it.

Marvin Olasky's *The Tragedy of American Compassion* provided the perfect complement to Sirico's testimony; whereas Sirico made his argument only to Congress, Olasky reached a popular audience, and whereas Sirico relied primarily on religious grounds, Olasky provided religious and historical rationales. Although Olasky's book realized only obscurity upon its initial publication in 1992, his ideas became a guiding force for welfare reform when, in 1995, former secretary of education William Bennett passed along a copy of the book to incoming speaker of the house Newt Gingrich, who in turn distributed it to all the House freshmen.[23] The book inspired a small group of Republican politicians to call themselves "compassionate conservatives," the moniker ultimately popularized by George W. Bush's 2000 presidential campaign.

For Olasky, the "tragedy of American compassion" is that we have replaced the successful private, charity-based poverty amelioration efforts common to this nation's first two centuries with the twentieth-century government-led New Deal and Great Society programs. Whereas those early programs inspired work and personal reform on the part of the recipients, the latter programs only bred dependency and entitlement. The early programs, because they recognized the fallen, sinful, or at the very least fallible nature of humans, sought to reform the individuals who populated the poor houses and the soup kitchens. The latter programs, however, began with what Olasky calls Social Universalist assumptions, that all humans are good and only a broken system inhibits their development; these assumptions have directed undue attention toward fixing the system.[24] The early programs held the possibility of ameliorating poverty because they allowed individuals to reform themselves, but the latter programs obliterated social mobility, ensuring that welfare recipients and their children would remain welfare recipients.

The success of early charitable efforts, Olasky argues, can be attributed to "the seven marks of compassion": affiliation, bonding, categorization, discernment, employment, freedom, and God. By affiliation, he refers to those programs' primary strategy of seeking out a needy person's natural affiliations, the family members and neighbors who should care for that person in place of the state or charity. If such affiliations are not available, a charity would engage in bonding, or linking needy individuals with families capable of caring for them. For instance, teenage boys abandoned on the crowded urban streets were sent to live with rural families who could incorporate the boys' labors into their farm-based economy. Third, early charity efforts attended to categorization; that is, dividing aid seekers between the worthy and unworthy poor, they only rewarded aid to the worthy poor, who were unable to support themselves or who only needed temporary assistance due to disastrous circumstances. This categorization depended upon discernment, which required charity workers to have such personal relationships with the impoverished of their neighborhoods that they could identify the worthy and unworthy poor. These early charity efforts also stressed employment, finding means of paying work for employable men wherever possible. Additionally, they prized freedom, by which Olasky refers to the freedom to work, a right that government subsidies to the poor inhibit.[25] Finally, these charitable efforts offered aid recipients access to God. More than simply fulfilling material needs, charities recognized and responded to spiritual ones, providing religious instruction and the opportunity for personal salvation in many cases. Olasky bemoans goverment welfare because its scale prevents it from engaging the first four marks of compassion, and the establishment clause makes the seventh unconstitutional. Thus, Olasky advocates shifting the burden to private charities precisely because those groups are capable of developing personal relationships with needy people as well as fostering moral and spiritual development.

Ultimately, Olasky's vision won out, and when the Republican Congress passed welfare reform and the Democratic president signed it into law, Americans of all political orientations were left to imagine new ways to care for the poor as well as alleviate other social problems, such as alcoholism, teenage pregnancy, and high school dropouts. The Clinton administration found one clear articulation of this position in First Lady Hillary Rodham Clinton's book and book tour, *It Takes a Village*, which remains a useful statement of liberal post-welfare ideology.[26] Although Clinton's book focuses on child health and touches on related social problems only by extension, she proposes the same types of voluntarism that Olasky praises. She does entertain a larger role for government in social reform than Olasky does, but she also recognizes its limitations and espouses family- and charity-based solutions in harmony with Olasky's "seven marks of compassion." Clinton fashions her position as a middle ground between, on the one hand, big government liberals who trust the state to solve all economic and social problems and, on the other hand, anti-government conservatives who became so frustrated by government's failure to solve those very problems that they "began to believe government itself was the problem."[27] In partnership with government, Clinton invests faith in families and communities as the institutions with the capacity to support and nurture healthy children. She asserts, "Home can—and should—be a bedrock for any child. Communities can—and should—provide the eyes and enforcement to watch over them, formally and informally. And our government can—and should—create and uphold the laws that set standards and safety for us all."[28]

Among the community institutions that Clinton charges with looking out for the well-being of America's children are religious organizations of all faiths. Noting studies that demonstrate that kids who regularly attend religious service are less likely to use drugs, Clinton urges that all kids be given the opportunity to participate in a religious community.[29] "Churches, synagogues, mosques, and other religious institutions," she explains, "not only give children a grounding in spiritual matters but offer them an experience in leadership and service roles where they can learn valuable social skills."[30] When those kids go on to become leaders working for the betterment of their own communities, those skills serve us all well.

In the years following welfare reform, a chorus of voices would join Sirico's, Olasky's, and Clinton's calls for fostering voluntarism and charity. George W. Bush announced his faith-based initiative in a July 1999 campaign speech, and Al Gore's campaign quickly countered that its candidate had also made similar proposals.[31] Then Bush made government funding for faith-based charities a marquee issue in his 2000 campaign and a hallmark of his early administration. On a wide range of issues—"problems like addiction and abandonment and gang violence, domestic violence, mental illness and homelessness"—faith-based charities can do much of the work that government has failed to do, Bush asserted.[32] According to the president, these charities "provide more than practical help to people in need. They touch and change hearts."[33] They do so because they reach needy men and women on an individual level, in a personalized manner. Less than a month into his presidency, Barack Obama reinstated Bush's program as the White House Office of Faith-Based and Neighborhood Partnerships, under the leadership of Pentecostal minister Joshua DuBois. In the midst of massive government bailouts and a trillion-dollar stimulus package, Obama acknowledged the ongoing role of private charities in economic recovery. "There is a force for good greater than government. It is an expression of faith, this yearning to give back, this hungering for a purpose larger than our own, that reveals itself not simply in places of worship but in senior centers and shelters, schools and hospitals, and any place an American decides," the president said.[34] Under both Democratic and Republican administrations, private charities have become a mainstay of the American social safety net.

As it promotes charitable organizations, this post-welfare discourse implies a revised model of civic participation. After welfare reform, citizens are no longer simply taxpayers whose wealth is redistributed by government bureaucracy; instead, the social safety net and the possibility for social reform depend on citizens giving voluntarily to charity. And more than just funding charities, the post-welfare model of civic participation encourages citizens to interact with the needy personally; to embody Olasky's marks of compassion, such as affiliation, bonding, and discernment; and to provide spiritual witness in addition to material sustenance. They must be Bush's "unsung heroes who do heroic acts on a daily and hourly basis."[35] They must be the men and women whose work Bush praised when he spoke at the Fishing School on the day he submitted his faith-based services proposal; because of them, "real change happens street by street, heart by heart, one soul, one conscience at a time."[36]

Religious leaders were quick to point out, as early as the 1994–1995 welfare debates in Congress, the potential limitations of volunteer-led charities to replace government welfare. Asen recounts how leaders of the largest and most influential religious charities, such as Fred Kammer of Catholic Charities USA, provided congressional testimony describing the constraints of their already-overburdened agencies.[37] Such concerns reached the press and were widely reported in newspapers across the country.[38] Although these charities were already providing millions of dollars worth of in-kind relief every year, they were stretched thin simply trying to compensate for the shortcomings of the existing welfare system. They were hardly equipped to respond to the fallout from massive rollbacks in that system. In the *Washington Post*, Laurie Goodstein reported Kammer's and others' fears that their agencies would find themselves unable to cope with the exponential growth in need prompted by welfare reform. She elaborated, for instance, upon the success of Rev. George Clements' One Church, One Child and One Church, One Addict programs, in which churches adopted individuals in need, but exposed his fear that such programs could never adopt all the needy families abandoned by welfare.

Other opinion leaders, religious and secular alike, expressed concern about whether Charitable Choice's government funding of religious organizations would threaten the constitutional separation of church and state. The problem was not entirely new; some large organizations like Catholic Charities USA had long relied on federal grants. Those organizations had accepted those grants, however, promising to conduct charity work free of religious bias or evangelizing. Charitable Choice, sponsored by Republicans Robert Dole and John Ashcroft, promised to loosen those restrictions. Religious agencies would be allowed to promote their sectarian creeds while doling out government-sponsored aid.[39] To ward against the establishment of religion, states disbursing some of their block grants to religious groups would have to ensure that those services were also available from nonsectarian groups. Providing aid to the needy in a secular, or at least ecumenical, fashion was just one of many challenges facing private charities in the wake of welfare reform.

7TH HEAVEN'S ARMY OF COMPASSION

In the midst of this national debate fixated upon both the promise and the uncertainty of volunteer-based religious organizations, *7th Heaven* offered a popular image of successful religious charity. By the show's depiction, Americans are capable of the model of civic participation demanded by welfare reform. Reaching out to the needy in their communities, individuals, especially Christians, can solve social problems such as poverty, divorce, and domestic violence by their own initiative. *7th Heaven* thus provides an optimistic portrayal of faith-based charity and volunteerism that was particularly reassuring in its post-welfare era.

Government Problems

In harmony with prevailing sentiments of the post-welfare era, *7th Heaven* conveys explicit skepticism of government's power to combat social ills. More than once, the show's story lines introduce problems that have either been created or compounded by government or, at the very least, that government has failed to solve. The government is most clearly a failure when it becomes the source of a social problem—in one clear case, poverty. In a second season episode, called "Red Tape," Eric encounters an elementary-school-aged boy named Clarence at the local food bank.[40] When Eric follows Clarence home, he discovers that Clarence and his mother live in terrifying poverty, even though she works full time as a high school teacher and part time as a waitress. Her wages, unfortunately, are garnished by the IRS because of back taxes owed by a former husband who left her saddled with his debt. The IRS, so incompetent in its bureaucracy—hence the episode title—has not been able to relieve this hard-working woman of this so clearly undeserved economic burden.

In another case, government was the source of a problem, which it later further exacerbated. When Eric's church receives a surprise gift of $20,000 from a member, he investigates to discover that an older woman, Sachiko, was simply passing along money that she had received as part of the government's reparations to Japanese internment victims.[41] She describes the horror of her childhood experience in an internment camp—having to live in a horse stall while her brother fought for the army of the same country that interned her—before concluding that she cannot accept what she considers "blood money" from the government. Eric listens sympathetically to her account of the internment and reparations, never challenging her interpretation of the government's original sin or of the reparations as blood money, implicitly agreeing that the government was wrong.[42]

Similarly, in a third-season episode, the family's interaction with a veteran named Millard further confirms their skepticism toward government handouts.[43] Annie finds Millard sitting outside the grocery store, homeless, in need of a shower and shave. When she brings Millard home, Eric investigates the type of veteran's administration support owed to Millard, only to discover that Millard is not interested in such government provisions. He is a self-reliant man happy to live on his own. Besides, as he describes to Eric and Annie, he has learned that he need not look to the government when there are plenty of kind citizens like the Camdens who will welcome him into their homes for a shower, shave, and meal when necessary. Millard's lesson for the Camden family is that self-reliance and neighborly spirit in proper doses can, and should, obviate government assistance.

The only significant exception to the show's fundamental skepticism toward government comes in its enduring respect for the police and the criminal justice system. Government may not be able to solve most problems, but the Camdens certainly respect the law, and they show high regard for the men and women who police illegal behavior. One of the most frequently recurring characters outside the Camden family is Sergeant Michaels, an officer on the local police force. Sergeant Michaels intervenes with the force of the law whenever Eric's work alone cannot solve a problem. For instance, when Eric rescues a female parishioner, Abby, from an abusive husband, and that abusive husband later angrily confronts Eric and Abby, Sergeant Michaels arrives to take the man away in handcuffs.[44] Another time, when Eric and Matt meet their friends Morgan and John Hamilton for lunch and the restaurant refuses to serve the Hamiltons because they are African American, Sergeant Michaels, who is himself African American, threatens the restaurant manager with legal action if he continues to refuse service.[45]

Aside from their profound respect for law enforcement officers, however, the Camdens have little need for government to confront social problems that well-meaning citizens are fully capable of solving.

Charitable Volunteerism

If individual citizens are capable of solving these social problems, the members of the Camden family are eager to help. Not only does the show pose one difficult social issue after another, but the characters express clear enthusiasm for personally contributing to their resolution. The father, Rev. Camden, is consistently characterized as a problem solver whose profession gives him the resources and skills to combat social ills. In a first-season episode, a pajama-clad teenage Matt comes into the kitchen to find his parents eating breakfast, and he gently chides them, "Solve the problems of the world yet?" Eric's answer—"No, but it's still early yet"—is only mildly sarcastic.[46] He and Annie and Matt all let on that the Camdens do devote their days to solving those problems. In another episode later that season, when Eric stops at home briefly, only to rush off again to confront a deadbeat dad, Annie teases him for being Superman. Looking down at her laundry basket, she remarks, "I think I have your cape in here somewhere, but you're on your own for the phone booth," to which Eric replies modestly, "I think my powers may have been overrated."[47] Of course, his powers have not been overrated: Eric's confrontation with the father is so successful that the man is inspired to catch up on his child support payments and recommit himself to his relationship with his daughter. Other times, Eric acknowledges his unique problem-solving abilities. When a parishioner wants him to confront the teenager who murdered her husband, Annie questions whether or not Eric will be able to get in to see the kid. Eric confidently responds, "Please. Me? I can do anything."[48] Eric's parishioners expect that their pastor will engage in this community work because they perceive it as part of the job they pay him to do. Once, when he is late for a church committee's meeting, one member of the group comments that Eric's tardiness is good because it suggests that the reverend is out working in the community, which is his gift.[49]

Rev. Camden hardly approaches these social problems alone; his wife and kids routinely join his charitable work. For instance, the youngest kids (in season one), Simon and Ruthie, are watching television when they see the breaking news that a neighboring church has been destroyed by racially motivated arson.[50] After they call the family together to watch the news report, Simon immediately asks, "What are we going to do?" Eric confirms his son's instinct, saying he does not yet know how they will respond, but they will. The Camdens collectively, following their patriarch's lead, are problem solvers, and they never hesitate to intervene when their work might combat a social ill or a community member's personal problem.

The most common episode structure, especially in the earliest seasons of *7th Heaven*, is for three to five story lines to run concurrently, one of which features a character from outside the Camdens' immediate family. That outside character either seeks out help from one of the Camdens or ends up the unwitting recipient of help from them. Sometimes this character is a member of the Camdens' extended family, such as Eric's sister Julie; other times this character is a member of the church congregation, such as the elderly ladies Mrs. Bink and Mrs. Hinkle, who recur across episodes; other times this character is a classmate of one of the Camden kids, such as a pregnant teenager befriended by Matt; and other times this outside character is simply a member of the Glen Oak community, such as an orphan named George who shows up in Eric's office. They enter the Camdens' universe with a wide range of problems—from divorce to alcoholism to depression to grief—and in nearly every case, the Camdens provide resources to alleviate the problem. Although Eric usually takes the lead in these community outreach narratives, all of the members of the Camden family take their turns helping him. Very often, one of the kids will introduce a needy friend to the family, and that kid will work with Eric to help the friend.

The prototype of this plotline is evident in the second episode of the very first season.[51] At first, Matt is secretive about a new friend who has been needing his help. When Annie calls Matt's bluff by subversively inviting this new friend, Renee, over to dinner, the whole family discovers that Renee is a pregnant teenager. As Matt explains it to Eric, Renee only had sex once, and as Renee explains to Annie, she and her boyfriend had used protection. Renee is, it seems, the victim of poor decisions and bad luck. Eric expresses to Matt that he is proud of him for befriending someone in need, but he reminds Matt that what Renee really needs is support from her parents and the baby's father. So, while Annie sets Renee up with childbirth classes, Eric seeks out her parents and the baby's father. Eric learns that Renee's mother ran off years ago, and he is initially unsuccessful with Renee's father, who refuses to speak to him. He is more successful with the baby's father, who takes Eric's lead on a job opportunity and secures the job. At the episode's conclusion, as Renee sings a solo in Sunday morning's church service, both her father and the baby's father are there to see her perform, and the two choke back tears as she does so. This episode displays the most typical elements of this basic plot structure: a member of the family brings home a needy person from the community. Together, Camden family members (in this case, three of them—Eric, Annie, and Matt) work together to provide resources to the person in need, and by the end of the episode, the problems have been resolved. Most of the time, these outside characters never appear again.[52]

Individual Solutions

For the wide range of social issues *7th Heaven* addresses, they are consistently framed in a remarkably similar way: as individual problems, experienced by individual citizens, which can be solved by individual volunteers. Whether an episode deals with alcoholism or divorce or teenage pregnancy, this complex social problem is always rendered in individual terms from the perspective of the character experiencing the problem at hand. Because these problems are solved by individual charitable efforts, their resolution displays Olasky's first four marks of compassion—affiliation, bonding, categorization, and discernment.

In the episode described above, the problem of teenage pregnancy is portrayed in clearly individual terms—through the story of this one teenage girl and her father and her boyfriend. This narrative exposes some of the problems that teenage pregnancy might produce for the individuals involved, such as abandonment and poverty. It also exposes the individual shortcomings that might lead to such a problem, such as the failure to use birth control correctly. It does not, however, address teenage pregnancy as a social phenomenon that might have collective bases or outcomes. It does not address collective bases such as media images, inadequate sex education curricula, and sexism, nor the collective outcomes of teenage pregnancy such as poverty, low birth weight infants, and increased high school dropout rates. *7th Heaven* treats other social problems in equally individualized terms. The frequent episodes about domestic violence typically treat only the personal problems created by this issue, such as the unsafe environments in which abused children live. One episode gives minor attention to the role that child abuse might play in creating more child abusers, and another demonstrates how sexist music might inspire violence toward women.[53] They still ignore so many other possible systemic causes of child abuse, such as poverty and lack of parent education and role models, as well as the social problems that it can create, such as an epidemic of teenage runaways and dropouts. Plus, treating each of these social issues separately, *7th Heaven* never shows how they might be interrelated, how child abuse and teenage pregnancy and poverty and low self-esteem and sexism might all be mutually reinforcing causes and results of each other.

Because these social issues are presented in such individual terms, they can also be solved in individual terms. The Camdens can solve teenage pregnancy by helping one needy girl rather than having to fight the state legislature to reform the sex education curriculum, for instance. They can solve domestic violence by removing a victimized child from his family rather than pressuring local officials to enforce existing laws. Dealing with these problems on individual terms, the Camdens' best resources are the strategies that Olasky called the "marks of compassion": affiliation, bonding, categorization, and discernment. Because the Camdens get to know so many needy people personally, they can easily discern what types of resources the various individuals need and deserve. Through their conversations with Renee, Eric and Annie can discern that she is simply an unfortunate teen whose problems are the result of poor decisions and bad luck. Because they know her personally, Eric and Annie can also pursue the strategies of affiliation and bonding. Eric seeks out her natural affiliations—her father and her baby's father—and he also welcomes her into the larger church community (which Olasky would call bonding).

Fostering affiliation and bonding is surely the most common charitable strategy the Camdens pursue, especially when they help the youth of their community. The clear majority of needy individuals introduced into the Camden family are children and teenagers—not only poor kids, drug-addicted kids, and pregnant kids, but also kids with learning disabilities, mental illnesses, gang affiliations, and other problems. In nearly every one of these cases, Eric or occasionally Annie immediately seeks out the child's parents. For instance, when Simon's friend Stan sleeps over at the Camden home, Eric and Annie discover that his nightmares stem from his fears about his sister's involvement in a gang.[54] Eric approaches Stan's parents, who are initially skeptical that their daughter, Karen, might belong to a gang. With some prodding from Eric, however, they do enough investigation into their kids' lives to discover that Stan's reports and Eric's instincts were correct, that Karen has joined a gang and is hiding a stash of weapons in their home. Although Karen initially refuses to accept Eric's and her family's offers to help her leave the gang, saying she can get out herself, her traumatic hospitalizing injuries from a gang fight later force Karen to realize that she needs the support of the minister and her family. In this case, like in so many others, Eric does not simply help the troubled person alone.

Instead, he intervenes with her and her whole family, nurturing the affiliations that can help solve her problem.

Although Eric always tries affiliation first, although he always seeks out the family members immediately responsible for a troubled individual, sometimes these family ties prove impossible to reconnect. In those cases, Eric routinely tries to establish alternate bonds. For instance, of the many teenage mothers that the Camden family encounters, one is a young woman named Theresa, whom they meet when she steals Matt's car—a crime she was desperate enough to commit because she was abandoned, alone, and poor.[55] At the same time, Eric has been counseling a parishioner, Elizabeth, who lost her son in a tragic accident not long before. Eric has tried to console her by introducing her to an organ transplant recipient, Carolyn, because Elizabeth and her husband had donated their son's organs upon his death. Ultimately, because it is clear that the pregnant Theresa's father will not relent and let her back into his life, Eric also introduces Theresa to both Elizabeth and Carolyn. Announcing that "it takes a village," the three form a bond that leads Theresa to move in with Elizabeth, and both Carolyn and Elizabeth look after Theresa while she awaits the baby.

Similarly, in a season five episode, the Camden family commits an act of bonding that takes a sacrifice on their part. Upon finding him homeless and alone, Eric invites Mary's ex-boyfriend Robby first to stay with the Camden family and ultimately to live with them.[56] Just months earlier, Robby had been chastised by the Camden family for cheating on Mary and trying to manipulate her into having sex with him. When Eric discovers that Robby's girlfriend has kicked him out and his mom has moved across the country without him, all while Robby was trying to go to school and develop into a responsible adult, the Camdens welcome him into their home. They adopt the strategy of bonding—creating new family ties—because affiliation is no longer possible.

Individual Victims

These strategies of affiliation and bonding are available because *7th Heaven* individualizes these social problems. They are *appropriate*, however, because of the way the show portrays human failings. When Olasky praises nineteenth-century Christian charities, he appreciates that those organizations understood human beings' sinful nature and the need for personal salvation and reform in order to solve poverty and social decay. He blames "social universalist" assumptions—beliefs that humans are fundamentally good and their failings can be blamed on unjust social structures—for the creation of failed government welfare systems. *7th Heaven* does not adopt either of these outlooks precisely; it tends to see individuals as mistaken or as the victims of other people's mistakes, or occasionally as the victims of larger structures, typically the government. Instead of assuming that the people in need are fundamentally bad or unredeemable, the reverend preaches, and the members of his family and community understand, that people are basically good and try to do good as much as possible, but that sometimes we all fall short. In one episode, when Ruthie asks why people do things that they know are wrong, Annie explains to her that she thinks "everybody does the best they can for whoever they are at each and every moment; unfortunately, sometimes who they are is a totally unconscious person, not thinking about right or wrong or the consequences of their actions."[57] Ruthie, admitting her recent wrongdoing, agrees with Annie and explains that "being good is a full time job and I just dozed off for a minute." Just as the Camdens recognize their own occasional mistakes as aberrations from their fundamental nature, they also give friends and community members the same benefit of the doubt.

Many of the problems encountered on *7th Heaven* either result from, or have been exacerbated by, the brokenness of an individual family. Children in particular become the victims of their families' dysfunction. For instance, when Lucy and Eric discover that Lucy's classmate Suzanne is poor, they also learn that her poverty is caused by her father's failure to pay child support, which is in turn caused by his own hurt feelings when Suzanne chose her mother over him in the divorce.[58] When Eric and Annie confront a teenage boy who is threatening to jump off of a building, their extensive negotiations with the boy reveal that his desperation was prompted by his belief that his mother failed to listen to him.[59]

Because these problems are so often caused by temporary failures of an individual or by family conflict, their resolution involves either an individual's recommitment to core values of clean, healthy living or a family's commitment to resolve its conflicts. In the case of drug addict Terry Daniels, Eric's pleading with him over the course of an episode does little good.[60] Terry insists that he does not need more rehab, that he was wise to check himself out of rehab previously, and that he is happy with his life on the streets. At the end of that episode, however, when Terry shows up on the Camdens' front porch with his face battered and bloody, it is clear that he has learned a lesson and is ready to straighten up his life. Many other episodes end with a family confronting the source of its conflict. For instance, when Eric confronts Suzanne's deadbeat dad, he is initially unable to convince the dad to pay what he owes in child support.[61] Instead, Eric wins the dad's money at pool, but when he goes to deliver it to Suzanne and her mother, Suzanne's dad meets him there, wanting to pay the child support himself. Suzanne and her mother's poverty, it seems, can be solved as long as their family can repair its brokenness. When poverty, addiction, and other problems result from individual mistakes, repairing for those mistakes resolves the larger problem.

Secular Salvation

Because human problems result from bad decision making, rather than an inherently sinful nature, appeals to individual reform are rare, and suggestions of religious-oriented reform, such as Christian salvation, are nonexistent. Even though *7th Heaven*'s chief problem solver is a minister, the assistance that he and the members of his family dole out to needy individuals is remarkably nonreligious, requiring nothing of its recipients in the way of religious faith, conversion, or education. To be sure, when Eric engages in social outreach, whether it be to a church member or one of his kids' classmates, he always treats his work as a professional obligation, and he consistently identifies himself as a minister. For instance, when the president of the local university where Matt attends faces scrutiny and possible firing by the board of trustees, Eric attends their meeting and speaks up on behalf of the president.[62] When he rises to speak, he introduces himself as the minister of the Glen Oak Community Church, not as the parent of a university student. His standing within this body, and his authority to speak on the issue at hand, comes from his credentials as a minister.

Eric's religion, however, is always *institutional* more than it is *theological* or *spiritual*. That is, Eric is a minister by profession, which entails having an office at the church and fulfilling the professional obligations of a minister, such as performing weddings, meeting with grieving families, and preaching on Sundays. The show's theological content is minimal. Only rarely does Eric reflect on his faith, and the kids do so only rarely as well. Annie once struggles to recite the familiar "to everything there is a season" Scripture passage, and she cannot identify that it comes from the book of Ecclesiastes.[63] Their images of God and other theological concepts are unsophisticated, and their infrequent prayers are simple. In general, the Camdens share a mild sense of God as someone who can and will deliver the things they want, and Simon especially vocalizes such request-oriented prayers to God. In the opening episode, he prays for God to deliver a new puppy, a prayer request granted with Annie's intervention.[64] In later episodes, Simon's prayers are answered when the twins turn out to be boys and when a mysterious Santa sighting renews Ruthie's faith in the magic of Christmas.[65] Lucy, too, knows a consumption-oriented God; when she chooses to wear her engagement ring after the engagement has been called off, she rationalizes, "If God didn't want me to have this ring, He wouldn't have had Jeremy give it to me."[66] In general, the show's theological content never advances beyond these immature images of God and their associated prayers, and, more often than not, the show simply avoids theological content.

Thus, maybe it should come as no surprise that the Rev. Camden's interventions into individuals' lives never come with any faith-based strings attached. He never offers food or money to a poor person if only she will right her relationship with God. He never tells an alcoholic that his admittance to or release from rehab will be dependent on a profession of faith. He never shares the good news of the gospel with a homeless, addicted, abused, or runaway teenager. Whether or not those individuals have spiritual needs, Eric only solves their material and relational needs, which are typically interrelated. He does occasionally invite community members to church, and often a family's problems are solved when they join together at a Sunday morning service. In one case, when Eric sets up an impoverished, alcoholic father with assistance from the church's Meals on Wheels program and a referral to an Alcoholics Anonymous group, he also invites the man to come to church.[67] He never, however, says that either of those services is conditional on the man's participation in church. And he never suggests that coming to church might entail spiritual transformation or renewal.

The Camdens also never intimate that their faith tradition is the best or truest path to social reform or spiritual enlightenment. To the contrary, they consistently demonstrate an ecumenical spirit and build relationships with other faith communities in their town. When Simon and Ruthie experience "guilt gut" for one of their transgressions, they go on a spiritual pilgrimage to the local houses of worship of a variety of faiths, hoping that one of the spiritual leaders will be able to give them an antidote for their feelings of remorse. After they talk to a Catholic priest, a Jewish rabbi, and a Buddhist monk, Simon and Ruthie arrive back at the Camden home, where they discover that all the men they have just met are their father's friends.[68] A sixth-season episode, which aired in the spring of 2002, deals with the issue of discrimination against Muslims, telling the story of an elementary school girl who is bullied on her walk home from school.[69] The Camdens defend her publicly in the name of religious freedom and they stage a protest when the local private school will not admit the girl. Finally, also in the sixth season, the oldest Camden son, Matt, marries a Jewish woman, who is the daughter of a rabbi. Although Eric and Annie struggle with this interfaith marriage, and especially Matt's possible conversion to Judaism, they ultimately give the wedding their blessing. Eric gives a short speech at the rabbi's Shabbat service, where he extols the values, such as love, shared by the two faiths.[70] Although Eric never wavers in his own faith, and he expects the members of his family to adhere to their nondescript Protestant Christianity, he never shows anything less than respect for other faith traditions, nor does he assert that his has a unique claim on truth or morality. Contrary to critics who fear that faith-based social services would show preference for one religion or discriminate against others, Eric's approach to Christian leadership and charity models a nonthreatening ecumenical spirit.

COMPASSION BEGINS AT HOME

On *7th Heaven*, these public acts of compassion grow out of the Camden family domestic sphere. Thus, *7th Heaven*'s model of civic participation forges important connections between the private and public spheres, connections that are necessary in the post-welfare era. The post-welfare era demands that, if government cannot impose a social safety net, the private sphere must instead foster the charitable spirit that is manifest in public acts of compassion. In the case of *7th Heaven*, civic participation, and specifically the show's model of individual, charitable social reform, is rooted in the private sphere because, on the one hand, Eric's professional life and its charity work are inextricable from his domestic life, and because, on the other hand, Eric and Annie's parenting is an outlet for social reform. Because *7th Heaven*'s ideal of civic participation has evident roots in the private sphere, it takes on the feminine characteristics typically fostered in the home.

Domesticated Clergy

Even if all the members of *7th Heaven*'s Camden family participate in providing social services and fostering social reform, their exemplar is Rev. Camden, whose civic participation grows out of his professional obligations as a minister. The role of the clergy has long bridged the private and public spheres, and, as a result, it has been defined by the conflicted gender codes of masculinity associated with the public sphere and femininity with the private. Although Rev. Camden's work spans the public and private spheres, and he occasionally demonstrates both masculinity and femininity, his ties to the domestic sphere are strongest and his feminine characteristics clearest. He thus models a uniquely feminized, domesticated form of charitable civic participation.

Whereas Ann Douglas has famously argued that the clergy is a feminized profession, and Roxanne Mountford has highlighted the appeals to masculinity commonly directed at members of the clergy, Muriel Mellow shows how clergy commonly traverse public and private spaces, which are defined by masculine and feminine norms.[71] Clergy perform the church's most public acts and serve as the church's public representative by blessing and serving the Eucharist, sharing the word of God, and even proclaiming the church's stance on public issues. Mountford argues that church architecture and homiletics instruction define the clergy's public roles by masculine norms. She explains, "Homileticians entreated preachers to develop themselves as *men* so that their congregations would recognize them as civic leaders in the mold of other great American statesmen" and so that they might have "membership in the national fraternity that produces civic leaders and presidents."[72] At the same time, however, clergy are also invited into the most intimate moments of their parishioners' private lives, leading young couples through premarital counseling, listening to an adulterer's emotional anguish, sitting at the bedside of a dying mother. In these private spaces, clergy are expected to perform the types of emotional labor so commonly deemed feminine. Ultimately, both Douglas and Mellow conclude that the role of the clergy has moved gradually from the masculine civic statesman to the feminine personal counselor. Mellow explains that as Protestant theology has de-emphasized the authoritative God with a hierarchical relationship to humans, it has obviated the clergyman who mediated between humans and the divine. Instead, clergy are now "counselors, dealing with people's personal problems rather than arbitrators of spiritual and transcendent concerns."[73]

7th Heaven's model of a clergyman falls squarely within this contemporary image of a feminized counselor capable of emotional labor, rather than a masculine civic statesmen. Rev. Camden is grounded in the domestic sphere, and his personal and professional duties are interrelated as they grow out of that domestic space. Although Eric pastors a church and keeps an office there, he also maintains a study at home, where he is frequently found meeting with parishioners or community members. Other parts of his professional role can also be conducted at home; Eric routinely works on his sermons in his study, and he often carries a yellow legal pad and a Bible around the house as he attends to other tasks, such as caring for the children. Sometimes he sets up his laptop, legal pad, and Bible at the kitchen counter and does his professional work from there. This consistent visual framing of Eric in the domestic sphere makes his professional work an extension of his domestic responsibilities, or it at least makes the two interrelated.

Not only is the Reverend Camden so comfortably situated in the domestic sphere, but he is even further feminized within that sphere.[74] He is feminized in part by his wife's acknowledged plumbing, carpentry, and electrical skills. In the show's opening episode, Annie crouches under the sink repairing the pipes, and when Eric comes and joins her, he admits his total ignorance about such things.[75] As the series progresses, Annie and her daughters rebuild a car and remodel the attic, both activities to which the patriarch of the house contributes nothing.[76] Once, when Eric is particularly frustrated and he expresses his emotion by banging his head against the wall, Annie scolds him, telling him not to damage the wall because she has no time to replaster.[77] Later in the episode, when the tables are turned, Eric scolds Annie not to damage the wall because he is unable to plaster. He is also feminized within the domestic sphere by his clear ability to perform typically feminine tasks. Although he cannot cook—a fact underscored repeatedly—he does perform much of the emotional labor in the house.[78] Also in the show's opening episode, Eric consoles an anguished Lucy, who is desperate to get her first period.[79] Even if she initially rebukes her sympathetic father, Lucy later celebrates with him when her period arrives. Eric is delighted when Lucy sends him to the drugstore to pick up tampons; he had been agonizing about whether or not Lucy would ever send him on such errands the way Mary had always done. In the many instances where Eric listens sympathetically or consoles his kids, he is never reluctant to share in their emotions of sadness, anxiety, or grief. His intimate conversations with the Camden kids often bring Eric to tears, and closure to these conversations usually comes when Eric and his kids hug and say "I love you."

Eric is thoroughly feminized by his framing within the domestic sphere and his comfort performing the feminine task of emotional labor, but even in more masculine public spaces, Eric's performance is often defined by feminine norms. The Reverend Camden's most common public performance is the Sunday morning sermon, where he does stand in the masculine fortress of a pulpit. Like the ones of nineteenth-century design that Mountford describes, Eric's pulpit is distant from and raised above the congregation he addresses. Any masculinity displayed by this visual dominance, however, is undercut by the feminized nature of his sermons. Whereas Mountford found in homiletics instruction the assertion that sermons should be a masculine display of intellect, Eric's sermons are often teary-eyed summaries of the lessons he learned from his interpersonal interactions over the course of the week. A sermon on prayer, for instance, begins with Eric's admission that his reflections grow out of his family's recent discussions about prayer.[80] He shares an anecdote about Ruthie and Matt, who were away riding horses as an answer to Ruthie's prayer. Then he elaborates upon his family's discussions about prayer—"what to pray for, how to pray, when to pray, whose prayers get answered, whose don't. . . ." As he describes an anonymous prayer request he received in the mail, the camera zooms closer and closer in on Eric's face, revealing the tears that well up in his eyes. By the time Eric has recounted the whole prayer request, from an adolescent boy worried about the crime in his community, and called for a moment of silence, Eric's eyes are nearly overflowing and his face quivers with emotion. His pleading, upward gaze is the episode's closing image before the screen fades to black. Here is Eric's most masculine performance, the public act of preaching, given over entirely to personal reflections and an overt display of emotions. He is hardly the rational, intellectual civic statesman that Mountford argues the homiletics tradition demands of the clergy.

If Eric is characterized by this femininity and domesticity more generally, his social reform work especially takes on these characteristics. Eric's approach to social service provision relies heavily on affiliation and bonding, strategies Olasky deems "compassionate," which depend on feminine skills such as nurturing relationships. Whenever Eric finds a child in need, and he approaches the child's parents, he does so cautiously, tenderly, and privately. He usually goes to the family home in the evening, presumably a time when members of his community would be available to host visitors. Thus, his interventions are personal and friendly, conducted in the safety of the domestic sphere. Other times, the Camdens conduct these interventions in their own home. For instance, when Ruthie brings home Yasmin, a hijab-wearing peer who is being harassed by older teenagers, Eric and Annie invite Yasmin's parents to their home that evening.[81] As they broach the difficult subject of anti-Muslim harassment, the four adults sit in the Camdens' living room, where Annie serves tea. They sit close together, lean in as they talk, and speak in affirming tones. These intimate domestic scenes often focus on facilitating reconciliation within estranged families; in this case, by alerting Yasmin's parents to the harassment she was experiencing, Eric fostered honesty and support within this family. Sometimes through this type of meeting, Eric encourages alcoholic parents to reconsider their behavior or unforgiving parents to pardon their kids' transgressions (such as pregnancy). Often at the end of these meetings, when Eric has ensured reconciliation between estranged parties, he stands off to the side and watches them hug. As he does so, his eyes well up as he sends a silent "thank you" upward.[82]

Not only does Eric conduct these interventions in a personal, feminine, domestic manner, but the strategies of affiliation and bonding are fundamentally private-sphere responses to public problems. Social issues such as poverty and alcoholism are solved within the confines of the private sphere when individual families agree to look out for their relatives who have gone astray, in the case of affiliation, or when they foster new familial relationships with a person in need, in the case of bonding. By *7th Heaven's* model, if each case of poverty, abuse, divorce, teenage pregnancy, or substance abuse can be solved by reconciliation within an individual broken family, they will not become social problems demanding collective solutions.

Parenting for Social Reform

Finally, *7th Heaven* fits the post-welfare privatization impulse because of the explicit faith it places in childrearing as a meaningful avenue for social reform. In this respect, it follows the liberal ideology that Hillary Clinton outlines in *It Takes a Village*. For as much as she wants community institutions, such as churches and schools, to take the lead in social reform, she rests ultimate responsibility for child welfare, and also for social betterment, with parents. According to Clinton, parents play the most crucial role in raising strong, healthy children. And if raising strong, healthy children is both a moral and a pragmatic obligation for America's future, then parenting is a civic duty. Clinton shares lessons gained from her own experience raising Chelsea, as well as abundant data from social scientific research, offering tips on a wide range of topics, from keeping kids safe to nurturing their intellects. She emphasizes, for instance, the importance of talking and reading to children even before they are ready to talk themselves, let alone read. She points to studies that link parental conversations with infants and toddlers to their early vocabulary and then links vocabulary and related analytic skills to professional success later in life.[83]

More than keeping children safe and stimulating their intellect, Clinton also charges parents with the responsibility of moral development in the nation's children. "One of the family's . . . most important tasks," she explains, "is to help children develop those habits of self-discipline and empathy that constitute what we call character."[84] Adequate character development in the home affords the potential to eradicate all sorts of social problems. Acknowledging America's contemporary racial conflict, she argues, "As always, the solution begins at home. Parents must learn to talk with children about the diversity of human experiences and traits, answering their questions simply and directly and giving them an appropriate vocabulary to describe what they see."[85] In part, her proposal is standard liberal American fare: if only we educate our children sufficiently, each generation will make this country better than the one before. But her framework is also unique to the post-welfare state: if we no longer trust government to solve social problems like racism, the stakes of parenting for the future of the country are much higher. Because she sees the family's integral role in raising healthy, productive children, Clinton joins Olasky in fretting over the deterioration of the American family. "There is much we can do," she asserts, "to encourage and strengthen marriages and to provide adequate support for children of divorced and single parents."[86]

Like Clinton's book, *7th Heaven* devotes significant attention to issues associated with childrearing. Among all the characteristics that set *7th Heaven* apart from similar television fare, one of the most distinct is its frank conversations about parenting. Eric and Annie discuss their childrearing strategies endlessly—not only the mundane details of parenting, such as how children should be punished for particular transgressions, but also how to instill values in their children.[87] For instance, as Eric reflects upon a shy teenager who approached him in his office one afternoon, he suggests to Annie that they make a renewed commitment to fostering communication with their children.[88] To do as much, they spend that evening in heartfelt conversations with Lucy, Simon, and Ruthie. Through these conversations, Eric and Annie remind their children of the values of openness and honesty.

Eric and Annie reiterate that they take parenting so seriously because they recognize that it is one contribution they make to improving the world. At the conclusion of one episode, the Camden parents sit together on the front porch and discuss their personal worries about the twins they are about to bring into the world.[89] Eric, reflecting on the discouraging day he has just endured, where he and his lunch companions were met with racism, admits, "After a day like today, I worry about bringing new souls into this world at this time." Annie counters, "I'm not worried. Their brothers and sisters will make a difference; they'll make it better. And so will [the twins]." Annie makes the same point again in a later episode.[90] After Ruthie delivers a passionate speech defending her Muslim friend Yasmin to the parent organization at her school, Eric and Annie reflect to each other how proud they are of their youngest daughter. Annie gushes, "When I feel like the world is getting a little crazy, I think of our kids and what nice and kind people they've turned out to be. It makes me happy knowing how they are making the world a better place."

Because they treat parenting as a strategy for social reform, the Camdens' childrearing practices prize moral lessons and character development. Oftentimes, the values taught in the Camden home are reinforced on multiple levels. In one episode, a given value, such as trust, forgiveness, or kindness, might become salient for one character on a personal level and for another character on a social or political level. Many episodes carry a value-based theme through four or five story lines, each one reinforcing the others. For instance, in a second-season episode titled "I Hate You," Simon and Eric encounter a neighbor whose numbered tattoos on her wrist reveal to them that she is an Auschwitz survivor.[91] Her testimony allows Eric the opportunity to teach Simon about the horrors of the Holocaust and specifically how this mass genocide resulted from Hitler's instilling hatred in the people of Germany. At the same time, Ruthie, Mary, and Lucy learn their own lessons about expressing hatred. When Ruthie yells "I hate you" at her mother, she learns the power of those words to hurt a loved one's feelings. And Mary and Lucy decide they hate Matt's new girlfriend for her perfect hair, perfect teeth, perfect grades, and other perfect qualities. When his girlfriend overhears their hateful banter about her, she breaks up with Matt. Mary and Lucy discover the consequences of their hatred—not only did they hurt this girl, but they cost Matt a relationship that he enjoyed. Thus, the story line involving Simon and the Holocaust survivor has demonstrated the dangers of hatred on a global scale, while the other Camden siblings have learned the dangers of hatred on a personal level. As is so common on *7th Heaven*, the values taught in the home have clear applicability to social problems larger than their family. And also like in so many *7th Heaven* episodes, the Camden parents played an integral role in instilling those values in their children.

On *7th Heaven*, it seems that almost no social problem is too big or too complex to be solved by thoughtful parenting. An episode aired early in the show's first season—and the first one to be billed as a "very special episode"—depicts how the problems of racism could be handled within the family setting.[92] When the Camden family discovers that a nearby African American church has been burned by arsonists, they invite the pastor and his family, the Hamiltons, to stay at their house until it is safe to return to their own. Rev. Morgan Hamilton has been a friend of Eric's since seminary, so their wives, Patricia and Annie, are also close. Their youngest kids— Lynn and Ruthie, Nigel and Simon—are closely matched in age, and they make easy playmates. Among the teenagers, Keisha Hamilton is close in age to Mary and Lucy, and John Hamilton to Matt, but the relationships between the teenagers are complicated by racial tension. The Camden teens are uneasy around the Hamiltons, seemingly never knowing what to say, and the Hamilton teens take offense at everything the Camdens manage to say. Over the course of the episode, however, and with the help of their parents, the Hamilton and Camden teenagers reconcile their differences and develop friendships. Initially, they all bond over a practical joke that each kid plays on the next. Then Keisha braids Lucy's hair in what she identifies as an African style. Lucy passes along Keisha's lesson about Rosa Parks, so that the Camden kids let the Hamiltons have the front seat in the car. Ultimately, when a white security guard harasses them all for loitering outside the elementary school as they wait for Simon and Nigel, the Camden teenagers, especially Matt, develop empathy for the racism that the Hamiltons endure regularly. By the end of the episode, the reconciliation between the families is evident when they all play Twister together, and when they lie in bed and say their goodnights in the style of *The Waltons*.

The Camdens and the Hamiltons are models of the families that the village needs to raise healthy, successful children. Their solution to racism begins just where Hillary Rodham Clinton suggested it should—in the home—as does the solution to so many other social problems confronted on *7th Heaven*. The Camden family home is just a starting point, however, because the lessons taught there are so often applied immediately to the numerous cases of people seeking their help.

CONCLUSION

Premiering in 1996, *7th Heaven* gave fictionalized shape to the model of civic participation necessitated by that year's dramatic welfare reform. Where welfare reform transformed citizens from welfare-supporting taxpayers into civic-minded volunteers, *7th Heaven* depicted well-meaning Americans looking out for the impoverished, abused, addicted, and otherwise downtrodden members of their communities. Articulating a clear disdain for government and its characteristic inefficient bureaucracy, *7th Heaven*'s characters demonstrated that Christians with good intentions can alleviate the social problems, such as poverty, alcoholism, and teenage pregnancy, that have eluded government programs. *7th Heaven*'s characters further fulfilled the promise of the post-welfare era because their social reform work bridged the public and private spheres. In doing so, it brought domestic, feminine characteristics to civic participation. Rev. Camden's professional civic work grew out of his domestic sphere responsibilities, and his and Annie's parenting served as an additional avenue for social reform. All told, by the end of *7th Heaven*'s eleven-year run, it had reached more than 40 percent of the American population with its ideal of individualized, secularized, and feminized charity work.

By making social service provision and social reform seem easy, and by depicting them as the natural province of religious organizations, *7th Heaven* only underscored the burden placed on churches in the popular imagination. As Ram A. Cnaan's survey research has demonstrated, church-going and non-churchgoing Americans alike assume that churches can and should provide a social safety net, a belief "so pervasive in our culture that it is a norm accepted by all members of society."[93] And indeed, religious organizations do provide significant social services to their communities.[94] Robert Wuthnow's national survey data reveals an almost unlimited range of services provided by religious organizations at the local and national levels, and he shows that recipients are generally happier with their experiences with civil sector organizations than with government. Unlike government, or even some nonprofit agencies, churches, Wuthnow notes, are able to function as "caring communities," which facilitate relationships over time, rather than simply handing out services.[95]

Cnaan and Wuthnow both demonstrate, however, that churches are not equipped to replace the social services once provided by government.[96] According to Wuthnow, although religious organizations respond well to short-term needs, such as clothing and shelter, they are ill prepared to respond to larger systemic patterns that produce poverty. Moreover, even if Olasky dreams of charity efforts of years past, when religious organizations built long-term transformative relationships with individuals in need, social scientists find that model of reform work rare among contemporary religious organizations.[97] Although congregations foster strong relationships among their members, they foster weaker affiliations between members and aid recipients, Wuthnow suggests.[98] In Putnam's terms, they facilitate bonding social capital more so than bridging. Thus, *7th Heaven*'s flawlessly simple example of Christian charity sets high, possibly unattainable, expectations for religious organizations.

7th Heaven's model of social reform also fits with the post-welfare ideology because it develops the image of welfare recipients as dependent wards. Asen has argued that prior to welfare reform, the popular image of welfare recipients shifted from contract signees to dependent wards of the state, and this notion of dependency fueled conservatives' fears about the welfare state. By 7th Heaven's depiction, needy individuals are no longer wards of the state, but they are instead wards of the community, whose needs must be addressed by more fortunate community members. Because 7th Heaven so commonly depicts social issues in terms of the experiences of children and teenagers, it infantilizes the recipients of charity, and it naturalizes their relationship with charity providers as one of dependence. When poor people, drug addicts, and single moms are depicted as children and teenagers, they are naturally naïve, weak, and desperate for the assistance of older and wiser community members. Because they are not independent, established, educated adults, whose self-worth might be undermined by paternalistic acts of charity, a pregnant teenager does not object when Annie chooses her childbirth classes, and a drug-addicted teen does not try to influence Eric's decision about his rehab program. So fully infantilized are these men and women, they need not assert agency over the forms of charity they accept in their lives.

Just as 7th Heaven's image of the feminized clergyman fits with long-standing characteristics of the clergy, it also resonates with common images of charity as feminine work. Charity work has commonly been the domain not only of nuns and members of other religious orders, but also of wealthy (female) socialites and other homemakers whose "leisure" time could be devoted to unpaid work. In the nineteenth century, these women formed church-related benevolent societies that fueled poverty relief and progressive reform efforts (such as the temperance movement). They held bake sales and bazaars that underwrote their churches' operating budgets and funded fledgling global missions. Women continued as the models of civic volunteerism into the twentieth century, donning candy striper uniforms and organizing parent-teacher associations.[99] A homemaker's flexible schedule made these activities possible, but they also grew out of domestic responsibilities, such as childrearing. 7th Heaven establishes a similar scenario, but gives the role of charity volunteer to the minister-father. He, too, has the sort of flexible schedule that allows him to visit needy people and attend community meetings in the middle of the day, often with little advance notice. And although his charity work technically relates to his professional work as a minister, very often he encounters needy people through his role as a father. Thus, although *7th Heaven* depicts a man performing this typically feminine charity work, it is his feminine characteristics that make him especially suited to do as much.

If *7th Heaven*'s model of private charity resonates with the burden placed on religious organizations and their leaders in the post-welfare era, its ideal of parenting for social reform resonates with two popular faith-based movements in that same era: Quiverfull and Christian homeschooling. Like *7th Heaven*, both imply that investing time and resources into Christian parenting not only demonstrates faithfulness but also yields social betterment through the work of the children raised in those families. Quiverfull proponents espouse the blessings of very large families, borrowing language from Psalm 127:[100]

> Sons are indeed a heritage from the Lord,
>   the fruit of the womb a reward.
> Like arrows in the hand of a warrior
>   are the sons of one's youth.
> Happy is the man who has
>   his quiver full of them.
> He shall not be put to shame
>   when he speaks with his enemies in the gate.

According to Quiverfull teaching, by raising a large family, Christians praise God and increase their own happiness. As some observers note, however, Quiverfull is driven by ambitions much larger than personal happiness and godly devotion. In Canada's *Globe and Mail*, Dorothy Woodend explains of the movement, "A religious war is being waged, not with bullets, but with babies."[101] Conservative Christians are raising up the army of Christ by literally raising more kids. She cites "breed to succeed" as their motto, making their practice of reproduction a direct fulfillment of the command in Genesis to "be fruitful and multiply."[102]

While Quiverfull encourages Christians to produce large families, the fast-growing Christian homeschool movement has given them resources for educating those broods at home. Although parents homeschool their children for a wide variety of reasons—geography, safety in the public schools, individual children's special needs, et cetera—since the 1980s, conservative Christian parents in particular have kept their kids out of public schools so that they could shield them from offensive subject matter such as Darwinism and sex education. Although statistics vary widely, estimates suggest that between one and two million children are homeschooled in the United States.[103] A 2003 study conducted by the Department of Education suggested that among those, nearly 30 percent choose to homeschool so that they can provide religious or moral instruction, and other numbers suggest that about two-thirds of homeschoolers identify as evangelical Christians.[104] With the recent surge in Christian homeschooling, an industry of resources has emerged; there are national organizations, Internet- and print-based curricula, and local cooperative associations that offer specialized supplementary classes for homeschooled students.[105] Although it is an individual or family decision, homeschooling has undeniable civic and political ramifications.[106] As Hanna Rosin revealed in the *New York Times*, the ultimate mission espoused by many homeschoolers is to "shape the culture and take back the nation."[107] As such, some homeschool families subscribe to the Generation Joshua curriculum, which encourages students to develop civic skills through hands-on participation in local campaigns and voter registration drives.[108]

Quiverfull and Christian homeschooling both exemplify *7th Heaven*'s principles exactly. By raising kids, especially lots of kids, and instilling morals in them, Christian parents equip a new generation for civic leadership. Not only do they pass on their faith tradition to their kids, and thereby provide their kids with resources for their own salvation and spiritual fulfillment, but they also contribute to their communities by raising kids committed to social betterment. Even if *7th Heaven*'s Camden parents never utter the term Quiverfull, their seven-child, five-bedroom, two-minivan household testifies to this lifestyle.[109] And although they do not homeschool their children (until the final seasons), the life lessons they routinely teach demonstrate the importance of moral instruction in the domestic sphere.

Finally, for all the characteristics *7th Heaven* shares with post-welfare ideology and with the spirit of charitable volunteerism more generally, its differences are equally striking. Because the show does not depict needy individuals as inherently fallen or sinful, as Olasky says previously successful charity did, it does not offer spiritual redemption as the solution to material problems. Individuals' fallen nature was what made religious organizations so well suited for social service provision and social reform in Olasky's scheme. In addition to doling out money and goods, religious charities have the moral authority to coax recipients out of their dependent behaviors, he argues. The danger, his opponents note, is that if religious charities use government money to exert that moral authority, they threaten the separation of church and state as well as the religious freedom of recipients.

By not articulating a moral or theological framework while its characters provide charity, 7th Heaven makes both proponents' hopes and skeptics' fears seem exaggerated. On the one hand, because 7th Heaven does not show needy people to be fallen or sinful, they do not need Christian salvation in order to reform their earthly ways. As such, every case of brokenness can be solved within the hour-long drama without a faith-based conversion experience. To be sure, sometimes 7th Heaven's needy people find spiritual, personal, or relational fulfillment along with the material solutions the Camden family provides. But because these individuals do not reform themselves through a conversion experience, 7th Heaven's model of social reform casts doubt upon Olasky's claim that social reform demands such opportunities for personal transformation. It also, however, casts doubt on skeptics' fears that, left in the hands of churches, charity work automatically becomes overtly religious. By Rev. Camden's example, it seems possible, even obvious, that faith-based charity efforts would focus more on reconciling interpersonal relationships than on fostering Christian faith. By his example, it seems possible, even obvious, that churches can provide charity and resolve social problems without ever imposing their religious values on the needy people they serve.

6

BIOLOGY, HETEROSEXUALITY, AND THE PRIVATIZATION OF FAITHFULNESS

The Da Vinci Code

God blessed them, and God said to them, "Be fruitful and multiply . . ."
Genesis 1:28

Then the man said, "This at last is bone of my bones and flesh of my flesh; this one shall be called Woman, for out of Man this one was taken."
Genesis 2:23

I will bless her, and moreover I will give you a son by her. I will bless her, and she shall give rise to nations; kings of peoples shall come from her.
Genesis 17:16

In their varied ways, *Amazing Grace, The Passion of the Christ, Left Behind,* and *7th Heaven* all depict faithful Christians engaged in the public lives of their communities. These Christians participate in a democratic legislative process, they gather in the public square to witness the public execution of a perceived criminal, they mobilize a global army, and they contribute to the volunteer organizations that keep their community intact. None of these activities is entirely foreign to American Christians, who have long endeavored to translate their faith commitments into their public, civic lives.

As Martin Marty has demonstrated, however, American Christianity has always felt an equal and competing pull toward the private sphere.[1] While Social Gospel Christians have oriented their attention to various forms of civic participation, the countering moral reform tradition has taught Christians to focus on their personal righteousness. The moral reform tradition posits not only that individual Christians should culti-vate Christian morality as a demonstration of faithfulness, but also that the private sphere of family and domestic life should exemplify Christian morality. According to Marty, this pull toward the private sphere has typified conservative Christianity, and in recent years, conservative Christians in the moral reform tradition have encouraged traditional nuclear families and have condemned a wide range of personal behavior deemed immoral—premarital sex, abortion, and same-sex intimacy, among others.

This moral reform tradition has not been absent from the contemporary media landscape. For as prominent as ideals of civic participation have been in such texts as *Amazing Grace*, *The Passion*, *Left Behind*, and *7th Heaven*, an equally popular text, *The Da Vinci Code (TDVC)*, exemplifies the moral reform tradition, providing a model of what might be called civic nonparticipation. Although the novel and its characters are not hostile to public life or civic participation, they express a clear preference for the private sphere, and especially human sexuality, as the domain of faithfulness.

That *TDVC* models the typically conservative moral reform impulse is made all the more remarkable by the firestorm that the novel, and later the film version, ignited upon its release. This controversy burned slowly upon the novel's publication but grew in intensity with its explosive popularity. Launched with an aggressive marketing campaign in March of 2003, the novel quickly ascended the *New York Times* bestseller list. By the time the film version was released in May 2006, the book had spent 162 weeks on the bestseller list—the full three years since its release.[2] The sixty million copies sold[3] had reaped $210 million in profit.[4] The book had been translated into forty-four languages and was issued in hardcover, illustrated, large print, audio, and two paperback editions, as well as a traveler's guide. All told, by winter of 2005, 28.5 percent of Americans claimed to have read the novel.[5] The movie, produced by Sony Pictures, directed by Ron Howard, and starring Tom Hanks and Audrey Tautou, would only add to the revenue totals and the story's popularity. It grossed $77 million when it opened on 3,735 screens and a total of $218 million through its three months in the theaters.[6]

The novel's sales derived from its popularity across religious sects, a phenomenon that Stark and his colleagues have called "the *Da Vinci Code* effect."[7] Whereas other Christian-themed popular media texts, including *The Passion* and *Left Behind*, found their largest audiences among regular churchgoers, especially evangelical Christians, *TDVC*'s audience not only crossed religious sects but also included both regular churchgoers and religiously unaffiliated individuals. The novel was read most widely by religious liberals, those who, according to Stark's questionnaire, consider the Bible an "ancient book of history and legends" (among whom 45 percent read the novel), and it was read least widely among religious conservatives, those who consider the Bible to be literally true (among whom 12 percent read the novel).[8] Although it may have been read across religious sects, and among both the religiously affiliated and unaffiliated, the novel owes its popularity to less orthodox believers.

The novel's popularity across religious sects, but also its relative disfavor among religious conservatives, may have been influenced by the reviews it received in wide-circulation newspapers as well as niche religious venues. Upon the novel's initial publication, reviews in the mainstream press were largely positive; for instance, the *New York Times*' Janet Maslin called the book a "gleefully erudite suspense novel."[9] She praised its plot, prose, and characters, but avoided the issues of Christian history and theology that would soon come to dominate public discourse about the novel. In successive months, as the book held steady atop the bestseller list, the mainstream evangelical periodical *Christianity Today* published multiple responses in its print magazine and on its Web site. Other critiques could be found on Web sites for smaller Christian publications such as www.cruxnews.com, the Institute for Religious Research, *Culture Wars*, and *Crisis* magazine.[10]

The reviews published in these conservative Christian outlets are unabashedly polemical, sharing a common belligerence toward the novel, its author, and its audiences. In *Culture Wars*, Anne Barbeau Gardiner says that Dan Brown means "to entrap young and uneducated readers," offering "an indoctrination into Gnosticism. The reader is intended to swallow the Gnostic poison while enjoying the murder mystery," and she even goes so far as to offer a psychiatric diagnosis, claiming that Brown's "obsessiveness of association is deviant and could well be a symptom of mental disorder."[11] Within a year of its publication, more thoughtful and systematic reactions to the book began appearing, and by now, at least thirty-four books and another twenty-three television and DVD specials have responded to *TDVC*.[12] As they explicitly take issue with the novel's characterizations of art history, church history, theology, and more, these responses do so on the grounds that the book is radical and dangerous. It "is nothing less than a conscious effort to obscure the uniqueness and vitality of the Christian faith and message," Darrell L. Bock accuses.[13] At "a time when catechesis and basic knowledge of the faith are so poor," the book proves especially dangerous, Carl E. Olson and Sandra Miesel assert, because it influences non-Christian readers and raises "difficult questions in the minds of many Christians."[14]

At the heart of this controversy is *TDVC*'s purportedly feminist message. The *Washington Post* explains that the book has set off a controversy over "women, sex, feminism, and the church."[15] The author's Web site claims that *TDVC* "is very empowering for women," and the *St. Petersburg Times* notes how the novel has won "kudos for tackling women's lib issues."[16] The *Milwaukee Journal Sentinel* assesses that the novel "may represent the tipping point for the far cosmic wing of modern feminism and predicts a tsunami of goddess-ness for the foreseeable future."[17] In contrast, its critics are concerned that *TDVC* is "laced with passages celebrating feminism" because it is "another infiltration by liberal cultural warriors."[18] According to Msgr. T. W. Young, writing in the newspaper of the Catholic Archdiocese of Atlanta, the novel includes "a radical feminist tirade."[19] Some of the book's critics even trace the entirety of its historical revision and theological challenges to a New Age ideology that emphasizes feminism, along with homosexuality, paganism, Gnosticism, and other radical ideas. Olson and Miesel, for instance, claim that the "sexual revolution" is what divides the culture from "serious Christians," and "*The Da Vinci Code* has more to do with abortion and homosexuality than it does with the origins of Christianity" because it invites people "to invent their own history, to replace the Gospel of Jesus Christ with scriptures that cater to contemporary preoccupations like feminism."[20]

As its critics suggest, the novel relays an unorthodox revision of Christian history, thick with discussions of gender and sexuality. Of the novel's two interwoven narratives, one immediate and one historical, the former probably explains the book's popularity and the latter its controversy. The immediate story takes place over twenty-four hours as eight characters, individually and in groups, follow a trail of clues across Europe. It combines romance, suspense, and conspiracy theories in 450 pages of short chapters, most with cliffhanger endings. The novel's historical narrative unfolds over hundreds of years as the primary characters uncover secrets that the church has kept since its fourth-century founding.[21]

The trail of clues that defines the immediate narrative is left by Jacques Sauniére, curator of the Louvre, who is murdered in the book's opening scene by an albino monk named Silas. Sauniére uses his dying strength and bleeding wounds to encode a message for his estranged granddaughter, Sophie Neveu, and a Harvard professor of symbology, Robert Langdon, whose pursuit of the curator's message sends them racing across Paris and to the British Isles. They are chased by a French law enforcement unit led by a proud Catholic, Bezú Fache, and his bumbling deputy, Lieutenant Collet.

Neveu and Langdon turn to Holy Grail enthusiast Sir Leigh Teabing for assistance with their code-breaking. He and his manservant, Rémy, also help Neveu and Langdon evade the police and the albino monk Silas, and they travel together by private plane to the British Isles. Once in London, however, their coalition crumbles when Teabing is revealed to be the mastermind behind the operation. His Grail fixation had led him to manipulate Opus Dei's Bishop Aringarosa, who used his assistant, Silas, to set this murderous chase in motion. Ultimately, Teabing is arrested, and Neveu and Langdon are left to unravel Sauniére's trail. They end up at the historic chapel at Rosslyn, where Neveu learns the secret Sauniére left for her—that her grandmother and brother, whom she believed died in a car accident when she was a young child, reside there. They have been in hiding to protect Western history's most powerful and hidden bloodline: Neveu and her brother are the most direct living descendants of Jesus Christ and Mary Magdalene.

As *TDVC*'s immediate narrative depicts these characters racing across Europe, the secondary narrative, and the one that has earned the novel its infamy, is the secret history of the church that their journey discloses. These revelations are sealed with the imprimatur of historical veracity found in the "fact" statement on the novel's first page, which claims, "All descriptions of artwork, architecture, documents, and secret rituals in this novel are accurate." The church, the novel reveals, has suppressed the venerated role held by the "sacred feminine" and "goddess worship" in pagan societies and early Christianity. It has done so in order to defame Mary Magdalene, who was Jesus Christ's companion throughout his ministry, the heir designated to lead his church, and his wife and the mother of his child, Sarah. The jealous male disciples wrested control of the church from Magdalene immediately following Jesus' ascension, prompting her to flee to France with Sarah and laying the groundwork for the male-dominated institution the church would become and remain throughout history. Through the centuries, however, the Priory of Sion has protected the legacy of Mary Magdalene and the traditions of goddess worship and the sacred feminine. The characters explain that when the church suppressed the sacred feminine, this secret society—through leaders like Leonardo da Vinci and Jacques Sauniére—celebrated it through art, architecture, and other symbolism. They have also protected the Holy Grail and the ancient ritual of Heiros Gamos, two of Western history's biggest secrets, both of which pay homage to the lost sacred feminine. Or so the story goes.

Surely the novel merited the public controversy it provoked. It questioned centuries-old church doctrines, such as the divinity of Jesus Christ. It cast doubt on the truthfulness of the canonical gospels, introducing extrabiblical gospels instead. And it made damaging accusations of sexism against the institutional church, providing little evidence for them. Indeed, the novel claims to recover the "sacred feminine" and "goddess worship," themes that I argue resonate with difference or cultural feminism's preference for celebrating women's uniqueness. When the novel succumbs to the excesses of that type of feminist ideology, however, it venerates women's biology and heterosexuality at the expense of any other feminine qualities. Ultimately, the novel's radical innovations in terms of gender politics lead it into a celebration of the private sphere, which has more affinity with the conservative moral reform tradition than any feminist platform. *TDVC*, I maintain, idealizes a model of civic nonparticipation for women and men alike.

DA VINCI'S UTOPIAN HERLAND?

When *TDVC* derides the Catholic Church for suppressing the "sacred feminine" and "goddess worship," and when it promises to reclaim these traditions, it resonates with the strand of feminist thought typically called cultural or difference feminism. Since its nineteenth-century advent, American feminism has always had one ideological strain committed to celebrating women, women's difference, and ostensibly unique female values such as collaboration, nurturing, caregiving, pacifism, cooperation, and the harmonious regulation of public life.[22] This strand of feminist thinking that emphasizes difference has consistently found itself at odds with other forms of feminism emphasizing sameness or equality; Ann Snitow identifies this divide recurring between maximizers and minimizers, cultural feminists and radical feminists, essentialists and social constructionists, cultural feminists and poststructuralists, motherists and feminists, and difference and equality feminism.[23] In each of these cases, one strain of feminist ideology is committed to discovering and celebrating women's uniqueness, while the other wants to deny, negate, or transcend any such uniqueness. Those who celebrate women's difference, Snitow notes, "argue that women have a special morality, or aesthetic, or capacity for community that it is feminism's responsibility to maximize."[24]

In the nineteenth-century woman's rights movement, notions of women's difference informed the expediency arguments proposing that women deserved the franchise because their uniquely moral nature would prompt social reform.[25] That line of thinking would lead not only to women's leadership of progressive reform movements but also to a celebration of the poten-

tial of a woman-led society.[26] Charlotte Perkins Gilman's 1915 utopian novel
Herland, for instance, portrays a fictive world where women live peacefully
and collectively according to women's values.[27] When this strain of feminist
thought resurfaced in the 1970s, it grew naturally out of radical feminism.
That is, as radical feminism's critiques of patriarchy grew sharper and the
tasks of revolution steeper, resorting to woman-identified safe havens—both
ideological and literal—was a natural progression.[28] The resulting cultural
feminism is evident in two landmark studies in psychology: Carol Gilligan's
In a Different Voice and Mary Field Belenky, Blythe McVicker Clinchy, Nancy
Rule Goldberger, and Jill Mattuck Tarule's *Women's Ways of Knowing,* which
both indicted the field of psychology for only studying men and thus producing theories that only explained men and found women lacking. They
suggested that women were a distinct group of people that could be defined
by shared—and valuable—characteristics. Sara Ruddick's influential essay
"Maternal Thinking" extended this argument to suggest that women could
be defined by their common experience of motherhood, which is characterized by the tasks of "preservation, growth, and acceptability."[29] "Out of
maternal practices," Ruddick claimed, arise "distinctive ways of conceptual-
izing, ordering, and valuing."[30]

Religious systems have proved especially rich targets for cultural/
difference feminist critique. One of the most forceful feminist challenges to
institutional religion has come from cultural feminist Mary Daly. Trained
as a Thomist theologian with Ph.D.s from the University of Fribourg in
Switzerland, Daly used her position as a tenured faculty member at Boston
College to accuse all religions of being patriarchal. By her third book,
Gyn/Ecology: The Metaethics of Radical Feminism, Daly had abandoned
all hope of reforming patriarchal religion and instead proposed creating
woman-oriented theology, developing sisterhood, and facilitating women's
journeys.[31] She encouraged women's "weaving world tapestries *of our own
kind,*" as well as "dis-covering, de-veloping the complex web of living/loving
relationships *of our own kind,*" and "living, loving, creating our Selves, our
cosmos."[32] Daly's very public forced resignation from Boston College also
won infamy for her brand of cultural/difference feminism: she was ousted
when the school declared unacceptable her twenty-year-old policy of teaching women-only classes.[33] In line with her feminist ideology, Daly had used
her classroom as a space to develop and promote specifically female energy.

Daly has not been the only one to critique institutional religion on
the grounds of its patriarchy or to introduce alternative woman-centered
theologies. Whereas Daly abandoned her Christianity, other feminists have

offered similar critiques and theological innovations from within the context of biblical religion. The more mainstream feminist theologian Elisabeth Schüssler Fiorenza, for instance, has promoted a feminist hermeneutic for biblical interpretation. Her groundbreaking *In Memory of Her* proposes that a feminist hermeneutic "must critically reveal patriarchal history for what it is and, at the same time, reconstruct the history of women in early Christianity as a challenge to historical-religious patriarchy."[34] Recognizing women's historic exclusion, she, too, perceives a need to discern women's unique contributions to Christian history.[35] Christian feminists outside academia have made similar overtures toward recovering women's roles within the church. In 1992, feminist clergywomen from the mainline Protestant denominations attracted national attention and public rebuke for their affirmations of womanhood at a national conference. There, they celebrated the Eucharist with milk and honey and called upon God using the Greek word for wisdom, *Sophia*.[36] Although, unlike Daly, these clergywomen had not abandoned Christianity entirely, they echoed her impulse to celebrate women specifically within a theological context. In line with Daly, contemporaries like Ruddick and Gilligan, and their historic foremothers like Gilman, they acknowledged that the central feminist goal is to repair centuries of patriarchy and male domination by celebrating women.

Sexism and the Single Girl

These high-profile feminist challenges to patriarchal religion had primed conservative critics for *TDVC*. Thus, when the novel purported to uncover the church's centuries-old suppression of the sacred feminine and goddess worship, those critics were equipped to view it as a "radical feminist tirade." Like these earlier cultural/difference feminists, *TDVC* exposes patriarchy and promises to replace it with woman-centered religion. Additionally, on top of this historical recovery effort, *TDVC* graphs a primary narrative equally explicit in its feminism. The lead female character, Sophie Neveu, is depicted from her entrance as strong, smart, and capable, and the novel's villains are unabashed in their sexism.

Neveu arrives on the murder scene, her presence unrequested, striding in with a "haunting certainty to her gait," only to interrupt the calculating interrogation session that Bezú Fache has under way with his primary suspect, Robert Langdon.[37] Although Neveu has justified her interruption on the grounds that she, a police cryptologist, has broken the numeric code that Saunière sketched in blood, she simultaneously has engineered

Langdon's escape. Recognizing that Langdon is the police's unwitting suspect who believes he has been called to the murder scene for his expertise in symbolism, Neveu has developed an elaborate ruse wherein she directs Langdon to call the U.S. embassy but provides a false number that leads him to a voice message she has recorded for him. Explaining that he is the suspect, the message details directions to the nearest bathroom, where Neveu meets Langdon and exposes the surveillance chip planted in his coat pocket. Throwing it out the window, she buys Langdon time to escape the French police. When Langdon realizes Sophie has just won his freedom, he "decided not to say another word all evening. Sophie Neveu was clearly a hell of a lot smarter than he was."[38] Neveu demonstrates her capabilities repeatedly as she and Langdon work together to complete the puzzle her grandfather left. She deciphers the initial numeric code as the Fibonacci sequence, and after Langdon solves the first two anagrams Saunière left, Sophie gets the third: "So dark the con of man" leads them to the painting *Madonna of the Rocks.*

Sophie Neveu, this confident and capable young woman, is the modern-day Mary Magdalene. The resemblance between the two is undeniable: not only does Magdalene's blood pulse through Neveu's veins, but the two share a common appearance. Neveu is everything the novel's men dream Magdalene to be; she is "healthy with an unembellished beauty and genuineness that radiated a striking personal confidence" and "her thick burgundy hair fell unstyled to her shoulders, framing the warmth of her face."[39] Neveu's burgundy hair is no coincidence: *TDVC*'s characters make the case that the redheaded disciple to Jesus' right in the *Last Supper* is Mary Magdalene.[40] In case these physical markers did not prove the similarity sufficiently, the novel describes Neveu's lifelong connection with Magdalene. As a child, Neveu recalls, when she played Tarot cards with her grandfather, she always drew a pentacle as her indicator card. If her grandfather was stacking the deck, he was doing so to ensure that Neveu always drew the indicator card that signified the sacred feminine and, by extension, Mary Magdalene. "An apropos inside joke," Langdon acknowledges.[41]

While Sophie Neveu, the modern-day Mary Magdalene, demonstrates the capabilities of a smart woman, her foes consistently underestimate women's potential. Police Chief Bezú Fache is disgusted by Neveu from the moment she arrives at the Louvre because he thinks "women not only lacked the physicality necessary for police work, but their mere presence posed a dangerous distraction to the men in the field."[42] He is the caricature of a sexist: a stocky man whom his inferiors call "the bull," Fache carries himself "like an angry ox with his wide shoulders thrown back and his chin tucked hard into his chest."[43] An immediate obstacle to the novel's protagonists, his sexism underscores his dislikability and sets him up to be the fool proved wrong by this strong duo that he assesses as only a "female cryptologist and a schoolteacher."[44] Additionally, Silas, the albino monk, demonstrates similar sexism, at least by association. This monk-turned-murderer is a member of Opus Dei, a Catholic group known for its sexist practices. Before Silas ruthlessly kills the nun who keeps watch over the Church of Saint-Sulpice, she reflects upon Opus Dei:

> their views on women were medieval at best . . . female numeraries were forced to clean the men's residence halls for no pay while the men were at mass; women slept on hardwood floors, while the men had straw mats; and women were forced to endure additional requirements of corporal mortification.[45]

Furthermore, the organization has just built new headquarters in New York, where not only do men and women come into the building through separate entrances, but they are "acoustically and visually separated" throughout the building.[46] By associating this antifeminist sentiment with the calculating murderer and the ox-like police chief, the novel makes little secret of its contempt for sexism.

Adoring the Magdalene

Although *TDVC*'s primary narrative conveys evident feminist themes by pitting a strong central female character against sexist villains, it is the novel's secondary narrative, the one concerned with rewriting Christian history, that carries out the work of cultural/difference feminism. Through information disclosed by the murdered Jacques Saunière, the heroic Robert Langdon, and even the vilified Sir Leigh Teabing, the novel exposes the secret history and symbolism of the sacred feminine, offering an alternative to the hegemonic narrative of Christian history. Jesus Christ, *TDVC* explains, "was the original feminist."[47] The characters describe his inclusion of women in the innermost circle of his ministry, and, drawing on passages from the gnostic gospels, specifically the Gospel of Mary Magdalene, they even assert that Jesus had left Mary Magdalene "instructions on how to carry on His Church after He is gone."[48] Jesus' plan to leave her in sole control of his ministry went unfulfilled, however, because Peter "was something of a sexist."[49] Peter never felt comfortable "playing second fiddle to a woman," so he wrested control of the church from Mary Magdalene.[50] Then, following Peter's lead, the sexist church fathers erased and even defamed Mary Magdalene's reputation as an early church leader. In their smear campaign, more than simply Mary Magdalene's history and legacy was lost; these men also managed to eradicate the fundamental respect for the feminine that had defined pagan and early Christian communities. In fact, by Teabing's description, Christian doctrine as we know it today was not formulated until Constantine's Council of Nicea in 325 C.E., when the church fathers settled on a canon of Scriptures that excluded the gnostic gospels that told Magdalene's story, such as the Gospel of Philip and the Gospel of Mary Magdalene. By the conclusion of that council, the church fathers had completely distorted Jesus' original feminist vision and erased the feminine from Christian theology.

Thus, the novel's heroes—Jacques Saunière, as Louvre curator and Priory of Sion Grand Master, and Robert Langdon, as professor of symbology—do the important work of preserving the early Christian traditions of goddess worship and the sacred feminine. Saunière was "the premiere goddess iconographer on earth," and he had a "passion for relics relating to fertility, goddess cults, Wicca, and the sacred feminine."[51] As curator, he had devoted his twenty-year tenure to helping "the Louvre amass the largest collection of goddess art on earth."[52] Langdon is, in many ways, both Saunière's heir and apprentice. Although the two never met— their scheduled meeting the night of Saunière's murder would have been the first time—Langdon was well aware of Saunière's work to preserve the sacred feminine, and Saunière knew of Langdon's book manuscript about the sacred feminine. Langdon's book, once published, would explain "the iconography of goddess worship—the concept of female sanctity and the art and symbols associated with it."[53]

These men celebrate the hidden ways that goddess imagery lives on in Western art and history. Two very common symbols—the rose and the five-pointed star—both represent the feminine, and *TDVC*'s characters show how they are found repeatedly in Western art. The five-pointed star, Langdon explains, embodies the principle of PHI, or the Divine Proportion. This magical number, 1.618, recurs throughout both art and nature, defining the proportion of female and male honeybees in a hive, the ratio of spirals on a sunflower's face, and the proportions of the human body. In the case of the five-pointed star, the ratios of the line segments necessarily equal PHI, "making this symbol the *ultimate* expression of the Divine Proportion. For this reason, the five-pointed star has always been the symbol for beauty and perfection associated with the goddess and the sacred feminine."[54] Thus, upon his death, when Jacques Saunière arranges his naked self with his arms and legs extended, his body forms a pentacle and pays tribute to the sacred feminine. Like the pentacle, the symbol of the rose further embeds the sacred feminine throughout Western art. Through its "five petals and pentagonal symmetry," the rose embodies these same characteristics of femininity.[55] Jacques Saunière accordingly filled his life with rose symbolism, including protecting the grail secret "sub rosa," under the sign of the rose in a rosewood box. The sacred feminine also lives on in the very architecture of Christian churches, where the entrance represents a woman's genitalia, "complete with labial ridges and a nice little cinquefoil clitoris above the doorway."[56]

Above all else, the sacred feminine is preserved through the work of Leonardo da Vinci. No friend of the Catholic Church, the painter hid subversive symbolism in many of his most famous paintings, including *Madonna of the Rocks*.[57] Even the *Mona Lisa* offers a subtle tribute to the sacred feminine, Langdon explains. As the left is historically associated with the feminine and the right with the masculine, by skewing the Mona Lisa so that she looks much larger from the left side than from the right, da Vinci offered homage to the feminine.[58] In his most subversive move, da Vinci painted Mary Magdalene into his *Last Supper* fresco, situating Jesus' closest disciple in her rightful place at his side. Like Jacques Saunière, Leonardo da Vinci had also served as Grand Master of the Priory of Sion, so Saunière's work to preserve the sacred feminine is an extension of da Vinci's sixteenth-century efforts. Through its frequent expositions on all of these symbols and artwork—the pentacle, the Divine Proportion, the rose, the *Mona Lisa*—TDVC pays tribute to its concept of the sacred feminine. It constructs a primitive Christianity and a subversive tradition within later Christianity that both demonstrate respect for the feminine.

With its celebration of Leonardo da Vinci's life and artwork, TDVC also wins its reputation for promoting homosexuality. The novel shows no reluctance to expose that Leonardo da Vinci was gay; it describes him as a "flamboyant homosexual."[59] TDVC further celebrates da Vinci for challenging traditional gender ideology. According to Langdon's account, the artist was invested in finding the male and female in everything, as "the human soul could not be enlightened unless it had both male and female elements."[60] He encoded male and female elements in harmony in his paintings, including the *Mona Lisa*. Although Langdon refuses to settle on one interpretation of the painter's best-known work, he suggests that whatever the painting may be, it is certainly androgynous. He entertains the possibility that *Mona Lisa* may be a self-portrait of da Vinci in drag, but suggests that, at the very least, it is a "fusing" of male and female. The name Mona Lisa, he explains, is an anagram of Amon and L'Isa, the Egyptian god and goddess of fertility.[61]

With all of this attention to women, femininity, and sex, it should come as no surprise that the novel's conservative critics labeled it a radical feminist danger. The book joins the work of cultural and difference feminists over the last two centuries, who have argued that because patriarchy, especially religious patriarchy, has suppressed women, women and femininity need liberation from their denigrated roles. The novel gestures toward such liberation by resuscitating a lost tradition of goddess worship, which grants the feminine the cultural legitimacy that comes with religious sanction. With its provocative revisionist history, *TDVC* has suggested an alternative role for women within Christian tradition, which has certainly warranted the resulting public controversy.

Da Vinci's Private Patriarchy

TDVC pursues this cultural/difference feminist ideology to its extreme limits, and this line of thinking ultimately leads the novel into its celebration of the private sphere and its ideal of civic nonparticipation. Not only does *TDVC* celebrate women, in line with cultural/difference feminism, but it celebrates them specifically for their unique biology and sexuality, characteristics particularly relevant to domestic life. Moreover, it celebrates women as a class of people in binary relationship to men as a class of people, which underscores the seemingly natural entailment of that binary: what Adrienne Rich has called "compulsory heterosexuality."[62] Because the novel gives religious sanction to this celebration of women, it makes biology and sexuality expressions of faithfulness. The novel thus privatizes faithfulness, modeling the highest expression of Christian discipleship as devotion to domesticity, sexuality, and procreation.

Mary (Magdalene) the Mother

TDVC's effort to restore the sacred feminine grows out of its characters' quest to find Mary Magdalene. Like the men who have sought her through the centuries, Sir Leigh Teabing considers Magdalene his "favorite mistress."[63] These men hope that their grail quest will lead them to the sarcophagus of

Mary Magdalene, as well as a crypt containing the records of her geneal-ogy. Finding her sarcophagus will allow Langdon and Teabing to worship Magdalene—as Langdon does in the book's final pages—and finding the associated documents will allow them to prove the church's historic sup-pression of women and replace it with their own celebration of her and all women. Thus, the men's devotion to Mary Magdalene is inextricable from their reverence for the sacred feminine.

Mary Magdalene's historical and religious significance, according to her suitors, centers almost entirely on her role in the private sphere—specifically her place as Jesus' wife and the mother of his children. TDVC makes the shocking assertion that the church has erased the revered place Mary Magdalene originally held in Christ's earthly church. By Langdon and Teabing's account, however, not only was Mary Magdalene Jesus' traveling companion in his ministry and the heir apparent designated to lead his church, but she was also his romantic, marital, and sexual partner. The two men tell her history by first introducing Mary Magdalene as Jesus' compan-ion; the two were "a pair," they explain.[64] Only after Magdalene is identified as Jesus' marital partner do the characters go on to explain her leadership role in the church. As they talk about her, these men consistently frame Mary Magdalene's standing in early Christianity in terms of her role as matriarch of Jesus Christ's bloodline. The early church was only troubled by Mary Magdalene, and only inspired to denigrate her publicly, because of her sexual relationship with Jesus and the offspring it had produced. Thus, she is a woman who derived her religious power through sexual relations with a man.

Magdalene's devotees throughout the years, even as they oppose the church for its smear campaign, revere her for the same quality that the church so feared: her motherhood. The Holy Grail they seek, so long thought to be the cup that Jesus used at the Last Supper, is not actually a cup at all, but rather a chalice, which the characters explain has long been the symbol for womanhood. According to Teabing, "When Grail legend speaks of 'the chalice that held the blood of Christ' . . . it speaks, in fact, of Mary Magdalene—the female womb that carried Jesus' royal bloodline." The chalice becomes simultaneously both more and less literal than it has customarily been. It is no longer the literal cup that held Jesus' metaphoric blood—out of which disciples drank at the Last Supper—but now the chalice becomes the metaphoric cup that held Jesus' literal blood. In the process, Mary Magdalene's symbolic significance is reduced to her reproductive functions. "Mary Magdalene was the Holy Vessel," Teabing explains. "She was the chalice that bore the royal bloodline of Jesus Christ. She was the womb that bore the lineage and the vine from which the sacred fruit sprang forth."[65] The simple verb construction here makes Mary Magdalene's role plain: she *was* simply the womb. All that Magdalene could have been as Jesus' companion in his ministry, as the heir to his church, has been reduced to the three predicate nouns that follow each iteration of the verb *was*: the Holy Vessel, the womb, and the chalice. Langdon suggests that the idea of a chalice, so firmly ensconced in grail legend, is a metaphor for Mary Magdalene.[66] But it might be fairer to call the relationship metonymy: the chalice does not simply stand in for Mary Magdalene; rather, she has been reduced to the blood-carrier, the chalice.

All women, and likewise the sacred feminine more generally, can be celebrated for these biological characteristics. For as much attention as the novel gives to the sacred feminine, this key term is given remarkably little definition, and the only characteristics ever associated with the sacred feminine are biological ones. For instance, the all-important rose symbol "has always been the premiere symbol of female sexuality, of female life—birth, menstruation, motherhood, menopause, and death . . . the blossoming flower resembles the female genitalia, the sublime blossom from which all mankind enters the world."[67] "Female life" has five stages, and the three that are definitively female all relate to women's reproductive cycles. Woman's significance is that all "mankind" is birthed from her genitalia.

The qualities of motherhood that Magdalene's suitors so revere differ markedly from the ones cultural/difference feminists have traditionally celebrated, especially in the case of Ruddick's "maternal thinking." These feminists revere motherhood for its social and psychological attributes, not simply the biological ability to reproduce. Moreover, they posit that these attributes have positive applications beyond the private sphere. Ruddick urges, for instance, that "all feminists must join in articulating a theory of justice shaped by and incorporating maternal thinking."[68] *TDVC* never allows Magdalene or the maternal to venture outside the private sphere. Her maternity is always, simply, the vehicle for Jesus' bloodline.

Male and Female Complementarity

When the novel celebrates women, it treats them as a class unified by biological characteristics in binary opposition to the characteristics of men. This binary pair of men and women, masculine and feminine, makes a perfect, complementary whole when united. Ultimately, the novel's repeated talk of this binary pairing of men and women leads *TDVC* to praise heterosexuality, heterosexual coupling, and biological reproduction as the highest expression of faithfulness to the divine.

When *TDVC*'s characters venerate the male/female binary, they do so following the tradition of the ancients, whose legacy da Vinci, Saunière, and the Priory of Sion have worked to preserve. The ancients, the novel explains, "envisioned their world in two halves—masculine and feminine. Their gods and goddesses worked to keep a balance of power. Yin and Yang. When male and female were balanced, there was harmony in the world."[69] Even the Hebrew Scriptures' name for God embodies this perfect balance. The tetragrammaton YHWH, Langdon explains, is the combination of the masculine Jah (as in Jehovah) and the feminine Havah, the pre-Hebraic name for Eve.[70] Art and symbolism also embody this principle of male and female balance, as in iambic pentameter, a favorite poetic rhythm of Jacques Saunière, which is formed by the successive coupling of balanced pairs.[71] Indeed, Saunière had a "passion for dualism." When the characters discover that he had nested a black cryptex inside a white one, it makes perfect sense:

> *Two cryptexes.* Everything in pairs. *Double entendres. Male female. Black nested within white.* Langdon felt the web of symbolism stretching onward. *White gives birth to black.*
>
> *Every man sprang from woman.*
>
> *White—female.*
>
> *Black—male.*[72]

Saunière, like the ancients whose legacy he worshiped and protected, believed that a perfect harmony could only be created when the male and female elements of the universe were in balance.

Through the ritual of Heiros Gamos, this dualistic thinking finds expression in heterosexual coupling. Outlasting even the novel's revealing of the true nature of the Holy Grail, Heiros Gamos is *TDVC*'s most enduring mystery. At least seven times the characters use vague terms to refer to a ritual. For Neveu, it is something shocking she once witnessed, and for Langdon it is a secret he must disclose to Neveu at the proper moment. The climax finally comes exactly two-thirds of the way through the novel—on page 307—when Neveu and Langdon compare notes, letting their audience members in on the secret of the ritual called Heiros Gamos. As Langdon and Neveu explain it, Priory of Sion members observe this two-thousand-year-old ritual each spring. Neveu describes the Heiros Gamos ritual she witnessed upon arriving at her grandfather's vacation house over spring break:

> Everyone in the circle rocked back and forth and chanted in reverence to something on the floor before them . . . the chanting grew steady again. Accelerating . . . Thundering now. Faster. The participants took a step inward and knelt.[73]

They knelt toward the sex act that was being performed at the center of the circle. As Grand Master of the Priory, Jacques Saunière was the celebrant of this ceremony, so he and a female partner were engaged in this focal sex act. Following the tradition of the Egyptians whose ritual is being replicated, these Priory members "celebrate the reproductive power of the female."[74] Like their Egyptian models, Priory members use the Heiros Gamos ritual to celebrate the human body.

Not only does Heiros Gamos grow out of the male/female binary, but its performance, and the characters' veneration of it, reinscribes this dualistic thinking. When Priory members engage in Heiros Gamos, the men wear black tunics, black shoes, and black masks; the women wear white gossamer gowns, white masks, and golden shoes, and they hold golden orbs. Participants are entirely covered up by these costumes, so that they are only distinguishable by sex. They have no other demographic characteristics—race, class, nationality—and they also have no personalities, no individual attributes, no distinguishing characteristics beyond gender. In this ritual, the most spiritual of all, each participant is categorized by his or her gender alone. Moreover, the participants are partnered in opposite-sex pairs, and the celebrated sex act is also between a man and a woman. The ritual itself is definitively heterosexual, and presumably even the "flamboyantly homosexual" Priory Grand Master Leonardo da Vinci would have celebrated Heiros Gamos with a female partner.

As it reinscribes the male/female binary, Heiros Gamos also gives men and women distinct roles in the sex act. For men, Heiros Gamos is a spiritual act and women become their spiritual/sexual vehicle. As Langdon explains it, Heiros Gamos was the ancients' route to glimpsing God, and the Priory has maintained that tradition. Heiros Gamos is based on the belief that

> the male was spiritually incomplete until he had carnal knowledge of the sacred feminine. Physical union with the female remained the sole means through which man could become spiritually complete and

> ultimately achieve *gnosis*—knowledge of the divine . . . By communing with woman . . . man could achieve a climactic instant when his mind went totally blank and he could see God . . . Physiologically speaking, the male climax was accompanied by a split second entirely devoid of thought. . . . A moment of clarity during which God could be glimpsed.[75]

There can be little doubt that Heiros Gamos venerates the feminine, but in doing so, it only celebrates the female body. Even then, it celebrates the female body specifically as a spiritual route to God only for men. Men need women's sexuality in order to see God. Within Langdon's lengthy description of Heiros Gamos, there is no attention to what the ritual might mean to women or how it might provide some spiritual or sexual satisfaction for them. Instead, women, reduced to their bodies, become physical instruments for satisfying men's spiritual needs.

All credit for preserving this ancient ritual of Heiros Gamos, as well as the secret legacy of Mary Magdalene and the Holy Grail, is due to the Priory of Sion.[76] As these men have worshiped the sacred feminine throughout the centuries, however, they have preserved the traditions that reduce women to their bodies and celebrate their reproductive sexuality. Importantly, the Priory members doing all this protecting are largely male. One character explains that women can be Priory members, and four have even served as Grand Master, but the *sènèchaux*, the "guardians," have traditionally been men. Thus, when *TDVC* reveals and reveres the historic work of the Priory in protecting the legacy of the sacred feminine, it celebrates a group of men who have reduced Mary Magdalene and all women to their wombs, who have used women's sexuality for their own spiritual fulfillment, and who have limited women's value to the private sphere.

Sophie Neveu and the Quest for Personal Fulfillment

While *TDVC*'s historical narrative reconstructs a Christian tradition that venerates the private sphere, its primary narrative further privatizes faithfulness. From the moment that the immediately sympathetic Sophie Neveu enters the story, the narrative commits itself to the private sphere. Even though the novel begins with the murder of Jacques Saunière—one of the most public men in Paris, who held all the shocking information about the church's historic sins—his granddaughter's introduction into the story transforms his death into a private matter. His trail of clues becomes a private message for Neveu, who embarks upon a journey toward personal fulfillment. The afternoon of his death, Jacques Saunière had left his estranged granddaughter a phone message that intimated that their lives might be in danger and offered to provide information about their family. She ignored her grandfather that afternoon, as she had been doing for ten years. Upon arriving at the murder scene, however, Neveu is filled with a sense of loneliness. Saunière had been her last remaining relative because her parents, brother, and grandmother had been killed in a car accident when she was a young girl. Thus, when Neveu discovers that her grandfather has left clues for her, she hopes these clues will take her to the family secrets that his phone message that afternoon had promised. There is a "motivation still burning within her. *The truth about my family.* Sophie still sensed something deeply personal entwined within this mystery."[77]

Neveu's instinct is proved correct when Saunière's trail of clues leads these grail seekers not to some grand new truth about the Holy Grail, but instead to private truths about Neveu's family—that her grandmother and brother are still alive and that she and her brother are the most direct living descendants of Jesus Christ and Mary Magdalene's bloodline. The final cryptex even takes Neveu and Langdon to the chapel at Rosslyn, where she reunites with her long-lost grandmother and brother. Along the way, Saunière's clues offer Langdon and Teabing plenty of opportunities to pontificate about the lost history of the Holy Grail, but these grail secrets always work in service of Neveu's private quest. Langdon and Teabing never uncover the documents proving Jesus and Mary Magdalene's bloodline, which threaten to discredit and destroy the Catholic Church if made public. Instead, the ultimate result of their grail quest, the conclusion of Saunière's trail of clues, is Sophie's family and the sense of fulfillment that finding them brings to her.

This personal narrative centers on Sophie Neveu, but the cast of characters around her makes the story even more personal. In the case of Sir Leigh Teabing, the blasphemy of this villain's public quest demonstrates by contrast the sanctity of Neveu's personal quest. Whereas Neveu only seeks individual fulfillment, Teabing wants to expose a public truth that could discredit the Catholic Church. During their journey, the two quarrel over whether or not to publicly reveal the grail truth they expect to find, which Teabing assumes will be a genealogical record of Jesus and Mary Magdalene's bloodline. Neveu's instinct is to follow her grandfather's reverence for secrets and keep the grail legend private.[78] Teabing, however, cannot comprehend any option other than making the grail truth public. As possession of the Holy Grail makes Neveu "the keeper of a truth that man has sought for centuries," Teabing believes that she "will be faced with the responsibility of revealing that truth to the world."[79] By the end of the novel, as the only truth revealed has been a personal one, Neveu does not end up holding the public power Teabing had anticipated. Even still, her newly discovered grandmother reaffirms Neveu's secrecy instinct. She knows that "the Priory has always maintained that the Grail should *never* be unveiled," as "it is the mystery and wonderment that serve our souls, not the Grail itself."[80]

TDVC's grail quest also becomes personal because it is framed as a love story. The romance between Neveu and Langdon is subtle but undeniable. Neveu is a lonely female seeking fulfillment, and even Langdon admits that his "lifelong affinity for bachelorhood" has been "replaced by an unexpected emptiness."[81] It should come as no surprise, then, that these two single lead characters find solace in their affection for one another. Initially, Langdon recognizes Sophie for her beauty, but as their journey together progresses, their mutual attraction grows deeper.[82] They fall into a routine of complementarity, where their unique skill sets make them a formidable clue-deciphering duo. Where Langdon knows symbolism and art history, Neveu's facility with letters and numbers helps her crack anagrams and codes. Along the way, both characters demonstrate gratitude for the other's role in this grail quest. As the two sit together en route to London, for instance, Langdon "watched her for a long while and felt an unexpected upwelling of contentment. Despite his troubles tonight, Langdon was thankful to have landed in such good company."[83] Later, Neveu verbalizes her appreciation for his role in their work together, and Langdon "felt an unexpected flicker of attraction between them."[84] The end of the narrative brings closure to this romance, in addition to the closure it brings to Neveu's search for her family. The final action of the story itself (before the epilogue) comes in a romantic exchange between the two. They agree to meet again soon, and "Sophie leaned forward and kissed him again, now on the lips. Their bodies came together, softly at first, and then completely. When she pulled away, her eyes were full of promise."[85]

The narrative concludes just as the romance must: the protagonists defeat their foe and find their treasure. This treasure is not the ordinary bounty of a grail quest—the cup from the Last Supper. Nor is it even the promised bounty of the revised grail legend—the sarcophagus of Mary Magdalene and the written records of Jesus and Magdalene's bloodline. Instead, these victors acquire the treasure of wisdom, which Northrop Frye notes is one of the ideal forms of wealth in mythopoeic romance.[86] They have become wise to the true nature of the grail, and Neveu has discovered her grandmother, herself a wise old crone. Together, Langdon, Neveu, her grandmother, and her brother settle into the safe space that Frye calls "cuddle fiction." The family home at Rosslyn "exuded a warm and inviting aura. The smell of bread wafted through the opened screen door, and a golden light shone in the windows."[87] There, outside the house on a bluff overlooking the Scottish countryside, Langdon and Neveu share the kiss that consummates their romance. At that moment, all the elements of the story have been resolved—the villain has already been revealed and the victims of his plot (the bishop, the monk, the police chief) have been redeemed. Now, with the kiss, the two central characters have found fulfillment through family and romance. That kiss marks the completion of the personal, private journey that defines this grail quest.

CONCLUSIONS AND IMPLICATIONS

Although *TDVC* caused controversy on a wide range of grounds—doubting Jesus' divinity, insulting the Catholic organization Opus Dei, revising church history—questions about its feminist implications persisted in critiques of the novel and in media coverage of the bestselling phenomenon. The novel's gender politics are not interesting simply because of their sheer popularity or controversy, however. They also have consequences because they lead directly to the novel's ideal of civic nonparticipation as the expression of faithful discipleship. *TDVC*'s explicit feminist platform is an avowed celebration of women, giving religious sanction to the "sacred feminine" and "goddess worship." It celebrates women, embodied as Mary Magdalene and Sophie Neveu, however, only for their private-sphere significance—specifically Mary Magdalene's sexuality and motherhood and Neveu's status as the descendant of this bloodline. Through its veneration of these women, the revised Holy Grail legend, and the ritual of Heiros Gamos, *TDVC* ultimately lauds biological sexuality and heterosexual reproduction as the natural expressions of faithfulness, so long suppressed by the Catholic Church. In direct contrast to contemporaneous Christian-themed mass media texts that model public, civic avenues for faithful discipleship, *TDVC* privatizes faithfulness.

TDVC's gender ideology brings the novel's political implications into sharp relief in part because it contrasts with the tradition of American feminism in three significant ways. First, *TDVC*'s reduction of women to biological sexuality and its preference for the private set the novel at odds with American feminism. Among feminists, only cultural/difference feminists have typically celebrated women as unique beings, and they have acknowledged a wide range of women's defining characteristics. Rather than limiting themselves to women's biology or sexuality, these feminists celebrate women for their social and interpersonal attributes. As they praise women's caring, nurturing, pacifist tendencies, they acknowledge that these traits may partially result from women's unique biology, but they also seek social and cultural explanations. The touchstone articulations of cultural/difference feminism in the field of psychology, by Gilligan and Belenky et al., both find gendered childhood socialization at least partially explanatory for women's difference.[88] Ruddick credits the experience of raising children for engendering the maternal characteristics she so values.[89] These feminists largely resist the temptation to essentialize women's difference, always admitting that both the causes and consequences of gender difference are larger than biology. By doing exactly the opposite—praising women for biological difference only—TDVC not only limits women to a narrow collection of valued characteristics, but it also makes those characteristics fixed and unchangeable, at least to the extent that biology is fixed and unchangeable.

Second, when TDVC reinscribes binary gender and compulsory heterosexuality, it also does so over and against the legacy of American feminism. In its primary narrative, the novel depicts the perfect complementarity of Robert Langdon and Sophie Neveu, whose skills as a formidable clue-deciphering duo imply the positive potential of harmonious and balanced bi-gendered pairings. And in its historical narrative, the novel's celebrations of male-female pairings in art and ritual reinforce the same point. This bi-gendered system hardly serves the ends of feminist politics, however. As Judith Butler has argued, it "imposes a duality and a uniformity on bodies in order to maintain reproductive sexuality as a compulsory order."[90] She could have been writing about TDVC precisely: its obsession with all things opposite—yin and yang, male and female—leads the novel to its climactic heterosexual coupling in Heiros Gamos. By imbuing this sexual rite with spiritual meaning, the novel gives religious sanction to the very sort of compulsory heterosexuality and compulsory reproduction from which feminism has sought to liberate women.

Third, TDVC's clear preference for the private sphere marks the novel's sharpest deviation from the tradition of American feminism. Cultural/difference feminists have typically celebrated women's unique attributes specifically for their public applicability. Acknowledging that women's culture has been fostered in the domestic sphere, cultural/difference feminism assumes that introducing it to the public sphere can transform politics. That is, this line of thought suggests that feminine values like cooperation, caregiving, and nonviolence, which have served women so well in the domestic sphere, "should be valued for their positive application in the public sphere."[91] Cultural/difference feminism has long informed feminist utopian fantasies like *Herland*, but even on a more modest scale, contemporary cultural/difference feminists "hold that women's political value system may be derived from traditional women's culture and applied to the public realm,"[92] even the "public, androcentric world."[93]

With this focus on the public sphere, cultural/difference feminism shares the more general feminist impulse toward publicity, as American feminists have always struggled to gain women wider access to the public sphere.[94] In the nineteenth century, that meant access to the legal sphere, including the rights to vote, practice law, and sit on juries. And in both the nineteenth and twentieth centuries, the move toward publicity has meant women's greater access to education and the professions. In twentieth-century feminism, the tendency toward publicity has been encapsulated by the pithiest statement of movement ideology: "The personal is political." Even what seem like the most private, individual matters for women, such as household distribution of labor, gendered socialization of children, and domestic violence, have social bases and public import. And the more recent gay liberation movement echoes this emphasis on publicity. Even the most individual, personal act, the act of coming out, is ultimately a celebration of publicity—the prerogative to be publicly gay.

In the religious context, feminists have been no less focused on publicity. Noting the persistent injustice that keeps women out of the highest ranks of the clergy in many denominations, feminists have urged the Roman Catholic Church, the Lutheran Church–Missouri Synod, and the Southern Baptist Convention to open their orders of priests and ministers to women. Because the priest or minister is the most public representation of the incarnate God-in-Christ to the members of the church, as well as the most public representative of the church to the world, these denominations remain patriarchal institutions as long as they exclude women from visible leadership. Other Christian feminist efforts have had similarly public import. The feminist project to create the *Inclusive Language Lectionary* sought to make Scripture texts free of male bias available to accompany the three-year lectionary cycle used in church services. Even Elisabeth Schüssler Fiorenza's feminist biblical hermeneutic aims to do more than empower women to read themselves into church history. She assumes that identifying women's roles in early Christianity, and demonstrating how traditional hermeneutics have obscured them, will enhance theological understandings of early

Christianity more generally. That is, rereading biblical religion through a feminist hermeneutic might change the church's understanding of itself as a public institution.[95]

These three deviations from feminist thought—the novel's affection for biological difference, compulsory heterosexuality, and the private sphere—not only reveal the absurdity of the public outcry over the novel's "radical feminism." More importantly, this analysis of the novel's gender politics suggests *TDVC*'s conservative political implications. The novel's preference for the private sphere typifies conservative thought in general, but it especially resonates with the religious impulse Martin Marty has called "private Protestantism." This way of thinking assumes that Christians should be most concerned with keeping their own personal affairs in order and helping their friends and neighbors right themselves with God, rather than working for public, social justice. In this worldview, individual, personal morality testifies to a believer's righteousness more than political, legislative, or charitable activism ever could. The novel's affection for heterosexual coupling especially resonates with the politics of personal morality, which have in recent years fixated upon issues associated with sexuality, such as abortion, homosexuality, and premarital sex. Posing as its central issues who should have sex with whom and what type of sex they should have, this moral reform tradition suggests that if we all have the right kind of sex with the right kind of people, we will find right relationships with God, and the world will be redeemed.

Over the last generation, some of conservative Christianity's most influential leaders have developed their public stature by articulating these ideals of personal morality and marriage and family life. Although James Dobson and Tim LaHaye may now be famous for their political organizing, both started their public careers dispensing marriage and family advice from a Christian perspective. As Dobson tells it, he was so disgusted by the feminists gathered in Houston for the 1977 U.N. Year of the Woman conference that he rededicated his life to promoting Christian family ideals.[96] In addition to publishing his first bestseller, *Dare to Discipline*, Dobson started a small local radio show that, thirty years later, is broadcast daily to millions of followers globally.[97] His organization, Focus on the Family, considers its task to be "to nurture and defend the family," and to that end, it distributes books, tracts, and videos, in addition to maintaining an Internet presence, that help Christians manage their marriages and families.[98] The organization's Colorado Springs headquarters also staffs a correspondence center that doles out advice, consolation, and resources in response to the hundreds of thousands of phone calls, letters, and e-mails it receives annually. Even as Dobson's political clout has grown, he has kept his organization largely free from politics, and he insists that supporting individual marriages and families remains his priority over influencing legislative or electoral politics.[99] Similarly, Tim LaHaye, one of the *Left Behind* coauthors, first published advice manuals related to personal psychology and marriage. In 1976, he and his wife, Beverly, wrote *The Act of Marriage: The Beauty of Sexual Love*, the first of nearly a dozen books the two would coauthor about sex and marriage. The LaHayes share Dobson's commitment to helping Christians strengthen their families, and they all promote the merits of the traditional, heterosexual nuclear family. For Dobson, the superiority of this family arrangement is self-evident: "The traditional family produces the healthiest children and greatest happiness for the most number of people."[100]

Although Dobson and the LaHayes may never depict anything as radical as *TDVC*'s ritual of Heiros Gamos, their public work embodies many of the novel's guiding assumptions. When they imply that marital sex is an act of Christian devotion, they echo the novel's respect for heterosexuality as a performance of faithfulness. When they instruct Christians to concentrate their energy on strengthening their families, they echo the novel's reverence for the private sphere as a venue for performing faithfulness. Thus, Christian marriage and family guidance, like that dispensed by Dobson and the LaHayes, provides believers with resources for performing exactly the model of faithfulness idealized by *TDVC*. The novel's vision of Christian discipleship, in short, is realized in these conservative Christian self-help discourses more so than in any feminist political agenda.

7

THE LIMITS AND POSSIBILITIES OF FAITH-BASED CIVIC PARTICIPATION

He has told you, O mortal, what is good: and what does the Lord require of you but to do justice, to love kindness, and to walk humbly with your God?

Micah 6:8

Jesus answered, "The first is, 'Hear, O Israel: the Lord our God, the Lord is one; you shall love the Lord your God with all your heart, and with all your soul, and with all your mind, and with all your strength.' The second is this, 'You shall love your neighbor as yourself.' There is no other commandment greater than these."

Mark 12:29-31

The Christian-themed media texts popular at the turn of the twenty-first century—not only *Left Behind, 7th Heaven, The Passion of the Christ, The Da Vinci Code*, and *Amazing Grace*, but also the dozens of other books, films, and television shows produced in that time period—earned their places in the national consciousness because they broke sales records, won awards, launched careers, and incited controversies. With their popularity among certain religious sects, they introduced evangelical Christians as a viable consumer demographic that would become attractive to media producers. Their significance does not end with their successes as consumable commodities, however.

These books, films, and television series drew attention because they dared to probe our beliefs and value systems. They offered what people of faith so commonly desire: access to God. Through the person of the bloodied Jesus in *The Passion*, along with his supposed descendants in *TDVC*, as well as the wise spiritual mentors in *Left Behind, Amazing Grace*, and *7th Heaven*, these texts offered us momentary glimpses of the divine. Their

181

images of God differed drastically, in keeping with the theology that produced them, from the low Christology of *The Passion* to the premillennial dispensationalism of *Left Behind* to the Gnosticism lurking behind *TDVC*. Although they did not name their theological predispositions, these media texts invited people of faith to navigate the various and competing theologies accessible in contemporary Christianity.

All five of these entertainment media texts also offered audience members opportunities to reflect on the faith-based obligations in their earthly lives, especially in relationship to any hope for another life in Christ. Indeed, these texts nearly fixated on civic life. *Amazing Grace* depicted its hero's lifelong crusade to win political reform through legislative channels. *The Passion of the Christ* portrayed its characters amidst one of the most public dramas of its historical era: the sentencing, torture, and execution of a presumed criminal. *Left Behind* celebrateed the militia of Christians who coalesce to combat a global dictator. *7th Heaven*'s characters struggled to alleviate some of the social issues that most tax our civic life today, such as teenage pregnancy, drug abuse, and poverty. And *The Da Vinci Code* arrived at its veneration for the heterosexual domestic sphere by first considering and then rejecting its villain's interest in the public import of religion. Even if the novel ultimately opted for the private over the public, it shares the overarching concern common to all these popular media: what are the civic consequences of our faithful lives as Christians?

Each of these texts answered that question in gendered terms. From the brutish masculinity and genteel masculinity portrayed in *Left Behind* and *Amazing Grace*, respectively, to the submissive femininity and charitable femininity more obvious in *The Passion* and *7th Heaven* and the heterosexuality celebrated in *TDVC*, all of these stories characterized their heroes along gendered lines. Not only did they construct models of faithful civic participation that were defined by gender, but they also reinforced the historic connections between gender and the various forms of civic participation.

These entertainment media were neither the first nor the last to introduce religious themes into popular culture. They were neither the first nor the last to offer audience members access to the divine, competing systems of Christian theology, or gendered ideals of civic participation. In the years since their successes, other books, films, and television shows have approached these topics exactly. Indeed, just months after *Amazing Grace* premiered in the theaters, William Paul Young published *The Shack*, which would become the Christian media publishing sensation of 2008. Within eighteen months of its release, *The Shack* had sold 5.4 million copies and had been translated into thirty languages.[1] Reports of life-changing encounters with the book fueled its popularity. The *Atlanta Journal-Constitution* described how a member of one of that city's larger churches found the book so moving that he purchased 750 copies to pass out to people in the pews around him on Easter Sunday.[2] Yet, like so many other Christian-themed mass media successes, *The Shack* has also provoked controversy. Albert Mohler, president of the Southern Baptist Theological Seminary, denounced the novel on his radio program.[3] Mark Driscoll, the leader of the Mars Hill megachurches in Seattle, instructed his congregants not to read the novel.[4] The LifeWay Christian bookstores, which are associated with the Southern Baptist Convention, had to remove the book from the shelves for a month to allow theologians to study it and make a recommendation. (With their blessing, the stores now sell the book again.)

In the model of recent Christian-themed media, *The Shack* articulates one narrow strand of Christian theology that has clear implications for gender and civic participation. It offers believers access to the divine when its protagonist, Mack, encounters the Christian trinity: a black woman named Papa, the Middle Eastern carpenter Jesus, and a mystical Asian woman, Sarayu.[5] He finds them when he accepts a mysterious invitation to return to the shack where his daughter was murdered. There, these three figures welcome him into a transformative weekend of theological conversations. Over the course of hours or possibly days, they teach Mack about love and relationships, which the novel depicts as the central lessons of Christian discipleship. When Mack discovers God's boundless love for all humans, he learns to extend that love to his own family, even going so far as to forgive his daughter's murderer. Through this main character's quest for healing, the novel struggles with questions that have haunted Christians for centuries—Why do bad things happen to good people? How can I forgive the one who has wronged me? and Does God love me even in the midst of my sin? It answers each of these questions with an affirmative and uplifting promise that God offers unconditional grace in response to the human evils of the world.

Although much of the novel's plot takes place in an otherworldly exchange between the protagonist and the divine trinity, *The Shack*'s theology offers not-so-subtle implications for human civic life on Earth. It teaches that because love and relationships should be humans' primary aspirations, we should be skeptical of institutions, which tend to inhibit the love and relationships that God wills for us. Those institutions demand hierarchy, and, as the novel's Jesus explains, "Once you have a hierarchy you need

rules to protect and administer it, and then you need law and the enforcement of the rules, and you end up with some kind of chain of command
or a system of order that destroys relationship rather than promotes it."⁶ In
particular, Jesus inveighs against the institutions of religion, politics, and
economics. He asserts, "They are the man-created trinity of terrors that rav-
ages the earth and deceives those I care about."⁷ He promises, however, "I
can give you freedom to overcome any system of power in which you find
yourself, be it religious, economic, social, or political."⁸

Because the institutions that most threaten loving relationships—
politics, economics, religion—are the basic structures of our civic life, *The
Shack*'s model of faithfulness puts Christians at odds with what Greg Boyd
would call the kingdom of the world.⁹ He encourages Christians to reject
the kingdom of the world, which values power, and to embrace the kingdom
of God, which values love. The kingdom of the world, according to Boyd,
manifests itself in tribalism and retributive justice and hierarchy, whereas
the kingdom of God models itself after Christ's self-sacrificial love for the
world. Boyd argues that Christians create the kingdom of God by enacting
Christlike dispositions, just as *The Shack*'s divine figures encourage Mack to
mimic their love for each other in his relationships with his loved ones. In
both schemes, earthly interactions with other humans figure prominently,
but the established civic sphere fares poorly as the structure that prohibits
the realization of God's kingdom.

The Shack, like so much Christian discourse, makes its gender politics
easily accessible. Even beyond its unconventional portrayal of a female God
and Holy Spirit, *The Shack* expresses God's desire for a gender-egalitarian
world. In conversation with Jesus, Mack learns that God does not desire
a hierarchy between men and women. Instead, "we want male and female
to be counterparts, face-to-face equals, each unique and different, distinctive in gender but complementary, and each empowered uniquely by Sarayu
from whom all true power and authority originates."¹⁰ The novel undercuts
these bold egalitarian moves in small ways. The God figure, even when
revealed as a black woman, is routinely called Papa. By the end of the novel,
God is revealed as a bearded white male, because God and Mack were going
on a journey where Mack was "going to need a father."¹¹ Moreover, the narrative stars a rugged outdoorsman on a personal quest to redeem himself
after failing to protect his vulnerable daughter. Typically a celebration of
male masculinity, the novel offers little glimpse at the role human females
and femininity might play in the relationships it so glorifies.

Beyond gender, *The Shack* engages many of the same theological issues that run through other recent popular media. Like *The Passion*, it keeps Jesus' sacrificial death at the center of Christianity. And, in its abiding desire for relationships of love and forgiveness and trust, it espouses many of the values that *7th Heaven* and *TDVC* both celebrate in private-sphere familial and sexual relationships. It contests, however, the popular image of the polarized good and evil so evident in the *Left Behind* books. Whereas those novels imagine a world order starkly divided between God and Satan, *The Shack* presents a world in which God has ordained all that is good, and humans have either created or imagined evil. Although God can make all things good, only humans distinguish between good and evil. Sarayu explains to Mack,

> It is *you* who determines good and evil. You become the judge. And to make things more confusing, that which you determine to be good will change over time and circumstance. And then beyond that and even worse, there are billions of you each determining what is good and what is evil. So when your good and evil clashes with your neighbor's, fights and arguments ensue and even wars break out.[12]

Good and evil exist in the human system, not the divine or cosmic one. The implication here is that if humans create evil, then we should not ask God to overcome it. Moreover, if we create evil by imagining it into being, then we need not eradicate it by punishment or retribution. Instead, we eradicate evil by our power *not* to imagine it into being.

I have dwelled upon this explanation of *The Shack* to make a simple point: these themes of civic participation and gender persist in popular Christian media and will presumably continue to do so into the future. They derive from a wide range of Christian theologies that find expression in books, films, television shows, and other mass media. Thus, the preceding five case studies are important individually, and I have tried to draw out their implications in the conclusion to each chapter. But because the recent popularity of *The Shack* reminds us that faith-based images of gender and civic participation are a phenomenon much larger than these five case studies, I would like to highlight six larger patterns, or lessons, derived from the preceding analyses that I believe speak to the intersections of gender, civic participation, and Christian media more generally. First, achieving a unified faith-based coalition for civic activism is an impractical dream and an unreasonable nightmare. Second, theoretical discussions of civic participation that focus narrowly on rational-critical deliberation and charitable volunteering miss the range of modes of civic participation widely available. Third, not only are ideals of civic participation still characterized by gender, but too often feminine dispositions are accessible to men and women alike while masculine dispositions remain exclusive to men. Fourth, popular images of civic participation reconstitute ideologies of race, often creating paternalistic relationships between white citizens and the black neighbors they help. Fifth, the conventions of entertainment media necessarily constrain the possible dispositions of civic participation they can depict, which makes entertainment media an imperfect source of cultural ideas about civic participation. Sixth, because Christianity promises to be a countercultural sphere separate from the state and market, it affords radical possibilities for facilitating civic participation.

THE LIMITS OF CHRISTIAN COALITIONS

These case studies make one point clear: the diversity of Christian belief systems makes a lasting, unified Christian political alliance impossible. Not only do these five media texts model five unique dispositions of faith-based civic participation, but they demonstrate how these unique dispositions stem from various Christian theologies. The low Christology common to liberation theologians and Mel Gibson alike facilitates the ideal of feminine submission in the face of divine will. Thus, *The Passion* is significant in part because it models this disposition for such a broad audience. But it is also significant because it shows us how the glorification of Christ's suffering death—wherever it is found—can lead to individual agency circumscribed as feminine submission. Similarly, the premillennial dispensationalism preached in the *Left Behind* novels leads to brutish masculinity as the celebrated model of civic participation, which I suspect premillennial dispensationalism has a tendency to do. And the example of *The Shack* reminds us that Christian media will only continue to proliferate with these varied and conflicting ideals for civic participation. Christian theology and Christian media are rich with resources for imagining faithful discipleship, but their very richness makes a unified coalition unlikely.

Contemporary political developments confirm the impossibility of building a unified faith-based civic coalition. In the aftermath of the 2004 election, when Christian leaders launched a backlash against the Falwell-inspired "values voters," they also questioned the conventional wisdom interpreting the election. Whereas popular narratives suggested that evangelical

Christians had reelected George W. Bush when they flocked to the polls to pass anti-gay marriage amendments, Christian leaders demonstrated how the relationship between religion and politics was not so simple. First, liberal Christians like Jim Wallis and Robin Meyers published their manifestoes, challenging the hegemony of those "values voters." Even conservatives like Greg Boyd and David Kuo added to the criticism of the Christian Right. In their own ways, all of them complicated the popular narrative by highlighting other forms of Christian activism aside from the "values voters."

In the following months and years, these men were proved correct when the Christian Right fractured internally. When Jerry Falwell died in May 2007, journalists and religious leaders alike seized upon that moment to mark a generational shift facing conservative Christianity, one with significant implications for faith-based civic engagement. They described the ailing health and impending retirements of most of the men and women who had politicized and mobilized conservative Christians and "set the movement's social agenda from Ronald Reagan's 1980 election through the 2004 general election."[13] Falwell was preceded in death by D. James Kennedy, the founder and leader of Coral Ridge Ministries, and followed in death by Paul Weyrich, while others, such as Pat Robertson and James Dobson, faced the ends of their careers.[14] Calling it the "evangelical crack-up," journalists noted that the 2004 election would be the movement's last triumph; although it had gained momentum over its more than twenty years of development, the Christian Right would never achieve the level of cultural power necessary to win definitive victories on signature issues like abortion and gay marriage.

Instead, the men commonly identified to succeed Falwell and his contemporaries seem poised to guide the movement in a new direction. These men, such as Rick Warren and Bill Hybels, reject any previous devotion or obligation to the Republican Party. As E. J. Dionne explained in the *Washington Post*, "A significant group of theologically conservative Christians no longer wants to be treated as a cog in the Republican political machine."[15] Rick Warren signaled his political independence when his Saddleback Church hosted bipartisan political events in the 2008 presidential election, and then he accepted the invitation to give the invocation at President Obama's January 2009 inauguration. Warren and like-minded Christian leaders also released their followers from single-minded devotion to the issues of same-sex marriage and abortion.[16] Even if they maintain their conservative opinions on these issues, they also show how Christian faith can lead to a larger agenda. Rick Warren's social focus, for instance, is the African AIDS crisis. Richard Cizik coaxed the National Association of

Evangelicals into affirming a platform plank opposing climate change (even if his political stances later cost him his standing with the organization). And other issues, such as poverty and the violence in Darfur, register in faith-based terms for these leaders as well.[17]

Along with rejecting partisan platforms, this new generation of Christian leaders eschews the narrow models of political organizing popularized by Falwell and his allies.[18] David Kuo explains that Ted Haggard's successor as pastor of Colorado Springs' New Life Church has promised to keep his pulpit "politics free."[19] Michael Luo and Laurie Goodstein describe Gabe Lyons' Fermi Project, which provides evangelicals with alternative outlets, such as the media and arts, for shaping the culture.[20] New York Times columnist Nicholas Kristof praises the scope of the work undertaken by Rick Warren and his Saddleback Church.[21] Committing themselves to fight poverty, malaria, and AIDS in sixty-eight countries, 7,500 of Warren's parishioners have traveled to volunteer in those countries, funding their trips with personal resources. Warren strives for Christians to be known as much for showing love as they are for staging political protests.[22] David Kirkpatrick cites Bill Hybels, leader of the Willow Creek Community Churches, as a model of the new generation of Christian leadership. Hybels calls for community involvement around issues such as racism, educational injustice, and poverty.[23] Kirkpatrick also describes an anti-abortion initiative akin to the one that Greg Boyd proposes: some of Wichita's pro-life activists, who earned a national reputation staging protests against abortion doctor George Tiller, have opened Choices, a medical center adjacent to an abortion clinic. There, they counsel women away from abortions by providing alternatives.

Each of these projects does important work on its own, and together they contribute to a public sphere where Christians, acting in the name of their faith, have a wide range of options for how they might participate in civic life. For Jerry Falwell and his ilk, the failure to create a permanent class of conservative Christian political leaders might be disappointing. Liberal Christians like Jim Wallis might also be disheartened not to coalesce a Christian majority willing to use its political influence to eradicate poverty or work on any of the other issues that interest them. Even Greg Boyd urges Christians universally to adopt his model of building the kingdom of God through loving acts of self-sacrifice. But the good news is that in what Rob Asen calls our "multiple public sphere," when some Christians work as political actors and some run charitable organizations and others perform individual acts of mercy, we have a civic life rich enough to encompass all these forms of engagement and flexible enough that individual people of faith can translate their religious commitments in the ways most meaningful to them.[24]

For liberals and anyone else worried about the political power of Christians, this diffused landscape should prove encouraging. Conservative Christians are not poised to grow into the behemoth political machine Ralph Reed and Jerry Falwell may have once promised, nor have they ever been such an impenetrable force. Activists who tend to blame the Christian Right for frustrating liberal political advances would be wise to reevaluate how uniform the evangelical Christian voting demographic ever was and whether or not it deserves the blame for the failure of liberal policy goals. Far short of being disciplined culture warriors, American Christians have tended to participate in our civic life in wide and varied ways, from praying to voting to volunteering.

THE LIMITS OF POPULAR IDEALS OF CITIZENSHIP

Although these entertainment media depict models of civic participation, their models barely resemble the ones popular in scholarly and theoretical discussions of civic life. This difference suggests, on the one hand, that entertainment media fail to promote the dispositions of civic participation that social theorists argue would benefit democracy most. On the other hand, this difference suggests that social theorists have a dangerously narrow view of the ways citizens might engage their communities.

The two dominant ideals of civic participation, at least in scholarly conversations, stem from Putnam's image of civic volunteerism and Habermas' image of rational-critical deliberation. It is probably safe to assume that neither of these is depicted perfectly in any entertainment media, and they certainly do not appear unproblematically in the five Christian-themed texts considered here. Of the five texts, 7th Heaven most nearly approximates Putnam's civic volunteerism. Because his surveys measure American rates of church attendance, organization membership, and charitable volunteering, among other behaviors, Putnam's engaged citizens are the ones who cook at soup kitchens, sponsor scout troops, and organize elementary school bake sales. 7th Heaven's characters perform some of these duties admirably: the minister-father stacks cans at a food pantry, the oldest son drives a Meals on Wheels van, and the whole family attends church together.

Yet 7th Heaven also highlights a major limitation of Putnam's perspective. Although its characters sometimes participate in civic institutions like churches and food pantries, their community involvement otherwise takes on renegade qualities. Working individually, the members of *7th Heaven*'s Camden family help the needy individuals in their community: the school-aged daughter brings an extra lunch for a hungry classmate, the older teenage son helps a pregnant friend find childbirth classes, the adolescent daughter intervenes with a teammate taking performance-enhancing drugs. These individual acts of charity do not register on surveys of civic behavior, nor do they figure into normative schemes for reinvigorating the health of the polis. They are, however, the "thousand points of light" and the "armies of compassion" so celebrated in political circles. And they are viable models of charitable giving for Americans who encounter poor, pregnant, or drug-dependent neighbors in their daily lives.

The other scholarly ideal of civic participation—rational-critical deliberation—also only appears in rough approximation in entertainment media. This ideal, often coupled with calls for "deliberative democracy" or "participatory democracy," has enjoyed renewed attention across academic disciplines in recent years, but especially in my home discipline of communication studies. Habermas' ideal of rational-critical deliberation came from the bourgeois public sphere, where citizens would gather together and, bracketing their personal interests and status differentials, deliberate for the common good, thus producing public opinion. In the two decades since *Structural Transformation of the Public Sphere* was first published in English, some responses have questioned the historical reality of the bourgeois public sphere Habermas glorified, and many others have questioned the possibility or desirability of such a public sphere within contemporary democracies.[25] Nancy Fraser, for instance, doubted that individuals could ever bracket their interests so as to deliberate for the good of the whole, and she wondered why a single public sphere was necessarily better than multiple public spheres.[26]

With critiques like Fraser's in mind, scholars have settled on these notions of deliberative or participatory democracy, which maintain Habermas' fundamental commitment: that the central act of our civic life together is deliberation. As Bill Keith notes, calls for deliberative democracy often indicate "a desire to make rationality and argumentation central to the practice of democracy."[27] They assume that citizens make democracy work because they gather together to talk about the issues of the day, and those discussions lead them to viable, workable, and agreeable solutions to the problems we face together. Deliberative democracy demands that citizens offer reasons and make arguments, and it trusts that the process of reason-giving ensures that better decisions are made. Kevin Mattson acknowledges, referring to Habermas' later work, that groups of citizens may never achieve an "ideal speech situation" or "communicative action," but he still affirms that the process of gathering to deliberate fuels democracy.[28]

If these theorists are right, if democracy demands deliberative discussions among citizens, then the Christian-themed media texts I have analyzed offer few resources for democratic citizens. None of them models this type of deliberative exchange. *Amazing Grace*'s dramatic portrayal of William Wilberforce's legislative crusade comes closest. Just like the thoughtful citizens Habermas imagined gathered in saloons, coffeehouses, and table societies, the film's Wilberforce and Pitt sip tea while they discuss antislavery activism. When activists gather at Wilberforce's stately home to share a meal, they discuss their political objectives. The men and women on both sides of the issue display their abilities to reason articulately about the slave trade, the impending wars across the continent, and other issues of the day. Surely, these are the engaged citizens whose deliberations can generate reasoned solutions to common problems.

And yet, *Amazing Grace*'s model of faith-based activism falls short of Habermas' ideal rational-critical deliberation, as well as more recent calls for participatory or deliberative democracy. The film's political operatives have personal interests in the topic of slavery—some members of Parliament are slave owners and others have personal relationships with slaves. They never try to bracket these personal interests, or any status differentials, in the interest of deliberating for the common good (as Fraser has said would be impossible anyway). Moreover, the film depicts deliberation, not between ordinary citizens, but between legislators with immediate political power. Habermas was interested in rational-critical deliberation in a civic sphere that could serve as a check against the state, and calls for participatory democracy assume that ordinary citizens need to deliberate with each other,[29] but the film only shows political elites engaged in this sort of discursive problem solving.

As these entertainment media fail to approximate the models of civic participation so celebrated in scholarly conversations, they also introduce alternative models that are viable in our contemporary public sphere. *The Passion*'s sympathetic characters practice feminine submission in response to the political drama of their day, and many Americans continue to do the same today. By the film's depiction, Mary, Mary Magdalene, and John participate by joining the crowds in the city streets and the public plaza to watch the torture and crucifixion of a perceived criminal. As they silently acquiesce to the proceedings, they trust that the seemingly unjust earthly rulers carry out God's will. If global prayer Web sites like the one hosted in Colorado Springs are any indication, contemporary Christians find this model of prayerful submission practical in today's complex political climate. As they gather electronically, they offer collective prayers for the nations of the world, whether or not they understand the various political dynamics of those nations. Surrendering themselves in prayer, they trust that God's wisdom is guiding civic affairs.

In a similar manner, *Left Behind*'s disposition of brutish masculinity also proves viable outside the novels' fictional world. As in *The Passion*, *Left Behind*'s heroes are confronted with an unjust and oppressive government. They arm themselves and respond to this global tyrant with coordinated violence. I have argued that such militarism has characterized United States foreign policy in the war on terror, where we divide the world into good and evil and judge the chasm to be so wide that it can be overcome only by violence, not by diplomacy. Such militarism also becomes the suitable disposition for civic engagement when we articulate our domestic policy disagreements as "culture wars." When liberals and conservatives treat disagreements over stem cell research, school prayer, and same-sex marriage as battles, then the fitting way to engage our neighbors and fellow citizens is with symbolic violence, rather than rational-critical deliberation.

Even *TDVC*'s heterosexual reproduction provides a model for how citizens might engage with their public sphere. In the novel, the characters demonstrate faithfulness to the restored Christian tradition by venerating women's sexuality, celebrating heterosexual intercourse, and reproducing the bloodline. When faithful Christians raise a brood, or even a quiverful, of children capable of propagating their parents' faith and values, they seek personal happiness for themselves, but they also contribute to the future of their community. Although *TDVC* itself shows a clear preference for the private sphere, its celebrated disposition of faithfulness—heterosexual reproduction—has clear implications for civic life.

None of these models of civic participation—feminine submission, brutish masculinity, or heterosexual reproduction—registers in normative discussions of the public sphere; they are not the desired behaviors that could supposedly reinvigorate our civic life. Yet they resonate in popular media and prove viable for contemporary Americans. None of these models of civic participation is flawless; indeed, I have tried to highlight their troubling implications in the conclusion to each case study chapter. As long as they circulate in popular consciousness, however, they merit thoughtful and sustained discussion of the role they should play in our civic life.

THE LIMITS OF MEDIA AND CIVIC PARTICIPATION

In addition to complicating narrow ideals of civic participation, these case studies also upend the fashionable lament that the mass media are destroying civic life. Although some optimistic voices have lauded the promise of new media for facilitating civic engagement, others have launched at least two complaints about the traditional media. Putnam has taken issue with the way television specifically turns Americans into passive consumers. Time that they once might have spent volunteering on behalf of a local organization, or at least socializing with their neighbors, Putnam claims they now spend watching television instead.[30] And Habermas decries the rise of the mass media as a market interest, which, in collusion with the state, eclipses the public sphere. Both may have valid points.

At the same time, however, the traditional entertainment media, which do shape popular consciousness, provide compelling images of civic life. They show attractive characters engaged in the political and civic questions of their day, working cooperatively alongside their neighbors. Even as sluggish Americans supposedly devote their free time to passively consuming media texts, they choose and popularize these films, books, and television shows so obviously concerned with civic activism. A skeptic might suggest that Americans consume stories about civic life rather than participating in it themselves. But a more optimistic analysis would suggest that Americans find civic life interesting and compelling, and their media choices both reflect and shape their civic participation.

Although I resist the dire warnings from social theorists who lament that the mass media are destroying our civic life, I recognize that these five case studies demonstrate the limitations of looking to entertainment media for models of exemplary behavior. Entertainment media, limited by the constraints of their technologies and genres, favor certain images of heroism over others. Each of these case studies shows how the combination of a particular medium and genre produces a model of civic participation that might not result from a different medium or genre. For instance, *The Passion*'s model of feminine submission results directly from its form as an R-rated feature length theatrical release. Only such a film could portray the unrelenting graphic violence that ultimately produces feminine submission as the suitable response. Such violence could not air on broadcast television, and even cable television would likely demand editing. Indeed, it is revealing that even for all the film's success in the theaters, it has not yet aired on U.S. television. Similarly, radio, print, or other media would not have proven capable of depicting the visceral, corporeal violence that results in feminine submission as a mode of civic participation.

Likewise, in the case of *Amazing Grace*, only a feature-length film could portray the prolonged contest between slavery and abolition; that story simply would not fit in a thirty- or sixty-minute television show. Nor would the costuming and sets necessary to depict the historical era fit within the budget of a typical television show. A television show, certainly a popular television show, seems unlikely to depict the historical scene necessary to produce British parliamentary genteel masculinity as its model behavior. In contrast, a serial television show lends itself easily to the individualized volunteerism featured on *7th Heaven*. Such programs thrive on simple, predictable plots with a limited number of familiar characters. Each episode promises narrative closure, which *7th Heaven* achieves with the easy resolution of the social issues it confronts weekly. A family drama, operating within a sixty-minute time frame and trying to appeal to a broad audience, simply lacks the capacity to deal with the social causes and political solutions of the issues it addresses.

Left Behind and *TDVC* illustrate especially well how the various media technologies and genres influence the stories produced. Both of these narratives, which found tremendous success as novels, later met failure upon their theatrical release. As a novel, *TDVC* owed its success to the conventions of the romantic grail quest. Adhering closely to those conventions, *TDVC*'s hero and heroine unravel a puzzle while they court each other romantically. The novel's happy ending brings sexual coupling as well as a solution to the puzzle. Given that *TDVC* is a romance novel, we should not be surprised to find that it glorifies heterosexual reproduction. Similarly, since *Left Behind* adheres to the conventions of an action-adventure narrative, we should not be surprised to discover that its heroes are brutish, masculine warriors. They live within the stock world order of such action-adventure sequences, where good and evil wage war against each other, so choosing violence over conciliation follows naturally.

These stories' failures as feature-length films dramatize their dependence on the novel as a form. Although their failures can be partly attributed to market dynamics and organized resistance, the difficulty of telling these stories on the big screen deserves some blame as well. Both of these films were produced to succeed. *TDVC* and the first *Left Behind* movie benefited from extensive and innovative marketing. *Left Behind*'s producers tried the unconventional tactic of prereleasing the film on DVD and video three months before it would arrive in the theaters. They hoped its early consumers would create a buzz that would drive sales upon the film's theatrical release.[31] They also recruited churches to serve as "sponsors," donating the $3,000 necessary to ensure the film's showing on one screen. And *TDVC* won mainstream press attention as early as the spring of 2004—more than two years before its release—when Akiva Goldsman agreed to write the screenplay and Ron Howard to direct the film.[32] It drew even more headlines when it signed an all-star cast, led by Tom Hanks and Audrey Tautou.[33] By the time of its release, *TDVC* was expected to garner as much as *Titanic*, or at least the largest receipts of the year.

Both films disappointed expectations. *Left Behind* earned little more than $4 million in domestic box office sales, and with $217 million in earnings, *TDVC* fell far short of *The Passion*'s $370 million or *Titanic*'s $600 million.[34] *Left Behind*'s dramatic failure might be attributed partly to its low budget and poor quality (much like its sequels). The film cost only $17 million to create, and its biggest celebrity draw was Kirk Cameron, of *Growing Pains* fame. *TDVC*'s success may have been hindered in part by the organized boycotts against it.[35] A top Vatican official, for instance, urged Christians to avoid the film, accusing it of blasphemy and heresy.[36]

TDVC's lackluster sales also resulted from the poor reviews the film received upon its release.[37] Indeed, *TDVC* and the *Left Behind* movies are lousy productions. The novels themselves have little literary merit, but they tell captivating stories in a familiar form that holds readers' attention. Those stories did not translate easily into feature films. *TDVC* had enjoyed the complexity possible in a fiction novel, and it found its plot twists reduced and simplified to fit into a screenplay. Without the measured revealing of the puzzle clues and the associated suspense, the film could not ascend to the level of climax that made the novel's revelations about female sexuality so titillating. Thus, the film did not achieve the shock value so integral to the novel's success, and it also did not arrive at the veneration for female (hetero)sexuality that defines the novel's mode of civic nonparticipation. In the case of *Left Behind*, the film's low budget did not allow for the special effects that would have been necessary to reproduce the novels' battle theatrics—especially the air missions, with their frequent crash landings and escape takeoffs. Without those gripping scenes, the film sacrificed the story's action-adventure dynamic, and its characters' masculinity seemed artificial and unnecessary. In their transformations into screenplays, both *TDVC* and *Left Behind* hemorrhaged their defining characteristics—historical puzzles and violent battles—and the resulting images of civic participation that depended on those characteristics, like the films themselves, were anemic.

Entertainment media privilege certain forms of storytelling—romance, mystery, drama—that produce limited images of heroism. Just as each of these five ideals of civic participation was limited individually by the specific combination of its medium and genre, so too are the possible models of civic participation in entertainment media limited by media technologies and genres more generally. Collectively, novels, films, and television shows lend themselves to modeling military heroism and romantic fulfillment much more easily than they do statesmanship or philanthropy, even if the latter ideals are not absent from popular culture entirely. It is hard to imagine a weekly television drama set in a local Red Cross chapter and focused on the mundane heroics of the volunteers who manage our blood supply, and it is equally difficult to imagine a feature film set in a food bank, where the protagonist is the retired gentleman who sorts pallets of canned vegetables. Even for all their limitations, entertainment media are our cultural currency. Social theorists may overstate the case when they berate the mass media for destroying our civic life, but these case studies illustrate how the media circumscribe the ways we can imagine civic participation.

GENDER AND THE LIMITS OF CIVIC PARTICIPATION

In the United States, legal reforms have stripped citizenship of the restrictions that once formally limited it to men alone: women now vote, sit on juries, and serve in the military. In 2008, less than one hundred years after women won the right to vote, a female candidate launched a serious and nearly successful national campaign for the presidency. So, too, cultural norms have loosened to allow men larger roles in voluntary and charitable civic activities. Ladies' aid societies no longer dominate foreign and domestic missions, and men contribute openly to these efforts, along with parent-teacher associations and hospital guilds and arts philanthropies. As these case studies make painfully clear, however, popular notions of civic participation have not lost their gendered conventions entirely. These texts suggest what may be true more generally: that men and women still find distinct avenues of civic participation open to them, and they find those avenues characterized by the norms of masculinity and femininity. Considered together, these texts suggest a pattern where the ideals of civic participation characterized by femininity are open to women and men alike, but the ones characterized by masculinity are restricted to men alone. In other words, male bodies continue to find more diverse opportunities for civic participation than female bodies do.

Masculinity and femininity, as I have defined them, are distinct from maleness and femaleness. Masculinity is a set of traits commonly associated with men, such as rationality, physical strength, and competitiveness, but not legally or scientifically limited to individuals with male bodies. Femininity is, likewise, the set of traits commonly associated with women, such as emotionality, submissiveness, and benevolence, but not limited to individuals with female bodies. If these traits are attached to bodies not by legal or scientific means, they develop their adhesion instead by rhetorical means. Entertainment media, like the books, films, and television series considered here, contribute to the popular discourse that reinforces (and sometimes troubles) the connections between masculinity and maleness, femininity and femaleness.

Gender constrains civic participation in the two texts that celebrate masculinity: *Amazing Grace* and *Left Behind*, both of which reinforce traditional connections between masculinity, maleness, and civic participation. Although they adapt distinct dispositions of masculinity—what I have called genteel and brutish masculinity—these texts both laud characteristics traditionally associated with men: rationality and intellect in the case of *Amazing Grace*, and courage and physical strength in the case of *Left Behind*. Importantly, both texts exclude women from these heroic versions of masculinity. In *Amazing Grace*, the celebrated form of activism—lawmaking— happens in an all-male sphere that women dare not enter. In *Left Behind*, female characters attempt to enter the masculine realm of civic participation—the battlefield—but there they find only failure. Where *Amazing Grace* simply excludes women from its civic centers of power, *Left Behind* makes martyrs of the female characters who inevitably fail at their earnest attempts to replicate the men's displays of masculinity. In both cases, the lesson is the same: only men can suitably perform the most prized form of citizenship.

Within the two narratives that praise femininity, *The Passion* and *7th Heaven*, male and female characters perform the favored disposition equally well. When *The Passion* visually affirms the characters who submit silently, it includes two women and one man among its heroes. Always depicted together, John, Mary, and Mary Magdalene are virtually indistinguishable. Although John sets himself apart momentarily because he begins the story in the garden with the men and he stands to the side as the women mop up Jesus' blood, his behaviors mimic his female companions as the three watch the unfolding drama and plead with God for mercy. *7th Heaven* blurs gender boundaries even more radically because its lead male character models feminine charitable volunteerism so admirably. Because the show depicts an educated, professional man volunteering in the community and taking shared responsibility for parenting, it illustrates that men are capable of performing these typically feminine behaviors. When his wife and daughters mimic the reverend's brand of community volunteerism, *7th Heaven* demonstrates that its disposition of civic participation does not discriminate based on sex.

By showing that femininity is fluid and accessible enough that men and women can perform it equally, *7th Heaven* and *The Passion* do progressive rhetorical work to loosen the connections between femininity and femaleness, thus easing the social pressures that discipline men's and women's public behaviors. More than just demonstrating that men are capable of feminine virtues such as emotional labor, charity, and obedience, these texts also suggest that women's historic contributions to the public sphere are so valuable that they should be practiced by men and women alike. At the same time, however, when taken in concert with *Amazing Grace* and *Left Behind*, it is clear that these entertainment media still protect the image of masculinity so fiercely as to exclude women. In concert, these five texts imply that men are capable of all the valued dispositions of civic participation, including those characterized by masculinity, femininity, and heterosexuality, whereas women are only suited to the ones characterized by femininity and heterosexuality.

Race and the Limits of Civic Participation

As with gender, these entertainment media also draw upon cultural ideologies of race and reinforce those very ideologies. Although the preceding analyses have not considered race systematically, a clear pattern emerges across these texts. Four of them—all but *TDVC*—depict racial or ethnic difference, and three of them—all the others but *The Passion*—depict peaceful resolution to racial difference. In each case, that peaceful resolution results from white citizens' paternalistic efforts on behalf of their black neighbors.

Among these texts, *TDVC* and *The Passion* are the outliers on this matter of racial difference. While *TDVC* eschews any discussion of race, *The Passion*'s treatment of ethnic difference prompted much of the public outcry about the film. Although Jewish and Christian leaders contested whether or not the film unfairly assigns Jews culpability for Jesus' death, I maintain that it depicts his torture and execution as the product of that ethnic conflict. When the overzealous Jewish leaders approach Pilate with the criminal they want crucified, Pilate's indifference to their internal religious/political squabbles gives way to his desire to quell the growing rebellion. Thus, the Roman governor's willingness to crucify a common Jew grows largely out of his distaste for the Jewish masses under his rule. The film vilifies ethnic conflict through these distasteful characters, but it makes heroes of the individuals who faithfully submit to the ethnic conflict that shapes their social order. By failing to resist this ethnic conflict, Mary, Magdalene, and John accept that God wills for them to live in a world where a member of their own ethnic group can be crucified because of their governor's contempt for them as a people.

In contrast, when *Amazing Grace*, *Left Behind*, and *7th Heaven* depict racial difference, they attempt reconciliation between the divided parties. Each of these texts stars white characters who, I have argued, serve as their heroes and models of faithful discipleship.[38] In each case, these white heroes come into contact with racial minorities, whose lives are somehow enriched by the efforts of their white neighbors. This archetypal narrative is clearest in *Amazing Grace*: the story of the legislative end of Great Britain's slave trade, it glorifies the small group of white men who saved a whole race of people from their oppression. The film's primary black character, Oluadah Equiano, exemplifies an alternative, but lesser, form of civic participation as he and other grassroots activists organize to educate leaders and commoners about slavery's evils. Taking Wilberforce on a tour of a slave ship, Equiano introduces Wilberforce, and by extension the film's white audience, to the horrors of the slave trade itself. He also, as the film describes but does not depict, travels around the countryside using his autobiography to educate whites about slavery. In this film, the black character's value is that he teaches white leaders about the oppression he has experienced, so that those white leaders can valiantly end this oppression.[39]

On *7th Heaven*, black characters teach their white friends about racial oppression in a contemporary U.S. context. Racial minorities figure only occasionally into *7th Heaven*'s narrative, and because of the show's basic structure, they are typically outside characters who benefit from the Camdens' charity (as do many needy white people). When black characters appear, the social issues they introduce typically relate to race. In the first season's very special episode, "The Color of God," the Camdens learn about racism from their friends, the Hamilton family, after the Hamiltons' church is destroyed by racially motivated arson. As the Hamiltons stay with the Camdens, the youngest kids struggle to understand racism so strong it would destroy a church, and the initially skeptical teenagers witness harassment directed by a white security guard at their black peers. With their newfound racial consciousness, the Camden teenagers work together with their younger siblings and parents to coordinate a community-wide ecumenical and interracial worship service. When that service signals the healing of the faith community destroyed by arson, it also intimates that racism has been solved because African Americans alerted whites to its existence, and whites assumed civic leadership to eradicate it.

Left Behind also depicts white people capable of saving needy minorities, but in less explicit ways. Its heroes—Rayford, Buck, and Chloe—are presumably white, if only because the books never mention their race while explicitly labeling racial minorities.[40] The fourth member of the founding Tribulation Force is the African American pastor Bruce, who dies early in the series. As the Tribulation Force expands into a global coalition, it naturally acquires members of multiple races, ethnicities, and nationalities, such as the Israeli chemist Chaim Rosenzweig and Rabbi Tsion Ben-Judah, as well as Ming Toy Wong, Laslos Mikos, Abdullah Smith, and David Hassid. These characters work together peacefully, suggesting the promise of inter-ethnic cooperation.

The dynamic is different when the Tribulation Force encounters a cell of Christian believers also hiding out in downtown Chicago, most of whom are working-class minorities. The pioneering Chloe discovers this group on one of her improvised missions, and she smuggles them back into the Tribulation Force's safe house.[41] There, her comrades greet these fellow believers and they share their faith testimonies, which has become common practice upon discovering other believers after the Rapture. After this initial meeting, however, this new cell of African Americans and Latinos is never fully integrated into the Tribulation Force, and they are always marked by their race and class difference. None of them ever earns a central role in any of the group's missions, and they appear only infrequently through the remainder of the books. Moreover, the books cast them as the beneficiaries of the white-led Tribulation Force's well-developed organization. Lucky that Chloe discovered them on a dark Chicago night, these minorities owe their survival to the Tribulation Force.

The pattern across Amazing Grace, 7th Heaven, and Left Behind is clear: whites must exercise civic leadership to protect blacks and other racial minorities, especially from racism. This message has its merits; to the extent that whites perpetuate racism, our interracial civic life benefits from racially conscious whites willing to counter racism. These media texts, however, depict whites doing so at the expense of racial minorities' agency. Black characters' possibilities for civic participation are limited to just one disposition: they can teach whites about racism, so that whites can eradicate it. These black characters cannot exercise agency to combat racism themselves, nor can they participate in civic life beyond the topic of race itself.

Of course, noting the common dynamic between black characters and white characters across these texts says little about the performances of blackness and whiteness therein. Although race and gender are an imperfect analogy, blackness can be separated from black bodies and whiteness from white bodies just as masculinity and femininity can be distinguished from male bodies and female bodies. Careful, sustained analysis of the racial dynamics within these entertainment media, and others, might reveal the ways that these texts trouble or reinforce the links between racialized bodies (black and white, for instance) and racial identities (blackness and whiteness), just as they both trouble and reinforce the links between sex and gender.

THE POSSIBILITIES OF FAITH-BASED CIVIC PARTICIPATION

Even for all the limitations inherent in each of these models of civic participation individually, and even for all their troubling implications in terms of gender and race, these five case studies still demonstrate the rich possibilities for faith-based civic participation. For as much as Jim Wallis and James Dobson and Greg Boyd may disagree about the proper role for Christians in civic life, they can all agree on one point, which these texts underscore: religious faith necessarily informs politics and civic life. Beginning with that premise, these competing models articulated by these leaders and these entertainment media entail a few lessons about the future of faith-based civic engagement.

First, religion is a natural locus for civic activism. Habermas desired to reinvigorate the bourgeois public sphere precisely because it was a space distinct from both the state and market. If the collusion of the state and market has made his public sphere impossible, churches and faith communities now provide a promising facsimile. Although churches entangle themselves with the state and market occasionally, Christians still hear the apostle Paul's call not to be conformed to such structures of the world.[42] When churches heed that call, they provide a space where Christians can organize against interests like the state and market. Churches have done as much throughout U.S. history. In the twentieth century, they provided the organizational space most famously for the civil rights movement, but also for opposition to the Vietnam War and nuclear armament.[43] Faith communities also train volunteers with the organizational skills necessary to lead oppositional movements. Many leaders of the nineteenth-century woman suffrage movement, for instance, honed their leadership skills in Quaker meetings, as well as through the mission and benevolence societies they ran in the mainline Protestant denominations. Churches have served similar purposes around the world—providing space and training leaders to oppose apartheid in South Africa and the dictatorial regimes throughout Latin America, for instance.

Left Behind and *7th Heaven* both provide compelling images of the church serving as such a civic space. On *7th Heaven*, civic volunteerism originates within the faith community because the church itself is a gathering place and Sunday morning services in the sanctuary often witness the resolution of a social problem. When the show's characters, especially the minister-father, volunteer in the community, they do so explicitly as representatives of the church. Likewise, civic activism in *Left Behind* also originates in the church. The series' core characters form their Tribulation Force in the church building where they find each other after the Rapture. Even as the Tribulation proceeds, and after that original building has been destroyed, they continue to organize from within the set of secret cells that compose their faith community. *Left Behind*'s church is definitively counter-cultural: it exists to oppose the regime that has taken over the global government and market, and the believers' allegiance to the church formally excludes them from the global market.

Left Behind and *7th Heaven* both model Christian faith communities as fecund spaces for fostering civic activism. They also, however, demonstrate the major limitations of the church as a civic sphere: its characteristic exclusivity. Just like Habermas' bourgeois public sphere, Christian faith communities necessarily only include a slice of a diverse population. As Wuthnow has noted, churches typically foster "bonding" social capital (creating bonds among similar individuals) rather than "bridging" social capital (creating bonds among diverse individuals).[44] *Left Behind*'s characters show no remorse about their exclusive community; their polarized world does not encourage them to collaborate with individuals of other faiths (except a few enlightened Jews). Even on *7th Heaven*, interfaith and interracial collaboration only happens on special occasions; usually, the family church is populated by white, middle-class, suburban families much like the Camdens themselves. These case studies demonstrate that, even as Christians find their faith communities fruitful grounds for civic organizing, they must guard against the church's tendency toward exclusivity.

Second, these books, films, and television series demonstrate the virtues of the nonpartisan impulse common to the new generation of Christian leaders. In response to the failures of Jerry Falwell's generation, Rick Warren, Greg Boyd, and Jim Wallis can all agree that partisanship does not serve the civic interests of faith communities. Importantly, these five media texts largely bypass the issue of political parties, and none of them models any sort of partisanship. *7th Heaven* is the only of these texts to mention political parties, and it does not do so until the sixth season, when the oldest son, Matt, reveals that he is a Republican, while his dad is a Democrat—hardly an overwhelming statement of partisanship.[45] *Amazing Grace*'s depiction of legislative activism reveals no obvious partisanship, instead depicting abolitionists as single-issue crusaders. In recent years, Christian leaders have traded their partisanship for precisely this sort of single-issue focus. Jim Wallis has chosen poverty as his signature issue, and Rick Warren devotes himself to AIDS in Africa, but both men pressure Democrats and Republicans alike to work on these issues. At Rick Warren's Civic Forum, for instance, the pastor asked both candidates, Barack Obama and John McCain, to commit to solving the world's orphan crisis.

Third, these case studies demonstrate that the future of faith-based civic participation demands breaking the links between sex, gender, and particular ideals of civic participation. Modeling gender-inclusive ideals of civic participation does not require stripping them of their masculine and feminine characteristics. Indeed, because men and women have made distinct civic contributions historically, gender equity entails incorporating all these various modes—voting and fundraising and picketing and letter writing and so many others. Gender equity also entails opening all these various modes of civic participation to male bodies and female bodies alike. We need more models of civic participation like *7th Heaven*'s, which makes the historically feminine duty of charitable volunteering accessible to both men and women. And we need fewer models of civic participation like *Left Behind*'s, which glorifies masculine battle heroism but shows women's inadequacies at performing this type of civic participation.

Finally, the most important lesson to emerge from these five case studies, as well as the examples of Christian leaders such as Wallis, Boyd, and Warren, is that every model of civic participation is necessarily inadequate. The Falwell-inspired "values voters" were obviously insufficient; not only did they reduce all of Christian theology and polity to two contemporary social issues (abortion and same-sex marriage), but their very hegemony shut down possibilities for alternative faith-based political positions. In response to this hegemony, the value of *Left Behind*, *The Passion*, and these other texts is that, taken together, they provide a multiplicity of options for faithful Christian civic participation. They intimate that Christians can be faithful when they submit to God's will, when they challenge the oppression around them, when they give to the needy in their communities, when they lobby for legislative reform, when they care for their children, or when they do any combination of these things. And these media texts are not alone; together with the models of civic participation available from other television shows, films, and books, as well as sermons, newspapers, interpersonal conversations, and other forms of communication, they challenge the hegemony of the "values voters" ideal. Providing multiple ideals of civic participation, these texts allow rich possibilities for people of faith as they articulate their own commitments to our shared public sphere.

NOTES

CHAPTER 1

1   Robert D. Putnam, "Bowling Alone: America's Declining Social Capital," *Journal of Democracy* 6, no. 1 (1995): 65–78; Robert D. Putnam, *Bowling Alone: The Collapse and Revival of American Community* (New York: Simon & Schuster, 2000).

2   Tracey Wong Briggs, "Can You Pass This History Test?" *USA Today*, September 18, 2007.

3   Putnam, *Bowling Alone*, 66.

4   Robert Wuthnow, "Mobilizing Civic Engagement: The Changing Impact of Religious Involvement," in *Civic Engagement in American Democracy*, ed. Theda Skocpol and Morris P. Fiorina (Washington, D.C.: Brookings Institution, 1999), 333, 338.

5   Wuthnow, "Mobilizing Civic Engagement," 360; Putnam, *Bowling Alone*, 77–78.

6   Ellen Goodman, "Winning Back Values Voters," *Washington Post*, November 6, 2004, A23; David Brooks, "The Values-Vote Myth," *The New York Times*, November 6, 2004, A19; Dana Milbank, "For the President, a Vote of Full Faith and Credit; Evangelical Christians Shed Their Reluctance to Mix Religion and Politics on Election Day," *Washington Post*, November 7, 2004, A07; Alan Cooperman, "Liberal Christians Challenge 'Values Vote,'" *Washington Post*, November 10, 2004, A07.

7   Erica Perez and Stacy Forster, "Election 2008; 25% of Young Voters Turn Out," *Milwaukee Journal Sentinel*, February 21, 2008, A12.

8   Eileen E. Flynn, "Voters Turn Out in Hordes for a 'Democracy Love Fest,' " *Austin American-Statesman*, March 5, 2008, A10; Cynthia Burton and Joseph A. Gambardello, "Turnout for N.J. Primary Highest in Half a Century," *Philadelphia Inquirer*, February 7, 2008, A15; Robert Mills, "Mass. Sets Record for Primary Turnout," *Lowell Sun*, February 6, 2008; Martha T. Moore, "Many New Voters Agree 'Time Has Come' for Obama," *USA Today*, February 6, 2008, 4A; Tim Craig and John Wagner, "Overeager Voters in Va., Md. Suffer a Super Letdown," *Washington Post*, February 6, 2008.

9   James O'Toole, "Happy Valley Turns into Obama country; Huge Crowd Turns Out at Penn State," *Pittsburgh Post-Gazette*, March 31, 2008, A1.

10   Karen E. Crummy, "CAMPAIGN 2008 State GOP Heals Rift, Gets Behind McCain," *Denver Post*, March 28, 2008, A1; Dennis B. Roddy, "Evangelicals Seen Warming to McCain," *Pittsburgh Post-Gazette*, September 7, 2008, A15.

11   Lynn Sweet, "Faith Forum Gives Debate Preview; McCain, Obama Field Queries on Abortion, Moral Failings, their Views of Court Justices," *Chicago Sun-Times*, August 17, 2008, A19; Sasha Issenberg, "Obama, McCain Air Views on Faith," *Boston Globe*, August 17, 2008, A1.

12   Daniel Gilgoff, "Why the Christian Right Fears Obama," *USA Today*, June 16, 2008, 12A; Kevin Drum, "John McCain, Semi-Baptist," *CBS News*, September 17, 2007, http://www.cbsnews.com/stories/2007/09/17/politics/animal/main3270400.shtml (accessed February 16, 2009).

13   Wayne Slater, "Conservative Christians Pleased Palin Adds Some Muscle to GOP Ticket," *Dallas Morning News*, October 4, 2008.

14   Sam Roberts, "Who's Black and Female and How Do They Vote?" *The New York Times*, January 29, 2008, B1.

15   David Beery, "The Women's Vote All for One?" *Chicago Daily Herald*, March 6, 2008, 1; Maureen Callahan, "Mothers & Daughters—Hillary Has Divided Them, Exposing a Rift between Feminist Generations," *New York Post*, February 17, 2008, 30.

16   Meghan Daum, "A Few PUMAs on the Loose," *Los Angeles Times*, August 30, 2008, A31.

17   Putnam, *Bowling Alone*, 194.

18   Putnam, *Bowling Alone*, 201. It is important to note that even while Putnam claims that women's entry into the paid work force has had a negative impact on community engagement, he is careful not to blame feminism or the women's movement for civic decline. He calls the feminist revolution "welcome and overdue" (194) and denies "the view that working women are 'to blame' for our civic disengagement" (201). His proposal with regard to paid labor is almost gender equitable; he suggests, "One practical way to increase com-

munity engagement in America would be to make it easier for women (and men too) to work part-time if they wished" (201).

19 Sharon Waxman, "Fox Unveils a Division for Religion-Oriented Films," *The New York Times*, September 20, 2006, E1.

20 Michael Ignatieff, "The Myth of Citizenship," in *Theorizing Citizenship*, ed. Ronald Beiner (Albany: State University of New York Press, 1995), 54.

21 J. G. A. Pocock, "The Ideal of Citizenship since Classical Times," in Beiner, *Theorizing Citizenship*, 31. George Armstrong Kelly's definition is also helpful because it specifies the citizen's relationship to the state: the citizen is the "city-dweller (a *bourgeois*) or [a] member of a state who exchanges political allegiance for the right to certain privileges and protections" (emphasis in original). George Armstrong Kelly, "Who Needs a Theory of Citizenship?" in Beiner, *Theorizing Citizenship*, 89.

22 Rogers M. Smith, *Civic Ideals: Conflicting Visions of Citizenship in U.S. History* (New Haven, Conn.: Yale University Press, 1997), 14.

23 Smith, *Civic Ideals*, 1997; Michael Schudson, "Good Citizens and Bad History: Today's Political Ideals in Historical Perspective," *The Communication Review* 4, no. 1 (2000): 1–19; Michael Schudson, *The Good Citizen: A History of American Civic Life* (New York: Martin Kessler Books, 1998).

24 Smith, *Civic Ideals*, 1.

25 Smith, *Civic Ideals*, 16.

26 Schudson, "Good Citizens," 1–19.

27 Kelly, "Who Needs?" 79.

28 Will Kymlicka and Wayne Norman, "Return of the Citizen: A Survey of Recent Work on Citizenship Theory," in Beiner, *Theorizing Citizenship*, 284.

29 Jürgen Habermas, "The Public Sphere: An Encyclopedia Article (1964)," *New German Critique* 3 (1974): 54.

30 Benjamin R. Barber, *A Place for Us: How to Make Society Civil and Democracy Strong* (New York: Hill & Wang, 1998), 38–39.

31 Jürgen Habermas, *The Structural Transformation of the Public Sphere: An Inquiry into a Category of Bourgeois Society* (Cambridge, Mass.: MIT Press, 1989), 3, 31–43; Habermas, "Public Sphere," 49; Craig Calhoun, "Introduction: Habermas and the Public Sphere," in *Habermas and the Public Sphere*, ed. Craig Calhoun (Cambridge, Mass.: MIT Press, 1989), 12. Nancy Fraser's fourfold critique of Habermas' ideal of the public sphere demonstrates the problems inherent in this disinterested rational-critical deliberation: "Rethinking the Public Sphere: A Contribution to the Critique of Actually Existing Democracy," in Calhoun, *Habermas and the Public Sphere*.

32 Habermas, *Structural Transformation*, 185, 188–95.

33 E.g., William Keith, "Democratic Revival and the Promise of Cyberspace: Lessons from the Forum Movement," *Rhetoric & Public Affairs* 5, no. 2 (2002): 311–26; idem, *Democracy as Discussion: Civic Education and the American Forum Movement* (Lanham, Md.: Lexington Books, 2007); Angela G. Ray, *The Lyceum and Public Culture in the Nineteenth-Century United States* (East Lansing: Michigan State University Press, 2005); Troy Murphy, "Deliberative Civic Education and Civil Society: A Consideration of Ideals and Actualities in Democracy and Communication Education," *Communication Education* 53, no. 1 (2004): 74–91; Rosa A. Eberly, "Rhetoric and the Anti-Logos Doughball: Teaching Deliberating Bodies the Practices of Participatory Democracy," *Rhetoric & Public Affairs* 5, no. 2 (2002): 287–300; G. Thomas Goodnight and David B. Hingstman, "Studies in the Public Sphere," *Quarterly Journal of Speech* 83 (1997): 351–99; Gerard A. Hauser and Chantal Benoit-Barne, "Reflections on Rhetoric, Deliberative Democracy, Civil Society, and Trust," *Rhetoric & Public Affairs* 5, no. 2 (2002): 261–75; Darrin Hicks, "The Promise(s) of Deliberative Democracy," *Rhetoric & Public Affairs* 5, no. 2 (2002): 223–60.

34 William Keith, "Introduction: Cultural Resources for Deliberative Democracy," *Rhetoric & Public Affairs* 5, no. 2 (2002): 219.

35 Putnam, *Bowling Alone*, 31–133.

36 Michael Walzer, "The Civil Society Argument," in Beiner, *Theorizing Citizenship*, 170.

37 Walzer, "The Civil Society Argument," 170.

38 Barber, *A Place for Us*, 58–61.

39 Putnam, *Bowling Alone*, 19.

40 Robert Asen, "The Multiple Mr. Dewey: Multiple Publics and Permeable Borders in John Dewey's Theory of the Public Sphere," *Argumentation and Advocacy* 39 (2003): 174.

41 Robert Asen, "A Discourse Theory of Citizenship," *Quarterly Journal of Speech* 90, no. 2 (2004): 191 (emphasis in original).

42 Asen, "A Discourse Theory," 194.

43 Asen, "A Discourse Theory," 194.

44 Compelling as Asen's framework is, his preference for the term *citizenship* is problematic because of the vast and diverse uses commonly made of the term. Asen is not able to solve the problem illuminated by Kymlicka and Norman: that citizenship as legal status often gets confused for citizenship as public participation. As such, for reasons of clarity, I tend to use the terms *civic participation*, *civic responsibility*, and *civic engagement* to refer to a citizen's public participation, whether or not it is state-oriented. Even though I choose a different term, I share Asen's discursive perspective.

45   Kevin Michael DeLuca and Jennifer Peeples, "From Public Sphere to Public Screen: Democracy, Activism, and the 'Violence' of Seattle," *Critical Studies in Media Communication* 19, no. 2 (2002): 125–51; Phaedra C. Pezzullo, "Resisting 'National Breast Cancer Awareness Month': The Rhetoric of Counterpublics and Their Cultural Performances," *Quarterly Journal of Speech* 89, no. 4 (2003): 345–65; Daniel C. Brouwer, "ACT-ing Up in Congressional Hearings," in *Counterpublics and the State*, ed. Robert Asen and Daniel Brouwer (Albany: State University of New York Press, 2001).

46   Elisabeth S. Clemens, "Organizational Repertoires and Institutional Change: Women's Groups and the Transformation of American Politics, 1890–1920," in Skocpol and Fiorina, *Civic Engagement in American Democracy*, 89.

47   Eleanor Flexner, *Century of Struggle: The Woman's Rights Movement in the United States* (Cambridge, Mass.: Belknap Press of Harvard University Press, 1975), 57–60.

48   Shannon L. Holland, "The Dangers of Playing Dress-Up: Popular Representations of Jessica Lynch and the Controversy regarding Women in Combat," *Quarterly Journal of Speech* 92, no. 1 (2006): 31.

49   Kristy Maddux, "When Patriots Protest: The Anti-Suffrage Discursive Transformation of 1917," *Rhetoric & Public Affairs* 7, no. 3 (2004): 290.

50   As Judith Halberstam notes in *Female Masculinity*, masculinity is an endlessly difficult concept to define. She resists the temptation to settle for it being "the social and cultural and indeed political expression of maleness," and by highlighting manifestations of masculinity outside the male body, Halberstam shows how masculinity can be broken from maleness (1). Masculinity and femininity are nothing, however, if they are not sets of traits historically related to male and female bodies, which have been kept stable by their constant reiteration as norms. According to Judith Butler, "Gender is the repeated stylization of the body, a set of repeated acts within a highly rigid regulatory frame that congeal over time to produce the appearance of substance, of a natural sort of being" (43–44). Bodies only come to be gendered, and genders only come to be coherent identities, because of this constant repetition of gender norms.

Butler would also question the natural existence of entities called "male bodies" and "female bodies," suggesting that bodies are no less performed than gendered identities are. For the simplicity of this discussion, however, I acknowledge that bodies are commonly construed as male and female and that social norms encourage those bodies to make themselves intelligible within the frameworks of femininity and masculinity.

Of course, neither femininity nor masculinity is constantly reproduced as a singular notion. Many competing images of femininity and masculinity circulate, and can often be distinguished by historical era, class, or race. Masculinity is sometimes the set of characteristics associated with the male bodies victorious in sports such as football and boxing, and other times it is the set of characteristics associated with the male bodies who dominate political leadership. The nuances of distinct masculinities and femininities deserve further analysis. Halberstam, *Female Masculinity* (Durham, N.C.: Duke University Press, 1998); see also Judith Butler, *Gender Trouble: Feminism and the Subversion of Identity* (New York: Routledge, 1999).

51   To be clear, these are not inherently male traits, nor are men uniquely capable of performing them. Instead, because they have so long been associated with maleness, women in the public sphere have commonly faced the "double bind" of trying to fulfill these expectations of public officials without violating the demands of femininity. See, for instance, Kathleen Hall Jamieson, *Beyond the Double Bind* (New York: Oxford University Press, 1995); Shawn J. Parry-Giles and Trevor Parry-Giles, "Gendered Politics and Presidential Image Construction: A Reassessment of the 'Feminine Style,'" *Communication Monographs* 63, no. 4 (1996): 337-53; Karlyn Kohrs Campbell, "The Discursive Performance of Femininity: Hating Hillary," *Rhetoric & Public Affairs* 1, no. 1 (1998): 1-19; Karrin Vasby Anderson, "From Spouses to Candidates: Hillary Rodham Clinton, Elizabeth Dole, and the Gendered Office of U.S. President," *Rhetoric & Public Affairs* 5, no. 1 (2002): 105-32.

52   Smith, *Civic Ideals*, 22.

53   Clemens, "Organizational Repertoires," 89.

54   Helen Irving, *Gender and the Constitution: Equity and Agency in Comparative Constitutional Design* (New York: Cambridge University Press, 2008), 91.

55   Irving, *Gender and the Constitution*, 93.

56   Sara M. Evans, *Born for Liberty: A History of Women in America* (New York: Free Press, 1997), 57.

57   Mary P. Ryan, "Gender and Public Access: Women's Politics in Nineteenth-Century America," in Calhoun, *Habermas and the Public Sphere*, 272.

58   Ryan, "Gender and Public Access," 267.

59   Ryan, "Gender and Public Access," 259-88.

60   Susan Zaeske, *Signatures of Citizenship: Petitioning, Antislavery, and Women's Political Identity* (Chapel Hill: University of North Carolina Press, 2003).

61   Susan Zaeske, "Little Magic: Martin van Buren and the Politics of Gender," in *Before the Rhetorical Presidency*, ed. Martin J. Medhurst (College Station: Texas A&M Press, 2008).

62   Karlyn Kohrs Campbell, *Man Cannot Speak for Her* (New York: Praeger, 1989), 1:12.

63   Campbell, *Man Cannot Speak for Her*, 1:13.

64   Jamieson, *Double Bind.*

65   Whether or not this reading is the most learned or faithful understanding of the original text, it has routinely been used to justify women's inferior sphere (Gen 2:18, 3:16); unless otherwise noted, all Bible passages are taken from the New Revised Standard Version.

66   1 Cor 14:34; Eph 5:22.

67   Elizabeth Cady Stanton, *The Woman's Bible* (New York: European Publishing Company, 1895). See especially letters 1–3 in Sarah Moore Grimké, *Letters on the Equality of the Sexes and the Condition of Woman, Addressed to Mary S. Parker, President of the Boston Female Anti-Slavery Society* (Boston: I. Knapp, 1838).

68   Michael W. Casey, "The First Female Public Speakers in America (1630–1840): Searching for Egalitarian Christian Primitivism," *Journal of Communication and Religion* 23 (2000): 1–28.

69   Phoebe Palmer justified her public speaking by relating the story of the day of Pentecost from the Acts of the Apostles. In that narrative, when the spirit fell upon men and women alike, Peter explained this odd occurrence by reference to this prophecy from Joel. Palmer, "Tongue of Fire on the Daughters of the Lord," in *Phoebe Palmer: Selected Writings*, ed. Thomas C. Oden (New York: Paulist, 1988), 33–34.

70   Maddux, "When Patriots Protest," 287–88.

71   Martha Solomon, "Stopping ERA: A Pyrrhic Victory," *Communication Quarterly* 31, no. 2 (1983): 109.

72   The full text of the Faith and Message statement is available at the Southern Baptist Convention's Web site: http://www.sbc.net/bfm/default.asp.

73   Wendy Cadge, "Vital Conflicts: The Mainline Protestant Denominations Debate Homosexuality," in *The Quiet Hand of God: Faith-Based Activism and the Public Role of Mainline Protestantism*, ed. Robert Wuthnow and John Hyde Evans (Berkeley: University of California Press, 2002); Randall Balmer and Lauren F. Winner, *Protestantism in America* (New York: Columbia University Press, 2002), 121–78.

74   Marty links these two tendencies within the Scriptures to the two Protestant parties he identifies, associating public Protestants with the Hebrew Scriptures and the Synoptic Gospels, and private Protestants with the Epistles of Paul. Martin E. Marty, *Righteous Empire: The Protestant Experience in America* (New York: Dial, 1970), 186.

75 Matt 25:31-46; Matt 21:12-17, 23-27; Mark 11:15-19, 27-33; Luke 19:45-48, 20:1-8; John 2:12-25.

76 Phil 3:20.

77 Rev 21:1.

78 Matt 22:16-22; Mark 12:13-17; Luke 20:20-26.

79 Importantly, these traditions have roots much deeper than the turn of the twenty-first century. Hoge, for instance, claims that both "were developments out of the earlier Puritan heritage, which embraced both the individual and social visions. But the link between piety and social reform was broken in the late nineteenth century." Dean R. Hoge, *Division in the Protestant House: The Basic Reasons behind Intra-Church Conflicts* (Philadelphia: Westminster, 1976), 25.

80 Marty, *Righteous Empire*, 179.

81 Marty, *Righteous Empire*, 179.

82 David O. Moberg, *The Great Reversal: Evangelism and Social Concern* (Philadelphia: Lippincott, 1972/1977), 22.

83 Moberg, *The Great Reversal*, 23.

84 Susan Curtis, *A Consuming Faith: The Social Gospel and Modern American Culture* (Baltimore: Johns Hopkins University Press, 1991), 3.

85 Curtis, *A Consuming Faith*, 2.

86 Hoge, *Division in the Protestant House*, 20.

87 Guth explains the Social Gospel's longevity thusly: "The Social Gospel was kept alive by the Great Depression and the activism of the New Deal until the 1960s, when it was again revived by the civil rights, antipoverty, and peace movements. By this time, social reform had become the primary mission of the church for a new generation of liberal clergy, who abandoned otherworldly religion altogether in favor of social transformation." James L. Guth, *The Bully Pulpit: The Politics of Protestant Clergy* (Lawrence: University Press of Kansas, 1997), 13.

88 Gary Selby, "Framing Social Protest: The Exodus Narrative in Martin Luther King's Montgomery Bus Boycott Rhetoric," *Journal of Communication and Religion* 24, no. 1 (2001): 68–93; idem, *Martin Luther King and the Rhetoric of Freedom: The Exodus Narrative in America's Struggle for Civil Rights* (Waco, Tex.: Baylor University Press, 2008).

89 Martin Luther King Jr., "Beyond Vietnam—A Time to Break Silence," speech given at Riverside Church, New York City, April 4, 1967, http://www.americanrhetoric.com/speeches/mlkatimetobreaksilence.htm.

90 William Sloane Coffin Jr., "Why Yale Chaplain Rode; Christians Can't Be Outside," *Life*, June 2, 1961, 54.

91 William Sloane Coffin Jr., "The Spirit of Lamech," sermon given January 9, 1966. My thanks to Ben Krueger, whose archival research has blessed us with the recovery of this and many other of Coffin's sermons.

92 Jerry Falwell, "Ministers and Marches," in *God's Bullies: Power Politics and Religious Tyranny*, ed. Perry Deane Young (New York: Holt, Rinehart, & Winston, 1965/1982), 313.

93 Falwell, "Ministers and Marches," 313.

94 Hoge, *Division in the Protestant House*, 75. Hoge also describes the way that this conflict played itself out in the pages of popular and Christian periodicals. The wealthy and influential Presbyterian J. Howard Pew penned a *Reader's Digest* editorial, titled "Should the Church 'Meddle' in Civil Affairs," in which he argued that the church should preach the gospel of Jesus Christ rather than involving itself in politics. The mainline/liberal periodical *Christian Century* countered that such calls for evangelism segregate the world unnaturally, dividing the economic, civil, political, and ecclesiastical realms. The gospel does not make such distinctions, the magazine claimed (Hoge, *Division in the Protestant House*, 37).

95 Donald K. Gorrell, *The Age of Social Responsibility: The Social Gospel in the Progressive Era, 1900–1920* (Macon, Ga.: Mercer University Press, 1988), ix.

96 Marty, *Righteous Empire*, 184–85.

97 Guth, *The Bully Pulpit*, 58.

98 Ram A. Cnaan and Stephanie C. Boddie, *The Invisible Caring Hand: American Congregations and the Provision of Welfare* (New York: New York University Press, 2002), 295.

99 See Quentin J. Schultze, ed., *American Evangelicals and the Mass Media* (Grand Rapids: Academie Books, 1990); idem, *Christianity and the Mass Media in America: Toward a Democratic Accommodation* (East Lansing: Michigan State University Press, 2003); Heather Hendershot, *Shaking the World for Jesus: Media and Conservative Evangelical Culture* (Chicago: University of Chicago Press, 2004); Stewart M. Hoover and Lynn Schofield Clark, *Practicing Religion in the Age of the Media: Explorations in Media, Religion, and Culture* (New York: Columbia University Press, 2002); Hal Erickson, *Religious Radio and Television in the United States, 1921–1991: The Programs and Personalities* (Jefferson, N.C.: McFarland, 1992); Daniel A. Stout and Judith M. Buddenbaum, "Genealogy of an Emerging Field: Foundations for the Study of Media and Religion," *Journal of Media and Religion* 1, no. 1 (2002): 5–12.

100 Matt 28:18-20 (see also Mark 16:14-18; Luke 24:36-39; John 20:19-23; Acts 1:6-8).

101 Peter Fraser, *Images of the Passion: The Sacramental Mode in Film* (Westport, Conn.: Praeger, 1998), 4–5.

102 Peter Fraser, *Images of the Passion*, 4–5.

103 See, for instance, Quentin J. Schultze, "Keeping the Faith: American Evangelicals and the Media," in Schultze, *American Evangelicals and the Mass Media*, 23; John P. Ferré, "The Media of Popular Piety," in *Mediating Religion: Conversations in Media, Religion, and Culture*, ed. Jolyon P. Mitchell and Sophia Marriage (New York: T&T Clark, 2003); Hendershot, *Shaking the World*, 5; Michele Rosenthal, " 'Turn it off!': TV Criticism in the Christian Century Magazine," in *Practicing Religion in the Age of the Media: Explorations in Media, Religion, and Culture*, ed. Stewart M. Hoover and Lynn Schofield Clark (New York: Columbia University Press, 2002); Michael Budde, *The (Magic) Kingdom of God: Christianity and Global Culture Industries* (Boulder, Colo.: Westview, 1997).

104 Mark Silk, *Unsecular Media: Making News of Religion in America* (Urbana: University of Illinois Press, 1995), 16–17.

105 Gerald E. Forshey, *American Religious and Biblical Spectaculars* (Westport, Conn.: Praeger, 1992), 1.

106 David Edwin Harrell, "Oral Roberts: Religious Media Pioneer," in *Communication and Change in American Religious History*, ed. Leonard I. Sweet (Grand Rapids: Eerdmans, 1993), 322–23.

107 Adam Piore, "A Higher Frequency: How the Rise of Salem Communications' Radio Empire Reveals the Evangelical Master Plan," *Mother Jones*, December 2005, 48.

108 Harrell, "Oral Roberts," 325.

109 Janice Peck, *The Gods of Televangelism: The Crisis of Meaning and the Appeal of Religious Television* (Cresskill, N.J.: Hampton, 1993), 1–2.

110 Razelle Frankl, *Televangelism: The Marketing of Popular Religion* (Carbondale: Southern Illinois University Press, 1987), 17–19; idem, "Transformation of Televangelism: Repackaging Christian Values," in *Media, Culture, & the Religious Right*, eds. Linda Kintz and Julia Lesage (Minneapolis: University of Minnesota Press, 1998), 165.

111 Stephen Prothero, *American Jesus: How the Son of God Became a National Icon* (New York: Farrar, Straus & Giroux, 2003), 42–123.

112 Theda Skocpol, "How Americans Became Civic," in Skocpol and Fiorina, *Civic Engagement in American Democracy*, 31.

113 Theda Skocpol and Morris P. Fiorina, "Making Sense of the Civic Engagement Debate," in Skocpol and Fiorina, *Civic Engagement in American Democracy*, 7–12.

114   In addition to the studies described, see also Andrew Kohut, *The Diminishing Divide: Religion's Changing Role in American Politics* (Washington, D.C.: Brookings Institution, 2000); Robert Wuthnow, *Saving America? Faith-Based Services and the Future of Civil Society* (Princeton: Princeton University Press, 2004); and J. Matthew Wilson, ed., *From Pews to Polling Places: Faith and Politics in the American Religious Mosaic* (Washington, D.C.: Georgetown University Press, 2007).

115   Hoge, *Division in the Protestant House*, 15. Similarly, Andrew Kohut, John C. Green, Scott Keeter, and Robert C. Toth draw upon data from a number of different surveys, including nationwide Pew Religion Surveys, National Election Studies, and Gallup Polls, in order to illuminate correlations between theological beliefs, religious affiliations, political commitments, and activist practices. Ram Cnaan and his colleagues conducted their own survey of 251 religious congregations in six urban areas, and they used the data gathered to draw conclusions about the quantity and types of social programs pursued by American congregations (Kohut, *Diminishing Divide*, 159–61; Cnaan and Boddie, *Invisible Caring Hand*, 299–304).

116   Rodney Stark, *What Americans Really Believe* (Waco, Tex.: Baylor University Press, 2008).

117   Justin Lewis, Sanna Inthorn, and Karin Wahl-Jorgensen, *Citizens or Consumers? What the Media Tell Us about Political Participation*, Issues in Cultural and Media Studies (New York: Open University Press, 2005), 5 (emphasis in original).

118   Kevin Michael DeLuca and Anne Teresa Demo, "Imaging Nature: Watkins, Yosemite, and the Birth of Environmentalism," *Critical Studies in Media Communication* 17, no. 3 (2000): 253.

119   Maurice Charland, "Constitutive Rhetoric: The Case of the Peuple Québécois," *Quarterly Journal of Speech* 73, no. 2 (1987): 138.

120   Stanley Eugene Fish, *Is There a Text in this Class? The Authority of Interpretive Communities* (Cambridge, Mass.: Harvard University Press, 1980), 3.

121   In some ways, my approach to close textual analysis echoes the traditional analytical method in rhetorical studies (e.g., Michael Leff, "Textual Criticism: The Legacy of G. P. Mohrmann," *Quarterly Journal of Speech* 72 [1986]: 377–89). Not only do I extend this approach to media texts, however I also disavow the "instrumentalist" approach that Jasinski claims drives so much of close textual analysis: James Jasinski, "Instrumentalism, Contextualism, and Interpretation in Rhetorical Criticism," in *Rhetorical Hermeneutics: Invention and Interpretation in the Age of Science*, ed. Alan G. Gross and William M. Keith (Albany: State University of New York Press, 1997).

122 Amy Johnson Frykholm's audience reception study of the *Left Behind* books is a useful complement, as it tries to explain how audience members made meaning out of those books. It also, however, demonstrates the limitations of audience research alone and the utility of textual criticism. For all of Frykholm's thoughtful reflections on audience reactions to the books, without any close textual analysis of the novels themselves, she cannot interrogate the features of narrative, plot, or character development that might have prompted any of these audience reactions. Frykholm, *Rapture Culture: Left Behind in Evangelical America* (Oxford: Oxford University Press, 2004).

123 For a related explanation of my perspective on rhetoric as discursive resource, see Kristy Maddux, "Feminism and Foreign Policy: Public Vocabularies and the Conditions of Emergence for First Lady Rosalynn Carter," *Women's Studies in Communication* 31, no. 1 (2008): 29–55. There, I build on Condit and Lucaites' concept of public vocabulary, which they argue forms a discursive resource bank from which individual rhetors borrow. Celeste Michelle Condit and John Louis Lucates, *Crafting Equality: America's Anglo-African Word* (Chicago: University of Chicago Press, 1993).

124 See Stuart Hall, "Encoding/Decoding," in *Culture, Media, Language*, ed. Stuart Hall, Dorothy Hobson, Andrew Lowe, and Paul Willis (London: Hutchinson, 1980); John Fiske, "Television: Polysemy and Popularity," *Critical Studies in Mass Communication* 3, no. 4 (1986): 391–408; Celeste Michelle Condit, "The Rhetorical Limits of Polysemy," *Critical Studies in Mass Communication* 6 (1989): 103–22; idem, "Hegemony in a Mass-Mediated Society: Concordance about Reproductive Technologies," *Critical Studies in Mass Communication* 11, no. 3 (1994): 205–30; idem, "Hegemony, Concordance, and Capitalism: Reply to Cloud," *Critical Studies in Mass Communication* 13 (1996): 382–84; Dana L. Cloud, "The Limits of Interpretation: Ambivalence and the Stereotype in *Spenser: For Hire*," *Critical Studies in Mass Communication* 9, no. 4 (1992): 311–24; idem, "Hegemony or Concordance? The Rhetoric of Tokenism in 'Oprah' Winfrey's Rags-to-Riches Biography," *Critical Studies in Mass Communication* 13 (1996): 115–37.

125 Philip Wander, "The Ideological Turn in Modern Criticism," *Central States Speech Journal* 34 (1983): 1–18. I am especially sympathetic and indebted to the ideological feminist criticism in the field of rhetorical studies, such as Bonnie J. Dow, *Prime-Time Feminism: Television, Media Culture, and the Women's Movement since 1970* (Philadelphia: University of Pennsylvania Press, 1996); Helene A. Shugart, "On Misfits and Margins: Narrative, Resistance, and the Poster Child Politics of Rosie O'Donnell," *Communication and Critical/Cultural Studies* 2, no. 1 (2005): 52–76; Kathleen Battles and Wendy

Hilton-Morrow, "Gay Characters in Conventional Spaces: *Will and Grace and the Situation Comedy Genre*," *Critical Studies in Media Communication* 19, no. 1 (2002): 87–105; Lisa M. Cuklanz, "The Masculine Ideal: Rape on Prime-Time Television, 1976–1978," *Critical Studies in Mass Communication* 15 (1998): 423–48; Brenda Cooper, "*Boys Don't Cry* and Female Masculinity: Reclaiming a Life & Dismantling the Politics of Normative Heterosexuality," *Critical Studies in Media Communication* 19, no. 1 (2002): 44–63.

126   Barbara Biesecker, "Michel Foucault and the Question of Rhetoric," *Philosophy and Rhetoric* 25 (1992): 351–64; Raymie E. McKerrow, "Critical Rhetoric: Theory and Praxis," *Communication Monographs* 56 (1989): 91–111.

CHAPTER 2

1   See Lucinda J. Peach, *Legislating Morality: Pluralism and Religious Identity in Lawmaking* (New York: Oxford University Press, 2002); Kent Greenawalt, *Private Consciences and Public Reasons* (New York: Oxford University Press, 1995); Robert Audi, *Practical Reasoning* (New York: Routledge, 1989); Robert Audi and Nicholas Wolterstorff, *Religion in the Public Square: The Place of Religious Convictions in Political Debate* (Lanham, Md.: Rowman & Littlefield, 1997); John Rawls, "The Idea of Public Reason Revisited," *University of Chicago Law Review* 64 (1997): 765–99; Jürgen Habermas, "Religion in the Public Sphere," *European Journal of Philosophy* 14, no. 1 (2006): 1–25; Melissa Yates, "Rawls and Habermas on Religion in the Public Sphere," *Philosophy and Social Criticism* 33, no. 7 (2007): 880–91.

2   See Jim Wallis, *God's Politics: Why the Right Gets It Wrong and the Left Doesn't Get It* (San Francisco: HarperSanFrancisco, 2005); David Kuo, *Tempting Faith: An Inside Story of Political Seduction* (New York: Free Press, 2006); Gregory A. Boyd, *The Myth of a Christian Nation: How the Quest for Political Power Is Destroying the Church* (Grand Rapids: Zondervan, 2005); Robin Meyers, *Why the Christian Right Is Wrong: A Minister's Manifesto for Taking Back Your Faith, Your Flag, Your Future* (San Francisco: Jossey-Bass, 2006); Kathleen Kennedy Townsend, *Failing America's Faithful: How Today's Churches Are Mixing God with Politics and Losing Their Way* (New York: Warner Books, 2007); Randall Balmer, *Thy Kingdom Come: How the Religious Right Distorts the Faith and Threatens America: An Evangelical's Lament* (New York: Perseus Books, 2006); Robert Edgar, *Middle Church: Reclaiming the Moral Values of the Faithful Majority from the Religious Right* (New York: Simon & Schuster, 2006); Michael Lerner, *The Left Hand of God: Taking Back Our Country from the Religious Right* (New York: HarperSanFrancisco, 2006); Tony Campolo, *Letters to a*

Young Evangelical (New York: Basic Books, 2006); John C. Danforth, *Faith and Politics: How the "Moral Values" Debate Divides America and How to Move Forward Together* (New York: Viking, 2006); Kristy Maddux, "Faithful Political Rhetoric," *Rhetoric & Public Affairs* 11, no. 1 (2008): 133–55.

3   It may be important to note here that the film is not always attentive to the details of the historical record. A historian, for instance, might object to Charles Fox taking the title Lord or might want to specify that the film's Pitt is William Pitt the Younger. In my analysis, I take the film at face value and read the characters and the narrative as they are presented, regardless of their consonance with standard histories of the era.

4   "What Would Wilberforce Do?" *Christianity Today*, March 2007, 28.

5   Charles Colson, "The Wilberforce Strategy," *Christianity Today*, February 2007, 132.

6   Sara Bakhshian, "New Film Explores Life, Legacy of Wilberforce," Religion News Service, February 14, 2007, available through LexisNexis. The rarity of collaboration between these four organizations cannot be overstated; whereas the National Council of Churches is an organization of mainline Protestant churches that regularly takes liberal stances on political issues, Sojourners is a coalition of Christians with more diverse beliefs theologically who also tend to take liberal political stances, while the National Association of Evangelicals and the Salvation Army tend to be more conservative, and the Salvation Army rarely stakes political positions publicly.

7   Senator Sam Brownback, announcement speech, January 20, 2007, Topeka, Kans.; transcribed from YouTube.com video, http://www.youtube.com/watch?v=xq1JGkevvXM (accessed March 26, 2008).

8   Sam Hananel, "Brownback Looks at Movie for Inspiration on Campaign Trail," Associated Press State and Local Wire, February 22, 2007, available through LexisNexis.

9   G. Jeffrey MacDonald, "Evangelicals Rally Around—and Disagree On—'Grace'; William Wilberforce's Faith Led to End of Slave Trade," *USA Today*, February 22, 2007.

10 World Vision Public Relations, "'Amazing Grace' Movie Is 'a Rallying Call to Combat Modern Slavery' Says World Vision Expert," February 22, 2007, available through LexisNexis; Operation Rescue, "He Could Have Been a Wilberforce," February 22, 2007, available through LexisNexis; Concerned Women for America, "Wilberforce: A Model for Today's Grassroots Activists," February 23, 2007, available through LexisNexis.

11 Habermas, "Religion in the Public Sphere," 3.

12 Rawls, "Idea of Public Reason," 767–68.

13   Rawls, "Idea of Public Reason," 783–84.

14   Kent Greenawalt is another outspoken advocate of delegitimizing religious rationales in political debate.

15   Peach, *Legislating Morality*, 118. To be fair, Peach is writing about Kent Greenawalt's proposal primarily and John Rawls' only secondarily. The distinctions she draws between the two, although interesting, are less significant here.

16   Habermas, "Religion in the Public Sphere," 9 (emphasis in original).

17   Habermas, "Religion in the Public Sphere," 10.

18   Habermas, "Religion in the Public Sphere," 7.

19   In recent years, many other books have lamented the sins and failures of the Christian Right and its influence on the Bush administration, but they have done so without articulating an alternative for Christian public influence. In that category of books, I would include Chris Hedges, *American Fascists: The Christian Right and the War on America* (New York: Free Press, 2006); Michelle Goldberg, *Kingdom Coming: The Rise of Christian Nationalism* (New York: W. W. Norton, 2006); and Kevin Phillips, *American Theocracy: The Perils and Politics of Radical Religion, Oil and Borrowed Money in the 21st Century* (New York: Viking, 2006).

20   Again and again, Jerry Falwell, Pat Robertson, and James Dobson emerge in these critiques as the villains who traded the loyalty of well-intentioned people of faith for connections and access within the Republican Party hierarchy. See, for instance, Meyers, *Why the Christian Right*, xii; Balmer, *Thy Kingdom Come*, 39; and Wallis, *God's Politics*, 65.

21   Campolo, *Letters*, 191 (emphasis in original).

22   Of course, well-meaning people of faith can disagree about how well Republican Party policies have exemplified Christian values. Controversy over the Iraq war is instructive: whereas prominent religious leaders, such as the United Methodist Church's Bishop Mel Talbert, decried the Iraq war for violating the tenets of just war theory, political philosopher Jean Bethke Elshtain identified the ways in which the broader war on terror did meet those very standards. Jean Elshtain, *Just War against Terror: The Burden of American Power in a Violent World* (New York: Basic Books, 2003); Alan Cooperman, "Church Leaders Propose Antiwar Plan," *Washington Post*, March 8, 2003, A15; Elizabeth Bumiller, "White House Letter; Religious Leaders Ask if Antiwar Call Is Heard," *The New York Times*, March 10, 2003, A16.

23   Balmer, *Thy Kingdom Come*, 33.

24   Campolo, *Letters*, 190.

25   Balmer, *Thy Kingdom Come*, 37–38.

26   Some critics also fret about the harm that partisanship and nationalism do to the faith itself. Because Christianity and right-wing politics are indistinguishable, "some of the best and brightest human beings alive today have run screaming out of the sanctuaries where they went looking for spiritual nourishment and a chance to serve God," Meyers laments. "They are wondering, *what happened to the Gospel?*" (*Why the Christian Right*, 31; emphasis in original). Boyd worries that Christian nationalism hurts the cause of global missions. When the world's image of Christianity becomes indistinguishable from American nationalism, people around the globe cannot hear the good news of Christ's gospel. Instead, Boyd explains, "they hear the gospel as *bad* news, as *American* news, *exploitive capitalistic* news, *greedy* news, *violent* news, and *morally decadent* news. They can't see the beauty of the cross because everything the American flag represents to them is in the way" (Boyd, *The Myth*, 110).

27   Reportedly, one thousand people left the church following his sermon series The Cross and the Sword, upon which his book is based. Boyd, *The Myth*, 10; Laurie Goodstein, "Disowning Conservative Politics, Evangelical Pastor Rattles Flock," *The New York Times*, July 30, 2006.

28   Given my feminist politics, I have serious reservations about using the term *kingdom*. Not only does it imply a male god, it also hearkens back to an antiquated form of patriarchy, where a male sovereign monarch ruled over powerless subjects. That is hardly a system of government I find promising, so it is certainly not an analogy to the divine I find meaningful. Because this term is so common in the contemporary debate over Christianity and civic engagement, however, I use it out of convenience and simplicity in this chapter. I also fear that avoiding the term kingdom would only obscure the sexism that haunts Christian thought.

29   Boyd, *The Myth*, 17–18.

30   Boyd, *The Myth*, 29–49.

31   Boyd, *The Myth*, 28.

32   Boyd, *The Myth*, 24–27.

33   Boyd, *The Myth*, 33.

34   In the parable of the mustard seed, as told in Matt 13:31-32, Jesus says, "The kingdom of heaven is like a mustard seed, which a man took and planted in his field. Though it is the smallest of all your seeds, yet when it grows, it is the largest of garden plants and becomes a tree, so that the birds of the air come and perch in its branches."

35   Boyd, *The Myth*, 61; he alludes to Phil 3:20, where Paul assures Christians that "our citizenship is in heaven."

36   Boyd, *The Myth*, 117.

37   Boyd, *The Myth*, 119.

38   Boyd, *The Myth*, 146 (emphasis in original).

39   Boyd, *The Myth*, 125.

40   Kuo, *Tempting Faith*, 207–11.

41   Kuo, *Tempting Faith*, 229.

42   Kuo, *Tempting Faith*, 241.

43   Kuo, *Tempting Faith*, 261.

44   Boyd and Kuo are not alone in recognizing the value of Christlike acts of self-sacrifice; their more liberal counterparts also hear God's call to perform mercy and charity work. Townsend, for instance, celebrates the Catholic Church's important history of running social service agencies, such as hospitals, orphanages, schools, and homeless shelters, all of which she praises for responding to material needs as well as creating a sense of community, especially among immigrant populations. Bob Edgar demonstrates Protestants' similar commitment to this sort of charity work, as exemplified by the homeless shelter that he and a colleague set up in Philadelphia in the early 1970s. Townsend, *Failing America's Faithful*, 71; Edgar, *Middle Church*, 146.

45   To be clear, these liberal religious leaders also see the value in the type of charity work that both Boyd and Kuo advocate. Townsend explains, for instance, that "to walk in God's path is not just to pray or give charity, but also to work for *justice* for every creature on His earth" (*Failing America's Faithful*, 4 [emphasis in original]). She, like Campolo and Edgar, sees justice and charity work as intertwined avenues for social reform. See also Campolo, *Letters*, 259; Edgar, *Middle Church*, 167.

46   Wallis, *God's Politics*, xvi.

47   Balmer, *Thy Kingdom Come*, 182 (emphasis in original).

48   Wallis, *God's Politics*, 71 (emphasis in original); see also Balmer, *Thy Kingdom Come*, 186.

49   Townsend, *Failing America's Faithful*, 85.

50   Danforth, *Faith and Politics*, 52, 124.

51   He refers to the commandment in Matt 22, Mark 12, and Luke 10.

52   Danforth, *Faith and Politics*, 31.

53   Danforth, *Faith and Politics*, 27.

54   On King, see Wallis, *God's Politics*, 22, 28, 60, 61; and Townsend, *Failing America's Faithful*, 85; on these other models, see Wallis, *God's Politics*, 38.

55   He is alluding to Jas 1:22.

56   Meyers, *Why the Christian Right*, 160.

57   Meyers, *Why the Christian Right*, 166–68.

58   A film's retrospective framing may or may not violate the historical record, but that is a matter best left for historians. I am concerned here not with whether or not the film's narrative is "true," but with how its framing allows it to appeal to contemporary audiences. Kristy Maddux, "Winning the Right to Vote in 2004: *Iron Jawed Angels* and the Retrospective Framing of Feminism," *Feminist Media Studies* 9, no. 1 (2009): 73–94.

59   MacDonald, "Evangelicals Rally Around."

60   In a 2005 cover story featuring the "25 most influential evangelicals in America," *Time* magazine included Charles Colson among such other dignitaries as Rick Warren and Tim LaHaye. His influence should not be underestimated.

61   Kuo, *Tempting Faith*, 266–67.

62   Balmer, *Thy Kingdom Come*, xviii.

63   An adaptation of Romans 12:2 and John 17:6-19, this saying saturates contemporary Christian discourse about earthly and heavenly obligations.

64   Digging further into the woman suffrage movement would, of course, reveal the complexity of its relationship with Christianity. Suffragists long alternated between arguing against the uses of the Christian Scripture that limited women's rights while relying on the Scriptures that granted women's equality and drawing on the organizational strength of churches for building a movement.

65   Campbell, *Man Cannot Speak for Her*, 1:12.

66   James Darsey, *The Prophetic Tradition and Radical Rhetoric in America* (New York: New York University Press, 1997), 16.

67   Danforth, *Faith and Politics*, 52–53.

68   Danforth, *Faith and Politics*, 27.

69   Kuo, *Tempting Faith*, 267.

70   Campolo, *Letters*, 147.

71   Wallis, *God's Politics*, 8–9.

72   MacDonald, "Evangelicals Rally Around."

73   World Vision Public Relations, "'Amazing Grace' Movie is 'a Rallying Call to Combat Modern Slavery' Says World Vision Expert," February 22, 2007, available through LexisNexis; Operation Rescue, "He Could Have Been a Wilberforce," February 22, 2007, available through LexisNexis; Concerned Women for America, "Wilberforce: A Model for Today's Grassroots Activists," February 23, 2007, available through LexisNexis.

74   Jen Waters, "The Force of Wilberforce," *Washington Times*, February 20, 2007.

CHAPTER 3

1   Frank Rich, "Mel Gibson's Martyrdom Complex," *The New York Times*, August 3, 2003, sec. 2, p. 1.

2   Internet Movie Database, "Box Office/Business for *The Passion of the Christ*," http://www.imdb.com/title/tt0335345/business (accessed March 25, 2007).

3   Internet Movie Database, "Trivia for *The Passion of the Christ*," http://www.imdb.com/title/tt0335345/trivia. It has since been bumped out of the top ten all-time grossing films.

4   Stark, *What Americans Really Believe*, 174.

5   Leon Wieseltier, "Mel Gibson's Lethal Weapon: The Worship of Blood," *New Republic*, March 8, 2004, 19.

6   Richard Corliss, "The Goriest Story Ever Told," *Time*, March 1, 2004, 65.

7   David Van Biema, "Why It's So Bloody," *Time*, February 7, 2005, 66.

8   Christy Lemire, "At the Movies: 'The Passion of the Christ,'" *The New York Times*, July 18, 2005.

9   A. O. Scott, "Good and Evil Locked in Violent Showdown," *The New York Times*, February 25, 2004, E1.

10   The most recent generation of Jesus films, such as *Jesus of Nazareth* and *Jesus Christ Superstar*, as well as earlier films, such as *King of Kings* and *The Robe*, focused on Jesus' life in totality, giving the crucifixion only passing attention. And within their limited depictions of the crucifixion, these films focused little attention on the violence itself.

11   Scott, "Good and Evil Locked in Violent Showdown."

12   Tom Tugend, "Film Could Revive 'Scurrilous Charges' against Jews," *New York Sun*, March 11, 2003, 2.

13   Christopher Nixon, "Is the Pope Catholic . . . Enough?" *The New York Times Magazine*, March 9, 2003, 50.

14   Michael Klein, "Gibson Screens 'Passion' for Clergy," *Philadelphia Inquirer*, July 27, 2003, B02; Jane Lampman, "Capturing the Passion," *Christian Science Monitor*, July 10, 2003, 11.

15   In the *Journal of Media and Religion*, Thomas Cooper has paid focused, scholarly attention to the portrayals of Jewish and Roman characters in the film. Thomas Cooper, "Of Anti-Semitism, Romans de Sade, and Celluloid Christianity: The Cases For and Against Gibson's Passion," *Journal of Media and Religion* 4, no. 4 (2005): 251–68.

16   William Booth, "Mel Gibson's Latest Drama Stars Himself," *Washington Post*, July 30, 2006, D01.

17   David Denby, "Nailed: Mel Gibson's 'The Passion of the Christ,'" *New Yorker*, March 1, 2004, 84; see also David Ansen, "So What's the Good News?" *Newsweek*, March 1, 2004.

18   Eric Harrison, "The Blood of Christ; Martyrdom Overwhelms 'The Passion,'" *Houston Chronicle*, February 25, 2004, 1.

19   Scott, "Good and Evil Locked in Violent Showdown."

20   S. T. Karnick, "Violence to Scripture?" *National Review Online*, February 27, 2004.

21   David Neff, "The Passion of Mel Gibson: Why Evangelicals Are Cheering a Movie with Profoundly Catholic Sensibilities," *Christianity Today*, March 2004, 30-35.

22   James B. Nickoloff, "Introduction," in *Gustavo Gutiérrez: Essential Writings*, ed. James B. Nickoloff, 1-22 (Maryknoll, N.Y.: Orbis Books, 1996).

23   Mary Potter Engel and Susan Brooks Thistlethwaite, "Making the Connections among Liberation Theologies around the World," in *Lift Every Voice: Constructing Christian Theologies from the Underside*, ed. Susan Brooks Thistlethwaite and Mary Potter Engel (Maryknoll, N.Y.: Orbis Books, 1998), 1.

24   Luke 4:18.

25   James H. Cone, *God of the Oppressed* (Maryknoll, N.Y.: Orbis Books, 1975/1997), 74.

26   Helen C. Orchard, *Courting Betrayal: Jesus as Victim in the Gospel of John* (Sheffield: Sheffield Academic Press, 1998), 262.

27   Cone, *God of the Oppressed*, 41.

28   Jon Sobrino, *Christ the Liberator: A View from the Victims* (Maryknoll, N.Y.: Orbis Books, 2001), 4.

29   Sobrino, *Christ the Liberator*, 4 (emphasis in original).

30   Rosemary Radford Ruether, "Eschatology and Feminism," in Thistlethwaite and Engel, *Lift Every Voice*, 129.

31   James Cone, "God is Black," in Thistlethwaite and Engel, *Lift Every Voice*, 103.

32   Cone, *God of the Oppressed*, 75, 130.

33   Jacqueline Grant, "Subjectification as a Requirement for Christological Construction," in Thistlethwaite and Engel, *Lift Every Voice*, 216.

34   Cone, *God of the Oppressed*, 128.

35   Joanne Carlson Brown and Rebecca Parker, "For God So Loved the World?" in *Christianity, Patriarchy, and Abuse*, ed. Joanne Carlson Brown and Carol R. Bohn (Cleveland, Ohio: Pilgrim, 1989), 1.

36 Colin E. Gunton, *The Actuality of Atonement: A Study of Metaphor, Rationality, and the Christian Tradition* (Grand Rapids: Eerdmans, 1989), 116.

37 Rita Nakashima Brock and Rebecca Ann Parker, *Proverbs of Ashes: Violence, Redemptive Suffering, and the Search for What Saves Us* (Boston: Beacon, 2001), 157.

38 Brown and Parker, "For God So Loved the World?" 156.

39 Marie Fortune, "The Transformation of Suffering: A Biblical and Theological Perspective," in Brown and Bohn, *Christianity, Patriarchy, and Abuse*, 145.

40 Carol R. Bohn, "Dominion to Rule: The Roots and Consequences of a Theology of Ownership," in Brown and Bohn, *Christianity, Patriarchy, and Abuse*, 114.

41 Brown and Parker, "For God So Loved the World?" 2 (emphasis in original).

42 Bohn, "Dominion to Rule," 107.

43 Brown and Parker, "For God So Loved the World?" 2.

44 Only in his crucifixion does Jesus make a transition into the divine world. Once Jesus acknowledges his own death with the words "it is accomplished," the camera angle changes drastically to an overhead shot looking down upon those gathered around the crosses—the only moment in the film with such a camera shot from above. The people below are like ants scurrying about, and suddenly the image of them below is contracted into a bubble, like a drop of water, which then falls to the earth, and the camera returns to its earlier position. Only at this point does Jesus join the divine realm, and only for this fleeting moment, as Jesus makes the transition, do we as audience members have access to the divine vantage point.

45 I base my argument about the film's preferred mode of citizenship in an opposition between "barbarous masculinity" and "feminine submission." In doing so, I assume that femininity and masculinity are only semi-stable constructs, which, as Judith Halberstam notes, are notoriously hard to define. They are rooted in the traditional role performances of women and men, as they have been reiterated across time. Masculine behavior thus is strong, commanding, and aggressive, while feminine behavior is weak, timid, and obedient. Masculinity and femininity are not entirely stable because, as Judith Butler notes, these genders are not naturally existing, but rather come to seem normal through their everyday iterations. Moreover, they become normative in dialectical opposition to each other—that is, what is feminine is necessarily what is not masculine, and vice versa. *The Passion* creates these gendered identities only in relationship to each other: the guards' masculinity only becomes apparent set in relief to the faithful disciples' femininity, and vice versa. Halberstam, *Female Masculinity*, 1; Butler, *Gender Trouble*, 3–44.

46 These numbers are slightly misleading, as there are only twenty shots of Mary, Mary Magdalene, and John, but the camera tends to dwell on those characters longer than it does on the guards or Jesus. In fact, just one of those shots of Mary lasts a full thirty-four seconds. Even still, the numbers suggest that the Roman guards receive considerable attention in this scene.

47 These three characters are also contrasted to the less faithful disciples, specifically Peter and Judas. In this narrative, these two are only depicted in their betrayals of Jesus—Judas turning him over for thirty pieces of silver and Peter denying him three times before the cock crows. Importantly, these traitorous disciples are depicted as very masculine, at least in comparison to the more faithful disciples. They are both tall, broad-shouldered men, and they have large, unkempt manes of dark, coarse hair with full beards. Moreover, they are significantly more aggressive than Mary, Mary Magdalene, and John. In the garden, for instance, when the temple guards approach to arrest Jesus, Peter fights back while John runs away to tell the women. When Peter cuts off Malchus' ear, Jesus scolds him, thus suggesting that John's act of running away was more faithful than Peter's violence. Judas' and Peter's performance of masculinity, even if is more subtle than the Roman guards' performance, still offers a pronounced contrast to the more faithful form of citizenship embodied by Mary, Mary Magdalene, and John.

48 Karen Armstrong has explicated this history in *The Gospel according to Woman: Christianity's Creation of the Sex War in the West* (Garden City, N.Y.: Anchor, 1987), 189–234.

49 John Macquarrie, *Mary for All Christians* (Edinburgh: T&T Clark, 2001), 40.

50 Macquarrie, *Mary for All Christians*, 40.

51 See, for instance, Longenecker and Gustafson, whose twelve-chapter book is divided thematically, each chapter focusing on a different aspect of Mary or of Marianism (such as "Holy Mary, Mother of God" and "Apparitions of the Virgin Mary"), but there is not one chapter devoted to Mary's place at the cross. Dwight Longenecker and David Gustafson, *Mary: A Catholic-Evangelical Debate* (Grand Rapids: Brazos, 2003).

52 Pope Benedict XVI, *Deus Caritas Est*, http://www.vatican.va/holy_father/benedict_xvi/encyclicals/documents/hf_ben-xvi_enc_20051225_deus-caritas-est_en.html.

53 Bruce Babington and Peter William Evans, *Biblical Epics: Sacred Narrative in the Hollywood Cinema* (Manchester: Manchester University Press, 1993), 108.

54 Their Web site is http://sites.capitalchristian.com/npc/.

CHAPTER 4

1   Lisa McMinn, "Y2K, the Apocalypse, and Evangelical Christianity: The Role of Eschatological Belief in Church Responses," *Sociology of Religion* 62, no. 2 (2001): 205–20; Nancy Schaefer, "Y2K as an Endtime Sign: Apocalypticism in America at the *Fin-De-Millennium*," *Journal of Popular Culture* 38, no. 1 (2004): 82–105.

2   Tim LaHaye and Jerry Jenkins' central roles in evangelical Christian circles surely enabled the success of these novels. In 2001, the Institute for the Study of American Evangelicals named LaHaye the most influential evangelical of the past twenty-five years, and in 2005, he and his wife Beverly were among *Time* magazine's twenty-five most influential evangelicals in America. In addition to developing a San Diego–area megachurch and its associated schools, LaHaye was also responsible for grassroots political organizing in California in the 1970s, ultimately leading to his participation in the founding of Jerry Falwell's Moral Majority. Prior to the *Left Behind* books, he was a well-published author of Christian tracts on marriage and family life, as well as nonfiction explanations of end-time prophecy. Although Jerry Jenkins had achieved comparatively less celebrity prior to *Left Behind*, he had ghostwritten and collaborated on various evangelicals' autobiographies, including Billy Graham's. From LaHaye's invitation, the two developed a successful working partnership: Jenkins writes each novel from start to finish, but he works from prophecy charts that LaHaye puts together—seventy to one hundred pages of outlines for each novel. The two split the profits from the books fifty-fifty. David Gates, "Religion: The Pop Prophets," *Newsweek*, May 24, 2004, 44; Craig Unger, "American Rapture," *Vanity Fair*, December 2005, 204; David Van Biema, "25 Most Influential Evangelicals in America," *Time*, February 7, 2005, 34.

3   Frykholm, *Rapture Culture*, 22.

4   Enthusiasm for the *Left Behind* books spanned cross sections of the American population: almost equal numbers of African American and white, as well as college-educated and high school-educated, respondents report having read the books. The books were more popular among women than men (23.7% to 13.6%), among eighteen-to-thirty-year-olds than those over sixty-five (25.8% to 11.7%), and in households with incomes over $100,000 than in households making less than $35,000 (24.6% to 18.6%). Although some of these differences are sizable, those disparities should not diminish the significance of these books being widely read across age, sex, education, income, and racial groups. Christopher Bader, Kevin Dougherty, Paul Froese, Byron

Johnson, F. Carson Mencken, Jerry Z. Park, and Rodney Stark, "American Piety in the 21st Century: New Insights to the Depth and Complexity of Religion in the U.S.," unpublished research made available September 2006, http://www.baylor.edu/content/services/document.php/33304.pdf (accessed March 25, 2007), 21; Stark, *What Americans Really Believe*, 172.

5   See the Internet Movie Database, "Box office/Business for *Left Behind*," http://www.imdb.com/title/tt0190524/business.

6   Paul S. Boyer, *When Time Shall Be No More: Prophecy Belief in Modern American Culture* (Cambridge, Mass.: Belknap Press of Harvard University Press, 1992), 56–68; Eugen Weber, *Apocalypses: Prophecies, Cults, and Millennial Beliefs through the Ages* (Cambridge, Mass.: Harvard University Press, 1999), 76; Richard Connors and Andrew Colin Gow, *Anglo-American Millennialism, from Milton to the Millerites* (Boston: Brill, 2004), xiv.

7   Kaplan suggests the centrality of apocalyptic thinking to European intellectual history, counting among its adherents Shakespeare, Dante, and Newton. Jeffrey Kaplan, *Radical Religion in America: Millenarian Movements from the Far Right to the Children of Noah* (Syracuse, N.Y.: Syracuse University Press, 1997), 12.

8   Boyer, *When Time Shall Be No More*, 68–71.

9   Stephen J. Stein, "Apocalypticism Outside the Mainstream in the United States," in *The Continuum History of Apocalypticism*, ed. Bernard J. McGinn, John J. Collins, and Stephen J. Stein, 493–515 (New York: Continuum, 2003), 497–503.

10   Frykholm, *Rapture Culture*, 15–17. The sixteenth-century English prophet Joseph Mede and the seventeenth-century Puritan Increase Mather are most often credited with developing Rapture doctrine. See Reiner Smolinski, "Apocalypticism in Colonial North America," in McGinn, et al., *The Continuum History of Apocalypticism*.

11   Tony Campolo claims, astonishingly, that even today the Scofield Bible earns more money for Oxford University Press than any other title. Campolo, *Letters*, 110.

12   Kaplan identifies a handful of fringe groups centered around unique eschatologies. In particular, he analyzes Christian Identity, Odinism and Ásatrú, and B'nai Noah. Kaplan, *Radical Religion*.

13   Frykholm, *Rapture Culture*, 18.

14   Stephen D. O'Leary, *Arguing the Apocalypse: A Theory of Millennial Rhetoric* (New York: Oxford University Press, 1994), 180–83.

15   Boyer, *When Time Shall Be No More*, 298.

16   Kaplan, *Radical Religion*, xiv; McMinn, "Y2K, the Apocalypse," 208.

NOTES TO PP. 93–97 ⤳ 229

17   Barry Brummett, *Contemporary Apocalyptic Rhetoric* (Westport, Conn.: Prae-
      ger, 1991), 17.
18   Matt 25:13.
19   Brummett, *Contemporary Apocalyptic Rhetoric*, 17.
20   Schaefer, "Y2K as an Endtime Sign," 84; Boyer, *When Time Shall Be No More*,
      75.
21   Boyer, *When Time Shall Be No More*, 75; Connors and Gow, *Anglo-American
      Millennialism*, xiv.
22   McMinn, "Y2K, the Apocalypse," 209.
23   Boyer, *When Time Shall Be No More*, 303.
24   Boyer, *When Time Shall Be No More*, 75–76.
25   Simon Coleman, "An Empire on a Hill? The Christian Right and the Right
      to Be Christian in America," *Anthropological Quarterly* 78, no. 3 (2005): 658;
      O'Leary, *Arguing the Apocalypse*, 12.
26   Elizabeth K. Rosen, *Apocalyptic Transformation: Apocalypse and the Postmodern
      Imagination* (Lanham, Md.: Lexington Books, 2008), xii.
27   O'Leary, *Arguing the Apocalypse*, 84; Boyer, *When Time Shall Be No Moree*, 95,
      96, 298.
28   Boyer, *When Time Shall Be No More*, 298–99.
29   In the case of Y2K millennial fever specifically, McMinn identifies three
      common strategies adopted by churches and other Christian communities.
      The three strategies, which she labels the Good Samaritan Strategy, the
      Joseph Strategy, and the Noah Strategy, range from continuing preexisting
      good works efforts, to evangelizing friends and neighbors, to divorcing soci-
      ety to live in the wilderness and await the impending storm. McMinn, "Y2K,
      the Apocalypse," 213–15.
30   Boyer, *When Time Shall Be No Moree*, 97.
31   O'Leary, *Arguing the Apocalypse*, 87–88.
32   Boyer, *When Time Shall Be No More*, 82.
33   O'Leary, *Arguing the Apocalypse*, 69.
34   O'Leary, *Arguing the Apocalypse*, 68.
35   O'Leary, *Arguing the Apocalypse*, 68.
36   O'Leary, *Arguing the Apocalypse*, 72.
37   James D. Faubion, *The Shadows and Lights of Waco: Millennialism Today*
      (Princeton: Princeton University Press, 2001), 8.
38   O'Leary, *Arguing the Apocalypse*, 75.
39   Frank Kermode, *The Sense of an Ending: Studies in the Theory of Fiction* (New
      York: Oxford University Press, 1967), 69.

40   Maxine Lavon Montgomery, *The Apocalypse in African-American Fiction* (Gainesville: University Press of Florida, 1996), 11.

41   Joshua Gunn and David E. Beard, "On the Apocalyptic Sublime," *Southern Communication Journal* 65, no. 4 (2000): 274.

42   Gunn and Beard, "On the Apocalyptic Sublime," 272.

43   Gunn and Beard, "On the Apocalyptic Sublime," 274.

44   Clyde Wilcox, Sharon Linzey, and Ted G. Jelen, "Reluctant Warriors: Premillennialism and Politics in the Moral Majority," *Journal for the Scientific Study of Religion* 30, no. 3 (1991): 254.

45   Tim LaHaye and Jerry B. Jenkins, *Left Behind: A Novel of the Earth's Last Days* (Wheaton, Ill.: Tyndale House, 1996), 309.

46   Tim LaHaye and Jerry B. Jenkins, *Assassins: Assignment: Jerusalem, Target: Antichrist* (Wheaton, Ill.: Tyndale House, 1999), 269.

47   As it turns out here, Jesus' work to separate the faithful from the unfaithful (the sheep from the goats) complicates the good/evil dichotomy slightly. Not only are there sheep and goats, there are also Jews, who are "Jesus' 'brethren,' the chosen people of God whom the sheep befriended." Jews who have accepted Christ become sheep with special status because of their origins as God's chosen people. Tim LaHaye and Jerry B. Jenkins, *Glorious Appearing: The End of Days* (Wheaton, Ill.: Tyndale House, 2004), 376.

48   LaHaye and Jenkins, *Glorious Appearing*, 28.

49   Tim LaHaye and Jerry B. Jenkins, *The Indwelling: The Beast Takes Possession* (Wheaton, Ill.: Tyndale House, 2000), 231–32; idem, *The Mark: The Beast Rules the World* (Wheaton, Ill.: Tyndale House, 2000), 141.

50   LaHaye and Jenkins, *Glorious Appearing*, 127, 389; see also p. 166.

51   Tim LaHaye and Jerry B. Jenkins, *Desecration: Antichrist Takes the Throne* (Wheaton, Ill.: Tyndale House, 2001), 86.

52   LaHaye and Jenkins, *Glorious Appearing*, 64.

53   LaHaye and Jenkins, *Left Behind*, 90–91.

54   LaHaye and Jenkins, *Left Behind*, 143.

55   Tim LaHaye and Jerry B. Jenkins, *Tribulation Force: The Continuing Drama of Those Left Behind* (Wheaton, Ill.: Tyndale House, 1996), 62.

56   The pope is one of the very few Catholic leaders who disappear in the Rapture. The novels explain that he was one of the most evangelical Catholic leaders in recent memory; LaHaye and Jenkins, *Tribulation Force*, 269, 276.

57   Carpathians also try to employ a similar dissociation in reverse. Cardinal Mathews, as the leader of Enigma Babylon One World Faith, explains, "I consider exclusivist, intolerant, one-way-only beliefs antithetical to true reli-

gion." Tim LaHaye and Jerry B. Jenkins, *Apollyon: The Destroyer is Unleashed* (Wheaton, Ill.: Tyndale House, 1999), 294.

58 LaHaye and Jenkins, *Tribulation Force*, 72.

59 LaHaye and Jenkins, *Tribulation Force*, 111.

60 Carpathia raised his lieutenant from the dead.

61 Tim LaHaye and Jerry B. Jenkins, *Soul Harvest: The World Takes Sides* (Wheaton, Ill.: Tyndale House, 1998), 307.

62 LaHaye and Jenkins, *Left Behind*, 176–77.

63 LaHaye and Jenkins, *Tribulation Force*, 50.

64 LaHaye and Jenkins, *Left Behind*, 309. See also pp. 155, 225, and 327.

65 LaHaye and Jenkins, *The Mark*, 77.

66 LaHaye and Jenkins, *Tribulation Force*, 65.

67 LaHaye and Jenkins, *Tribulation Force*, 236.

68 LaHaye and Jenkins, *Apollyon*, 100.

69 LaHaye and Jenkins, *Glorious Appearing*, 246.

70 LaHaye and Jenkins, *Glorious Appearing*, 333.

71 LaHaye and Jenkins, *The Mark*, 60.

72 LaHaye and Jenkins, *Left Behind*, 303–4.

73 LaHaye and Jenkins, *The Mark*, 178–79.

74 LaHaye and Jenkins, *Apollyon*, 98.

75 Tim LaHaye and Jerry B. Jenkins, *The Remnant: On the Brink of Armageddon* (Wheaton, Ill.: Tyndale House, 2002), 45.

76 LaHaye and Jenkins, *Apollyon*, 94; see also LaHaye and Jenkins, *Assassins*, 2.

77 LaHaye and Jenkins, *Apollyon*, 68–69.

78 This soteriology is not unique to the *Left Behind* books, and it certainly resonates with the Arminianism so common among American evangelicals. Named for Jacob Arminius, Arminianism is the doctrine that asserts that God's grace is available to all who seek it, as opposed to Calvinist doctrine that suggests God chooses whom to bestow grace upon. George M. Marsden, *Fundamentalism and American Culture: The Shaping of Twentieth Century Evangelicalism: 1870–1925* (New York: Oxford University Press, 1980), 37.

79 LaHaye and Jenkins, *Glorious Appearing*, 32.

80 LaHaye and Jenkins, *Left Behind*, 146 (emphasis in original).

81 LaHaye and Jenkins, *Apollyon*, 77.

82 LaHaye and Jenkins, *Apollyon*, 111.

83 LaHaye and Jenkins, *Apollyon*, 160.

84 LaHaye and Jenkins, *Apollyon*, 50; see also p. 331.

85 LaHaye and Jenkins, *Left Behind*, 4, 278, 285.

86 LaHaye and Jenkins, *Left Behind*, 74.

87   LaHaye and Jenkins, *Left Behind*, 172.

88   LaHaye and Jenkins, *Left Behind*, 294.

89   LaHaye and Jenkins, *Apollyon*, 19.

90   LaHaye and Jenkins, *The Remnant*, 275.

91   Tim LaHaye and Jerry B. Jenkins, *Armageddon: The Cosmic Battle of the Ages* (Wheaton, Ill.: Tyndale House, 2003), 309.

92   LaHaye and Jenkins, *Glorious Appearing*, 113.

93   LaHaye and Jenkins, *Left Behind*, 210. The significance of Buck's name becomes apparent in the thirteenth installment of the *Left Behind* books, where the character has given up the nickname and goes by his given name, Cameron, instead, because in Christ's millennial kingdom, "there's nothing to buck" (available at http://www.leftbehind.com/channelbooks.asp?pageid=1320&channelID=227). One of the major failures of the *Left Behind* movie came in the tragic miscasting of Kirk Cameron in the role of Buck. Whereas the Buck of the novels and the graphic novels is sturdy and tough, Kirk Cameron achieves little more brawn than Mikey Seaver, the twerpy high school student he earned his fame playing on *Growing Pains*.

94   LaHaye and Jenkins, *Left Behind*, 1.

95   LaHaye and Jenkins, *Tribulation Force*, 89.

96   LaHaye and Jenkins, *The Mark*, 106-7.

97   LaHaye and Jenkins, *Apollyon*, 11. Keeping in mind that this book was published in 1999, this technology was fairly futuristic at the time.

98   LaHaye and Jenkins, *Glorious Appearing*, 218 (from Rev 12:5).

99   LaHaye and Jenkins, *Glorious Appearing*, 208.

100   LaHaye and Jenkins, *Glorious Appearing*, 204-5.

101   LaHaye and Jenkins, *Glorious Appearing*, 306.

102   The books explain that the antichrist must be sentenced to the lake of fire, rather than simply being eliminated, because even in Jesus' millennial reign, humans must be able to make the choice for good, which means not choosing evil. The antichrist will return again at the end of those one thousand years, and he will be punished again, along with anyone who has chosen to follow him.

103   LaHaye and Jenkins, *Apollyon*, 89; *Left Behind*, 264-65.

104   LaHaye and Jenkins, *Assassins*, 183.

105   LaHaye and Jenkins, *Desecration*.

106   Tim LaHaye and Jerry B. Jenkins, *Nicolae: The Rise of Antichrist* (Wheaton, Ill.: Tyndale House, 1997).

107   LaHaye and Jenkins, *Desecration*.

108   LaHaye and Jenkins, *Armageddon*.

109   Asen, "A Discourse Theory," 200.

110   George W. Bush, "Address to a Joint Session of Congress," September 20, 2001.

111   Bush, "Address to a Joint Session of Congress."

112   George W. Bush, "Remarks at the National Day of Prayer and Remembrance," September 14, 2001; George W. Bush, "State of the Union," January 29, 2002.

113   See John M. Murphy, "'Our Mission and Our Moment': George W. Bush and September 11th," *Rhetoric & Public Affairs* 6, no. 4 (2003): 623–25.

Chapter 5

1   Jerry Krupnick, "Spelling Goes to Bat for '7th Heaven,'" *Star-Ledger*, October 14, 1996, 27; Lon Grahnke, "Bucking TV Trends; Actress Plays At-Home Mom in '7th Heaven,'" *Chicago Sun-Times*, October 7, 1996, 33.

2   Bader et al., "American Piety," 20; Stark, *What Americans Really Believe*, 174.

3   Bob Longino, "TV Review: 7th Heaven," *Atlanta Journal-Constitution*, August 26, 1996, 01E.

4   Eric Mink, "'Special' Look at Race on 'Heaven,'" *New York Daily News*, October 14, 1996, 75.

5   John J. O'Connor, "Critic's Notebook: A Do-Good Family, Sort of Like the Waltons," *The New York Times*, October 14, 1996, C16.

6   Renee Graham, "A Sort-Of 'Brady' Sequel; WB's Newest Family Fare is Sickeningly Sweet," *Boston Globe*, August 26, 1996, C5.

7   Devoted *7th Heaven* fans on the show's Internet bulletin boards would surely quibble with these ages and grades. I have made these estimates based on deduction from clues in various episodes, but *7th Heaven*'s writers take enough creative liberty with such details that precision is impossible.

8   Although this cast would remain stable for the first six seasons, contract renegotiations at the end of season six dramatically reduced Jessica Biel's and Barry Watson's participation in the show, and David Gallagher would depart not long after. As a result, later seasons saw the addition of other teenage characters informally adopted into the Camden family. Those seasons also evidence a change in the show's tone as it replaces its typical episodic plotlines with longer story arcs. Given this radical shift in the show's nature, this analysis focuses on the first six seasons, only making claims about the patterns that define those early years.

9   Because my analysis focuses on the first six seasons of the show, I make this claim only for those seasons.

10 Episode 5.08, "Gossip."

11 Episode 4.21, "Love Stinks (Part 1)."

12 Episode 1.05, "The Color of God."

13 Matt gets teased in episode 2.04, "Who Knew?"; Simon gets teased in 6.02, "Teased," and 6.03, "Sympathy."

14 Episode 1.02, "Family Secrets."

15 Episode 2.20, "Boyfriends."

16 Episode 1.07, "Saturday."

17 Episode 3.04, "The Legacy."

18 Episode 3.05, ". . . And a Nice Chianti."

19 Episode 2.16, "It Takes a Village."

20 Episodes 1.04, "No Funerals and a Wedding"; 1.21 "Dangerous Liaisons (Part 1)"; 4.11, "Forget Me Not."

21 Episode 2.11, "Lead, Follow, or Get Out of the Way."

22 Robert Asen, *Visions of Poverty: Welfare Policy and the Political Imagination* (East Lansing: Michigan State University Press, 2002), 167.

23 David Grann, "Where W. Got Compassion," *New York Times Magazine*, September 12, 1999, 62.

24 Marvin Olasky, *The Tragedy of American Compassion* (Washington, D.C.: Regnery Gateway, 1992), 50, 121.

25 Olasky, *Tragedy of American Compassion*, 111.

26 I use the term post-welfare era to refer to the time period since the 1996 reforms. I recognize that the legislation passed that year did not eliminate government welfare all together; it did leave us with Temporary Assistance for Needy Families (TANF) and other social programs, after all. At the same time, it also reduced government-sponsored welfare so dramatically that it left other community organizations scrambling for ways to compensate for the gaps left by the reduction in the government's role.

27 Hillary Rodham Clinton, *It Takes a Village and Other Lessons Children Teach Us* (New York: Simon & Schuster, 1996), 306.

28 Clinton, *It Takes a Village*, 145.

29 Clinton, *It Takes a Village*, 165.

30 Clinton, *It Takes a Village*, 173.

31 Scott S. Greenberger, "Who Came Up with It First, Bush or Gore?" *Austin American-Statesman*, July 29, 1999, A16.

32 George W. Bush, "Remarks by the President in Announcement of the Faith-Based Initiative," in the Indian Treaty Room at the Dwight D. Eisenhower Executive Office Building, January 29, 2001.

33   George W. Bush, "Remarks by the President in Announcement of the Faith-Based Initiative."

34   The White House Press Office, "Obama Announces White House Office of Faith-based and Neighborhood Partnerships," February 5, 2009, http://www.whitehouse.gov/the_press_office/ObamaAnnouncesWhiteHouseOfficeofFaith-basedandNeighborhoodPartnerships/ (accessed April 8, 2009).

35   George W. Bush, "Remarks by the President in Announcement of the Faith-Based Initiative."

36   George W. Bush, "Remarks by the President in Submission of Faith-Based Services Proposal," at the Fishing School, January 30, 2001.

37   Asen, *Visions of Poverty*, 203.

38   See, for instance, Laurie Goodstein, "Churches May Not Be Able to Patch Welfare Cuts," *Washington Post*, February 22, 1995, A01; Mike McManus, "Churches Oppose GOP Cuts," *Seattle Post-Intelligencer*, February 26, 1995, D3; Gail Perry-Daniels, "Clergy: GOP Welfare Reform Cruel," *Madison (Wis.) Capital Times*, February 8, 1995, 7A; Larry Witham, "Charities Call 'Contract' Cruel to Poor," *Washington Times*, December 21, 1994, A4.

39   Jeffery Rosen, "Unholy Orders; Separating Church and State Is Not Easy in Welfare Reform," *Pittsburgh Post-Gazette*, November 27, 1995.

40   Episode 2.14, "Red Tape."

41   Episode 4.09, "Dirty Laundry."

42   Of course, most people would now agree that the government's internment of Japanese-Americans was wrong. This plot simply allows *7th Heaven* the opportunity to opine about government shortcomings.

43   Episode 2.06, "And the Home of the Brave."

44   Episode 1.08, "What Will People Say?"

45   Episode 2.13, "The Tribes that Bind."

46   Episode 1.14, "Seven is Enough."

47   Episode 1.16, "Brave New World."

48   Episode 2.01, "Don't Take My Love Away."

49   Episode 1.18, "Faith, Hope, and the Bottom Line."

50   Episode 1.05, "The Color of God."

51   Episode 1.02, "Family Secrets."

52   Renee is among the minority who do appear again—in her case, once more, just two episodes later.

53   Episodes 3.04, "The Legacy"; 5.09, "Tunes."

54   Episode 2.07, "Girls Just Want to Have Fun."

55   Episode 3.05, ". . . And a Nice Chianti."

56   Episode 5.10, "Surprise."

57   Episode 4.17, "Twelve Angry People."
58   Episode 1.16, "Brave New World."
59   Episode 2.02, "See You in September."
60   Episode 1.07, "Saturday."
61   Episode 1.16, "Brave New World."
62   Episode 2.18, "We the People."
63   Episode 1.01, "Anything You Want."
64   Episode 1.01, "Anything You Want."
65   Episodes 2.14, "In Praise of Women"; 3.10, "Here Comes Santa Claus."
66   Episode 6.11, "Pathetic."
67   Episode 2.19, "Time to Leave the Nest."
68   Episode 4.08, ". . . And Expiation."
69   Episode 6.12, "Suspicion."
70   Episode 6.17, "Lip Service."
71   Ann Douglas, *The Feminization of American Culture* (New York: Noonday, 1977); Roxanne Mountford, *The Gendered Pulpit: Preaching in American Protestant Spaces* (Carbondale: Southern Illinois University Press, 2003); Muriel Mellow, *Defining Work: Gender, Professional Work, and the Case of Rural Clergy* (Montreal: McGill-Queen's University Press, 2007).
72   Mountford, *Gendered Pulpit*, 41, 59 (emphasis in original).
73   Mellow, *Defining Work*, 121.
74   Importantly, Eric's masculinity is simultaneously shored up by his clear heterosexual desire. He and Annie exchange frequent passionate kisses, and there are many allusions to their active sex life.
75   Episode 1.01, "Anything You Want."
76   Episodes 3.02, "Drunk Like Me"; 4.04, "Come Drive with Me."
77   Episode 2.22, ". . . And Girlfriends."
78   Episode 1.05, "The Color of God."
79   Episode 1.01, "Anything You Want."
80   Episode 4.16, "Say a Little Prayer for Me."
81   Episode 6.12, "Suspicion."
82   See, for instance, episodes 2.03, "I Love You," and 2.14, "Red Tape."
83   Clinton, *It Takes a Village*, 100.
84   Clinton, *It Takes a Village*, 147.
85   Clinton, *It Takes a Village*, 188.
86   Clinton, *It Takes a Village*, 41. Clinton is not as concerned as Olasky is with preserving the traditional nuclear family in all cases. She explains, "Although the nuclear family, consisting of an adult mother and father and the children to whom they are biologically related, has proved to be the most durable and

effective means of meeting children's needs over time, it is not the only form that has worked in the past and the present" (50).

87 For its frank discussions of parenting, *7th Heaven* especially stands apart from so many of the other television dramas of its era. The other ones featuring teenagers, such as *Beverly Hills, 90210* and *Dawson's Creek*, featured absent parents whose role in their children's lives was minimal.

88 Episode 4.19, "Talk to Me."

89 Episode 2.13, "The Tribes that Bind."

90 Episode 6.12, "Suspicion."

91 Episode 2.09, "I Hate You."

92 Episode 1.05, "The Color of God."

93 Cnaan and Boddie, *Invisible Caring Hand*, 226, 281.

94 Wuthnow, *Saving America?*

95 Wuthnow, *Saving America?* 65.

96 Cnaan and Boddie, *Invisible Caring Hand*, 291.

97 Wuthnow, *Saving America?* 35.

98 Wuthnow, *Saving America?* 65.

99 Putnam, *Bowling Alone*, 194–95.

100 Of course, some Christian sects, such as the Roman Catholic Church and the Church of Jesus Christ Latter-day Saints, have always valued large families. In this age of birth control, Quiverfull is repopularizing this trend among other Protestant sects. Kathryn Joyce, "Arrows for the War," *The Nation*, November 9, 2006, http://www.thenation.com/doc/20061127/joyce (accessed July 25, 2008).

101 Dorothy Woodend, "A Holy War in Which the Weapons Aren't Bullets but Babies," *Globe and Mail*, November 25, 2006, F4.

102 Gen 1:28.

103 Amy Fagan, "Teach Your Children Well," *Washington Times*, November 26, 2007, A1.

104 Amy Fagan, "Teach Your Children Well"; David D. Kirkpatrick, "College for the Home-Schooled Is Shaping Leaders for the Right," *The New York Times*, March 8, 2004.

105 Amy Fagan, "Teach Your Children Well."

106 Many of the homeschooled elite will go on to cultivate their political skills at Patrick Henry College. Located in the furthest suburbs of Washington, D.C., in Purcellville, Va., Patrick Henry College is an avowedly conservative institution designed for homeschooled students, to train them for political leadership. David D. Kirkpatrick notes that the college has found remarkable success at winning its students politically prestigious internships—in the

White House, on President Bush's reelection campaign, and in Republican congressional offices. The school is too young—it was founded in 2000—for its political impact to be clear yet, but its early successes in recruiting students and winning them access to politics suggest that Patrick Henry College will play an integral role in translating the private sphere act of childrearing and homeschooling into public significance.

107 Hanna Rosin, "God's Harvard," *The New York Times*, September 9, 2007.

108 David D. Kirkpatrick, "College for the Home-Schooled."

109 To be precise, in early seasons, the family drives a minivan and a station wagon. The station wagon is later replaced by an electric minivan.

CHAPTER 6

1 Marty, *Righteous Empire*, 178–79.

2 Wesley Morris, "'Da Vinci' Surprise: Both Sides of the Controversy May Win," *Boston Globe*, May 14, 2006, N11.

3 Daniel Henninger, "Holy Sepulchre! 60 Million Buy 'The Da Vinci Code,'" *Wall Street Journal*, May 19, 2006, A10.

4 Stuart Laidlaw, "Even Detractors Can't resist Adding to the Buzz," *Toronto Star*, May 20, 2006, L02.

5 Bader et al., "American Piety," 21.

6 Internet Movie Database, "Box Office/Business for *The Da Vinci Code*," http://www.imdb.com/title/tt0382625/business (accessed November 28, 2006).

7 Stark, *What Americans Really Believe*, 169–71.

8 Stark, *What Americans Really Believe*, 172.

9 Janet Maslin, "Spinning a Thriller from the Gallery at the Louvre," *The New York Times*, March 17, 2003, E8.

10 Darrell L. Bock, "The Good News of Da Vinci," *Christianity Today*, January 5, 2004; Chris Armstrong, "Thanks, *Da Vinci Code*," *Christian History*, http://www.christianitytoday.com/history/newsletter/2003/nov14.html (accessed June 19, 2008); Michael S. Rose, "The Greatest Story Ever *Sold*," *Cruxnews.com*, October 15, 2003; Ronald V. Huggins, "Cracks in the Da Vinci Code," Institute for Religious Research, http://www.irr.org/da-vinci-code.html (accessed March 25, 2007); Anne Barbeau Gardiner, "Book Review: Dan Brown, *The Da Vinci Code*," *Culture Wars*, February 2004, http://www.culturewars.com/2004/DaVinci.html (accessed June 19, 2008); Carl E. Olson and Sandra Miesel, "Christ, the Early Church, Constantine, and the Council of Nicaea," *Planet Envoy*, http://www.envoymagazine.com/planetenvoy/review-davinci-part2-full.htm (accessed November 19, 2004);

James Patrick Holding, "Not InDavincible: A Review and Critique of *The Da Vinci Code*," *Answers in Action*, 2003, http://www.answers.org/issues/davincicode.html (accessed March 25, 2007); Timothy Maurice Reidy, "Breaking the Code," *Commonweal*, September 12, 2003; Sandra Miesel, "Dismantling *The Da Vinci Code*," *Crisis*, September 2003, http://www.crisismagazine.com/september2003/feature1.htm (accessed November 19, 2004); Collin Hansen, "Breaking The Da Vinci Code," *Christianity Today*, January/February 2004.

11   Anne Barbeau Gardiner, "Book Review: Dan Brown, *The Da Vinci Code*."

12   Kristy Maddux, "*The Da Vinci Code* and the Regressive Gender Politics of Celebrating Women," *Critical Studies in Media Communication* 25, no. 3 (2008): 243–44.

13   Darrel L. Bock, *Breaking the Da Vinci Code: Answers to the Questions Everyone's Asking* (Nashville: Nelson Books, 2004), 95.

14   Carl E. Olson and Sandra Miesel, *The Da Vinci Hoax: Exposing the Errors in The Da Vinci Code* (Fort Collins, Colo.: Ignatius, 2004), 29.

15   Roxanne Roberts, "The Mysteries of Mary Magdalene: Bestseller Renews Interest in a Misunderstood Figure," *Washington Post*, July 20, 2003, D01.

16   Sharon Tubbs, "The Gospel according to Dan Brown," *St. Petersburg (Fla.) Times*, January 25, 2004, 1E.

17   Kathleen Parker, "Ga-ga over Goddessness," *Milwaukee Journal Sentinel*, August 3, 2003, 04J.

18   Laurie Goodstein, "Defenders of Christianity Rebut 'The Da Vinci Code,'" *The New York Times*, April 27, 2004, A22.

19   T. W. Young, "'The Da Vinci Code' Is All Fiction, Keep in Mind," *Georgia Bulletin*, December 11, 2003, http://www.georgiabulletin.org/local/2003/12/11/Da_Vinci_Code_Is_All_Fiction/ (accessed November 19, 2004).

20   Olson and Miesel, *Da Vinci Hoax*, 15.

21   It might be helpful to acknowledge here that I do not accept Brown's narrative of church history in total. The purpose of this analysis is not, however, to question his Christian history; there are plenty of books and articles that do just that. Those arguments contest the book's major claims, especially Magdalene's role as Jesus' wife and sexual partner and the authority of Constantine's Council of Nicea in defining Christian doctrine, as well as the book's more minor claims, such as the number of witches burned at the stake and the number of panes of glass in the Louvre. Given that my purpose is to consider the function of this narrative in its contemporary context, I treat it as neither true nor false historically, but in a certain sense real for its readers.

22   Josephine Donovan, *Feminist Theory: The Intellectual Traditions of American Feminism* (New York: Continuum, 1992), 32.

23   Ann Snitow, "A Gender Diary," in *Conflicts in Feminism*, eds. Marianne Hirsch and Evelyn Fox Keller (New York: Routledge, 1990), 14–28.

24   Snitow, "A Gender Diary," 24.

25   Aileen Kraditor, *The Ideas of the Woman Suffrage Movement, 1890–1920* (New York: Columbia University Press, 1965), 43–74.

26   Bonnie J. Dow, "The 'Womanhood' Rationale in the Woman Suffrage Rhetoric of Frances E. Willard," *Southern Communication Journal* 56, no. 4 (1991): 298–307; Evans, *Born for Liberty*, 125–30.

27   Donovan, *Feminist Theory*, 48.

28   Alice Echols, *Daring to Be Bad: Radical Feminism in America, 1967–1975* (Minneapolis: University of Minnesota Press, 1989), 243–65.

29   Sara Ruddick, "Maternal Thinking," in *Mothering: Essays in Feminist Theory*, ed. Joyce Trebilcot (Totowa, N.J.: Roman & Allanheld, 1983), 220, 225.

30   Ruddick, "Maternal Thinking," 224.

31   Mary Daly, *Gyn/Ecology: The Metaethics of Radical Feminism* (Boston: Beacon, 1990); see also Mary Daly, *The Church and the Second Sex* (New York: Harper & Row, 1968), and Mary Daly, *Beyond God the Father: Toward a Philosophy of Women's Liberation* (Boston: Beacon, 1985).

32   Daly, *Gyn/Ecology*, 27–29, 11 (emphasis in original).

33   Pamela Ferdinand, "Feminist Ethics Course: No Place for Men," *Washington Post*, February 26, 1999, A1.

34   Elisabeth Schüssler Fiorenza, *In Memory of Her: A Feminist Theological Reconstruction of Christian Origins* (New York: Crossroad, 1994), L.

35   To be clear, Elisabeth Schüssler Fiorenza is not an extreme cultural feminist the way that Mary Daly is. She does not assume that women are wholly unique creatures whose spiritual experience necessarily differs from men's. She does, however, share the basic cultural/difference feminist impulse to recover women and women's contributions.

36   Lynn Schofield Clark and Stewart M. Hoover, "Controversy and Cultural Symbolism: Press Relations and the Formation of Public Discourse in the Case of the Re-Imagining Event," *Critical Studies in Mass Communication* 14 (1997): 310–31.

37   Dan Brown, *The Da Vinci Code* (New York: Anchor, 2003), 50.

38   Brown, *The Da Vinci Code*, 87.

39   Brown, *The Da Vinci Code*, 50.

40   One of more egregious failures of the film adaptation, although there were many, was to cast the brunette Audrey Tautou in the role of Sophie Neveu.

Her character never exuded the likeness of Mary Magdalene, and its attendant sexuality, the way the book's Neveu did.

41 Brown, *The Da Vinci Code*, 92.
42 Brown, *The Da Vinci Code*, 50.
43 Brown, *The Da Vinci Code*, 21.
44 Brown, *The Da Vinci Code*, 156 (emphasis removed for clarity).
45 Brown, *The Da Vinci Code*, 41.
46 Brown, *The Da Vinci Code*, 28.
47 Brown, *The Da Vinci Code*, 248.
48 Brown, *The Da Vinci Code*, 247–48.
49 Brown, *The Da Vinci Code*, 248.
50 Brown, *The Da Vinci Code*, 248.
51 Brown, *The Da Vinci Code*, 23.
52 Brown, *The Da Vinci Code*, 23.
53 Brown, *The Da Vinci Code*, 23.
54 Brown, *The Da Vinci Code*, 96 (emphasis in original).
55 Brown, *The Da Vinci Code*, 202.
56 Brown, *The Da Vinci Code*, 326.
57 Brown, *The Da Vinci Code*, 138.
58 Even though historians and art aficionados customarily refer to Leonardo
da Vinci as Leonardo, since da Vinci simply refers to his home town, I have
chosen to use the name da Vinci, in keeping with the novel's pattern.
59 Brown, *The Da Vinci Code*, 45.
60 Brown, *The Da Vinci Code*, 120.
61 Brown, *The Da Vinci Code*, 121.
62 Adrienne Rich, *Blood, Bread, and Poetry: Selected Prose 1979–1985* (New York: W. W. Norton, 1986).
63 Brown, *The Da Vinci Code*, 243.
64 Brown, *The Da Vinci Code*, 244–48.
65 Brown, *The Da Vinci Code*, 249; see also p. 255.
66 Brown, *The Da Vinci Code*, 238.
67 Brown, *The Da Vinci Code*, 255.
68 Ruddick, "Maternal Thinking," 226.
69 Brown, *The Da Vinci Code*, 36.
70 Brown, *The Da Vinci Code*, 309.
71 Brown, *The Da Vinci Code*, 303.
72 Brown, *The Da Vinci Code*, 323.
73 Brown, *The Da Vinci Code*, 142–43.
74 Brown, *The Da Vinci Code*, 308.

75 Brown, *The Da Vinci Code*, 308–9.
76 Brown, *The Da Vinci Code*, 257. The novel even ties Walt Disney into this effort to preserve the sacred feminine, which he has achieved through the films *Cinderella*, *Sleeping Beauty*, *Snow White*, and *The Little Mermaid*. All four deal "with the incarceration of the sacred feminine," which finds liberation through the symbolism in these films. As Snow White's eating of the apple is an allusion to Eve, and *The Little Mermaid* includes "blatant symbolic references to the lost sanctity of Isis, Eve, Pisces the fish goddess, and, repeatedly, Mary Magdalene," these films are yet another way that the sacred feminine lives on in art and symbolism (Brown, *The Da Vinci Code*, 262).
77 Brown, *The Da Vinci Code*, 294 (emphasis in original).
78 Brown, *The Da Vinci Code*, 101.
79 Brown, *The Da Vinci Code*, 294.
80 Brown, *The Da Vinci Code*, 444 (emphasis in original).
81 Brown, *The Da Vinci Code*, 33–34.
82 Brown, *The Da Vinci Code*, 70.
83 Brown, *The Da Vinci Code*, 287.
84 Brown, *The Da Vinci Code*, 340.
85 Brown, *The Da Vinci Code*, 449.
86 Northrop Frye, *Anatomy of Criticism: Four Essays* (Princeton: Princeton University Press, 1957), 103.
87 Brown, *The Da Vinci Code*, 440.
88 Carol Gilligan, *In a Different Voice: Psychological Theory and Women's Development* (Cambridge, Mass.: Harvard University Press, 1982), 7–9; Mary Field Belenky, Blythe McVicker Clinchy, Nancy Rule Goldberger, and Jill Mattuck Tarule, *Women's Ways of Knowing: The Development of Self, Voice, and Mind* (New York: Basic Books, 1986), 45.
89 Ruddick, "Maternal Thinking," 224.
90 Judith Butler, "Contingent Foundations: Feminism and the Question of 'Postmodernism,'" in *Feminists Theorize the Political*, ed. Judith Butler and Joan W. Scott (New York: Routledge, 1992), 15.
91 Dow, *Prime-Time Feminism*, 165.
92 Donovan, *Feminist Theory*, 62.
93 Donovan, *Feminist Theory*, 59.
94 Importantly, American feminism has felt a reciprocal pull to protect the private sphere. As it has tried to guarantee women's participation in the public sphere, it has also valued the sanctity of private decisions, including the privacy ideology so basic to the *Roe v. Wade* decision. Safeguarding privacy has been similarly important in the gay liberation movement, as it

has celebrated the *Lawrence v. Texas* ruling that sexual privacy is guaranteed by the due process clause of the Fourteenth Amendment.

95   Fiorenza, *In Memory of Her*, xlvi.

96   Patricia Rice, "James Dobson Is an Evangelical Agenda-Setter," *St. Louis Post-Dispatch*, September 3, 1995, 7B.

97   Karen E. Crummy, "Dobson: Husbands Get Final Say," *Denver Post*, August 1, 1999, B01.

98   Eric Gorski, "Focus on the Family Revels in Nurturing, Defending Families," *Chattanooga (Tenn.) Times Free Press*, July 10, 2005, A10.

99   Gorski, "Focus on the Family Revels"; Esther Diskin, "Family Doctor; James Dobson's Radio Show Blends Common-Sense Psychology with a Christian Foundation," *Virginian-Pilot*, July 25, 1995, E1.

100   Terri Cotton, "Focus on the Family Marks 25 Years," *Denver Post*, July 26, 2002, B02.

Chapter 7

1   Jeff Strickler, "Shack Author to Speak in Twin Cities," *Minneapolis Star Tribune*, February 7, 2009, 3E.

2   Christopher Quinn, "'The Shack': Trip to Top a Page Turner," *Atlanta Journal-Constitution*, June 28, 2008, 1E.

3   Kristen Campbell, "A Novel Approach to God," *Mobile (Ala.) Register*, July 12, 2008.

4   Julia Duin, "Story about Accessible God Becomes Best-Seller," *Washington Times*, August 7, 2008, A01.

5   William P. Young, *The Shack* (Newbury Park, Calif.: Windblown Media, 2007), 65.

6   Young, *The Shack*, 122–23.

7   Young, *The Shack*, 179.

8   Young, *The Shack*, 181.

9   Boyd, *The Myth*, 17–28.

10   Young, *The Shack*, 148.

11   Young, *The Shack*, 219.

12   Young, *The Shack*, 135 (emphasis in original).

13   William McKenzie, "Younger Evangelicals are Taking Movement in a New Direction," *Dallas Morning News*, March 18, 2008.

14   Alan Cooperman, "Evangelicals at a Crossroads as Falwell's Generation Fades," *Washington Post*, May 22, 2007; David D. Kirkpatrick, "The Evangelical Crackup," *New York Times Magazine*, October 28, 2007.

15   E. J. Dionne, "Message from a Megachurch," *Washington Post*, December 5, 2006.

16   David Kuo, "It's Not Your Father's Religious Right," *Washington Post*, February 24, 2008.

17   McKenzie, "Younger Evangelicals"; Nicholas Kristof, "Evangelicals a Liberal Can Love," *The New York Times*, February 3, 2008.

18   Michael Luo and Laurie Goodstein, "Emphasis Shifts for a New Generation of Evangelicals," *The New York Times*, May 21, 2007.

19   David Kuo, "It's Not Your Father's Religious Right," *Washington Post*, February 24, 2008.

20   Luo and Goodstein, "Emphasis Shifts."

21   Kristof, "Evangelicals a Liberal Can Love."

22   Kirkpatrick, "The Evangelical Crackup."

23   Kirkpatrick, "The Evangelical Crackup."

24   Asen, "A Discourse Theory," 191.

25   Ryan, "Gender and Public Access."

26   Nancy Fraser, "Rethinking the Public Sphere."

27   Keith, "Introduction: Cultural Resources," 219.

28   Kevin Mattson, "Do Americans Really Want Deliberative Democracy?" *Rhetoric & Public Affairs* 5 (2002): 327.

29   Mattson, "Do Americans Really Want?"; Michael Sproule, "Oratory, Democracy, and the Culture of Participation," *Rhetoric & Public Affairs* 5 (2002): 301–10.

30   Putnam, *Bowling Alone*, 228.

31   As absurd as it now seems, movie executives assumed that an audience for Christian-themed films did not exist. Thus, *Left Behind*'s promoters needed donors to underwrite showings in theaters that otherwise would not screen the film. Steve Rabey, " 'Left Behind: The Movie' at the Center of Controversy," *San Diego Union-Tribune*, October 27, 2000, E-4; Rebecca Sodergren, "Producers Hope Video Release Gives 'Left Behind' a Boost at Box Office," *Pittsburgh Post-Gazette*, October 31, 2000, E-5.

32   Jack Mathews, "And Next . . . the Anti-'Passion,' " *New York Daily News*, March 21, 2004, 16.

33   Bill Thompson, "An Impressive Cast of Hollywood Heavies Gets 'The Code,' " *Charleston (S.C.) Post and Courier*, June 16, 2005, 14F.

34   These numbers are taken from http://www.imdb.com/, not adjusted for inflation.

35   Laurie Goodstein, "Christian Foes of 'Da Vinci Code' Debate How to Fight It," *The New York Times*, May 11, 2006, 25.

36 Ian Fisher, "Vatican Official Urges Boycott of 'Da Vinci' Film," *The New York Times*, April 29, 2006, 8.

37 For instance, Ann Hornaday, "No Masterpiece Here: The Biggest Mystery of 'The Da Vinci Code': Why Is It So Dull?" *Washington Post*, May 19, 2006, C01.

38 These white characters may not be heroes for all audience members. Significant cultural studies research has shown that oppressed groups often develop reading strategies that allow them to identify with minorities or villains in popular culture texts. Hall, "Encoding/Decoding," 117–27; Justin Lewis, *The Ideological Octopus: An Exploration of Television and Its Audience* (New York: Routledge, 1991); David Morley, *The Nationwide Audience: Structure and Decoding* (London: British Film Institute, 1980).

39 This stock narrative of racial reconciliation parallels the easy resolution that gay coming out narratives so often find in television and movies. As Bonnie J. Dow and others have argued, gay characters and their coming out stories tend to serve straight audiences. Tailored toward educating straight audiences, stories such as Ellen DeGeneres' coming out on her sitcom, *Ellen*, educated heterosexuals about queer sexualities and assuaged their fears about gay lifestyles. Bonnie J. Dow, "*Ellen*, Television, and the Politics of Gay and Lesbian Visibility," *Critical Studies in Media Communication* 18, no. 2 (2001): 129.

40 In the three *Left Behind* movies, all three characters are played by white actors.

41 LaHaye and Jenkins, *Desecration*, 241–42, 245–47, 249–50, 260–62, 271.

42 Rom 12:2.

43 Aldon Morris, *The Origins of the Civil Rights Movement: Black Communities Organizing for Change* (New York: Simon & Schuster, 1986); Steven R. Goldzwig, "A Rhetoric of Public Theology: The Religious Rhetor and Public Policy," *Southern Speech Communication Journal* 52 (1987): 128–50; George Cheney and Steven R. Goldzwig, "The U.S. Catholic Bishops on Nuclear Arms: Corporate Advocacy, Role Redefinition, and Rhetorical Adaptation," *Central States Speech Journal* 35 (1984): 8–23.

44 Wuthnow, *Saving America?* 65; Putnam, *Bowling Alone*, 78.

45 Episode 6.15, "I Really Do."

References

Anderson, Karrin Vasby. "From Spouses to Candidates: Hillary Rodham Clinton, Elizabeth Dole, and the Gendered Office of U.S. President." *Rhetoric & Public Affairs* 5, no. 1 (2002): 105–32.

Armstrong, Karen. *The Gospel according to Woman: Christianity's Creation of the Sex War in the West.* Garden City, N.Y.: Anchor, 1987.

Asen, Robert. "A Discourse Theory of Citizenship." *Quarterly Journal of Speech* 90, no. 2 (2004): 189–211.

———. "The Multiple Mr. Dewey: Multiple Publics and Permeable Borders in John Dewey's Theory of the Public Sphere." *Argumentation and Advocacy* 39 (2003): 174–88.

———. *Visions of Poverty: Welfare Policy and Political Imagination.* East Lansing: Michigan State University Press, 2002.

Audi, Robert. *Practical Reasoning.* New York: Routledge, 1989.

Audi, Robert, and Nicholas Wolterstorff. *Religion in the Public Square: The Place of Religious Convictions in Political Debate.* Lanham, Md.: Rowman & Littlefield, 1997.

Babington, Bruce, and Peter William Evans. *Biblical Epics: Sacred Narrative in the Hollywood Cinema.* Manchester: Manchester University Press, 1993.

Bader, Christopher, Kevin Dougherty, Paul Froese, Byron Johnson, F. Carson Mencken, Jerry Z. Park, and Rodney Stark. "American Piety in the 21st Century: New Insights to the Depth and Complexity of Religion in the U.S." Unpublished research made available September 2006. http://www.baylor.edu/content/services/document.php/33304.pdf (accessed March 25, 2007).

Balmer, Randall Herbert. *Thy Kingdom Come: How the Religious Right Distorts the Faith and Threatens America: An Evangelical's Lament.* New York: Perseus Books, 2006.

Balmer, Randall Herbert, and Lauren F. Winner. *Protestantism in America.* New York: Columbia University Press, 2002.

Barber, Benjamin R. *A Place for Us: How to Make Society Civil and Democracy Strong.* New York: Hill & Wang, 1998.

Battles, Kathleen, and Wendy Hilton-Morrow. "Gay Characters in Conventional Spaces: *Will and Grace* and the Situation Comedy Genre." *Critical Studies in Media Communication* 19, no. 1 (2002): 87–105.

Beiner, Ronald, ed. *Theorizing Citizenship.* Albany: State Univrsity of New York Press, 1995.

Belenky, Mary Field, Blythe McVicker Clinchy, Nancy Rule Goldberger, and Jill Mattuck Tarule. *Women's Ways of Knowing: The Development of Self, Voice, and Mind.* New York: Basic Books, 1986.

Biesecker, Barbara. "Michel Foucault and the Question of Rhetoric." *Philosophy and Rhetoric* 25 (1992): 351–64.

Bock, Darrell L. *Breaking the Da Vinci Code: Answers to the Questions Everyone's Asking.* Nashville: Nelson Books, 2004.

Bohn, Carole R. "Dominion to Rule: The Roots and Consequences of a Theology of Ownership." In Brown and Bohn *Christianity, Patriarchy, and Abuse,* 105–16.

Boyd, Gregory A. *The Myth of a Christian Nation: How the Quest for Political Power Is Destroying the Church.* Grand Rapids: Zondervan, 2005.

Boyer, Paul S. *When Time Shall Be No More: Prophecy Belief in Modern American Culture.* Cambridge, Mass.: Belknap Press of Harvard University Press, 1992.

Brock, Rita Nakashima, and Rebecca Ann Parker. *Proverbs of Ashes: Violence, Redemptive Suffering, and the Search for What Saves Us.* Boston: Beacon, 2001.

Brouwer, Daniel C. "ACT-ing Up in Congressional Hearings." In *Counterpublics and the State,* edited by Robert Asen and Daniel C. Brouwer, 87–110. Albany: State University of New York Press, 2001.

Brown, Dan. *The Da Vinci Code.* New York: Anchor, 2003.

Brown, Joanne Carlson and Carole R. Bohn, eds. *Christianity, Patriarchy and Abuse: A Feminine Critique.* Cleveland, Ohio: Pilgrim, 1989.

Brown, Joanne Carlson, and Rebecca Parker. "For God So Loved the World?" In Brown and Bohn, *Christianity, Patriarchy, and Abuse,* 1–30.

Brummett, Barry. *Contemporary Apocalyptic Rhetoric.* Westport, Conn.: Praeger, 1991.

Budde, Michael. *The (Magic) Kingdom of God: Christianity and Global Culture Industries.* Boulder, Colo.: Westview, 1997.

Butler, Judith. "Contingent Foundations: Feminism and the Question of 'Postmodernism.' " In *Feminists Theorize the Political,* edited by Judith Butler and Joan W. Scott, 3–21. New York: Routledge, 1992.

———. *Gender Trouble: Feminism and the Subversion of Identity.* New York: Routledge, 1999.

Cadge, Wendy. "Vital Conflicts: The Mainline Protestant Denominations Debate Homosexuality." In *The Quiet Hand of God: Faith-Based Activism and the Public Role of Mainline Protestantism,* edited by Robert Wuthnow and John Hyde Evans, 149–78. Berkeley: University of California Press, 2002.

Calhoun, Craig, ed. *Habermas and the Public Sphere.* Cambridge, Mass.: MIT Press, 1996.

———. "Introduction: Habermas and the Public Sphere." In Calhoun, *Habermas and the Public Sphere,* 1–48.

Campbell, Karlyn Kohrs. "The Discursive Performance of Femininity: Hating Hillary." *Rhetoric & Public Affairs* 1, no. 1 (1998): 1–19.

———. *Man Cannot Speak for Her.* 2 vols. New York: Praeger, 1989.

Campolo, Tony. *Letters to a Young Evangelical.* New York: Basic Books, 2006.

Casey, Michael W. "The First Female Public Speakers in America (1630–1840): Searching for Egalitarian Christian Primitivism." *Journal of Communication and Religion* 23 (2000): 1–28.

Charland, Maurice. "Constitutive Rhetoric: The Case of the Peuple Québécois." *Quarterly Journal of Speech* 73, no. 2 (1987): 133–50.

Cheney, George, and Steven R. Goldzwig. "The U.S. Catholic Bishops on Nuclear Arms: Corporate Advocacy, Role Redefinition, and Rhetorical Adaptation." *Central States Speech Journal* 35 (1984): 8–23.

Clark, Lynn Schofield, and Stewart M. Hoover. "Controversy and Cultural Symbolism: Press Relations and the Formation of Public Discourse in the Case of the Re-Imagining Event." *Critical Studies in Mass Communication* 14 (1997): 310–31.

Clemens, Elisabeth S. "Organizational Repertoires and Institutional Change: Women's Groups and the Transformation of American Politics, 1890–1920." In Skocpol and Fiorina, *Civic Engagement in American Democracy,* 81–110.

Clinton, Hillary Rodham. *It Takes a Village and Other Lessons Children Teach Us.* New York: Simon & Schuster, 1996.

Cloud, Dana L. "Hegemony or Concordance? The Rhetoric of Tokenism In 'Oprah' Winfrey's Rags-to-Riches Biography." *Critical Studies in Mass Communication* 13 (1996): 115–37.

———. "The Limits of Interpretation: Ambivalence and the Stereotype in *Spenser: For Hire.*" *Critical Studies in Mass Communication* 9, no. 4 (1992): 311–24.

Cnaan, Ram A., and Stephanie C. Boddie. *The Invisible Caring Hand: American Congregations and the Provision of Welfare.* New York: New York University Press, 2002.

Coleman, Simon. "An Empire on a Hill? The Christian Right and the Right to Be Christian in America." *Anthropological Quarterly* 78, no. 3 (2005): 653–71.

Condit, Celeste Michelle. "Hegemony, Concordance, and Capitalism: Reply to Cloud." *Critical Studies in Mass Communication* 13 (1996): 382–84.

———. "Hegemony in a Mass-Mediated Society: Concordance about Reproductive Technologies." *Critical Studies in Mass Communication* 11, no. 3 (1994): 205–30.

———. "The Rhetorical Limits of Polysemy." *Critical Studies in Mass Communication* 6 (1989): 103–22.

Condit, Celeste Michelle, and John Louis Lucaites. *Crafting Equality: America's Anglo-African Word.* Chicago: University of Chicago Press, 1993.

Cone, James. "God Is Black." In Thistlethwaite and Engel, *Lift Every Voice,* 101–14.

———. *God of the Oppressed.* Maryknoll, N.Y.: Orbis Books, 1975/1997.

Connors, Richard, and Andrew Colin Gow. *Anglo-American Millennialism, from Milton to the Millerites.* Boston: Brill, 2004.

Cooper, Brenda. "*Boys Don't Cry* and Female Masculinity: Reclaiming a Life & Dismantling the Politics of Normative Heterosexuality." *Critical Studies in Media Communication* 19, no. 1 (2002): 44–63.

Cooper, Thomas. "Of Anti-Semitism, Romans de Sade, and Celluloid Christianity: The Cases For and Against Gibson's Passion." *Journal of Media and Religion* 4, no. 4 (2005): 251–68.

Cuklanz, Lisa M. "The Masculine Ideal: Rape on Prime-Time Television, 1976–1978." *Critical Studies in Mass Communication* 15 (1998): 423–48.

Curtis, Susan. *A Consuming Faith: The Social Gospel and Modern American Culture.* Baltimore: Johns Hopkins University Press, 1991.

Daly, Mary. *Beyond God the Father: Toward a Philosophy of Women's Liberation.* Boston: Beacon, 1985.

———. *The Church and the Second Sex.* New York: Harper & Row, 1968.

———. *Gyn/Ecology: The Metaethics of Radical Feminism.* Boston: Beacon, 1990.

Danforth, John C. *Faith and Politics: How the "Moral Values" Debate Divides America and How to Move Forward Together.* New York: Viking, 2006.

Darsey, James. *The Prophetic Tradition and Radical Rhetoric in America.* New York: New York University Press, 1997.

DeLuca, Kevin Michael, and Anne Teresa Demo. "Imaging Nature: Watkins, Yosemite, and the Birth of Environmentalism." *Critical Studies in Media Communication* 17, no. 3 (2000): 241–60.

DeLuca, Kevin Michael, and Jennifer Peeples. "From Public Sphere to Public Screen: Democracy, Activism, and the 'Violence' of Seattle." *Critical Studies in Media Communication* 19, no. 2 (2002): 125–51.

Donovan, Josephine. *Feminist Theory: The Intellectual Traditions of American Feminism.* New York: Continuum, 1992.

Douglas, Ann. *The Feminization of American Culture.* New York: Noonday, 1977.

Dow, Bonnie J. "*Ellen,* Television, and the Politics of Gay and Lesbian Visibility." *Critical Studies in Media Communication* 18, no. 2 (2001): 123–40.

———. *Prime-Time Feminism: Television, Media Culture, and the Women's Movement since 1970.* Philadelphia: University of Pennsylvania Press, 1996.

———. "The 'Womanhood' Rationale in the Woman Suffrage Rhetoric of Frances E. Willard." *Southern Communication Journal* 56, no. 4 (1991): 298–307.

Eberly, Rosa A. "Rhetoric and the Anti-Logos Doughball: Teaching Deliberating Bodies the Practices of Participatory Democracy." *Rhetoric & Public Affairs* 5, no. 2 (2002): 287–300.

Echols, Alice. *Daring to Be Bad: Radical Feminism in America, 1967–1975.* Minneapolis: University of Minnesota Press, 1989.

Edgar, Robert. *Middle Church: Reclaiming the Moral Values of the Faithful Majority from the Religious Right.* New York: Simon & Schuster, 2006.

Elshtain, Jean. *Just War against Terror: The Burden of American Power in a Violent World.* New York: Basic Books, 2003.

Engel, Mary Potter, and Susan Brooks Thistlethwaite. "Making the Connections among Liberation Theologies around the World." In Thistlethwaite and Engel, *Lift Every Voice,* 1–29.

Erickson, Hal. *Religious Radio and Television in the United States, 1921–1991: The Programs and Personalities.* Jefferson, N.C.: McFarland, 1992.

Evans, Sara M. *Born for Liberty: A History of Women in America.* New York: Free Press, 1997.

Falwell, Jerry. "Ministers and Marches." In *God's Bullies: Power Politics and Religious Tyranny,* edited by Perry Deane Young, 310–17. New York: Holt, Rinehart, & Winston, 1965/1982.

Faubion, James D. *The Shadows and Lights of Waco: Millennialism Today.* Princeton: Princeton University Press, 2001.

Ferré, John P. "The Media of Popular Piety." In *Mediating Religion: Conversations in Media, Religion, and Culture,* edited by Jolyon P. Mitchell and Sophia Marriage, 83–92. New York: T&T Clark, 2003.

Fiorenza, Elisabeth Schüssler. *In Memory of Her: A Feminist Theological Reconstruction of Christian Origins.* New York: Crossroad, 1994.

Fish, Stanley Eugene. *Is There a Text in This Class? The Authority of Interpretive Communities.* Cambridge, Mass.: Harvard University Press, 1980.

Fiske, John. "Television: Polysemy and Popularity." *Critical Studies in Mass Communication* 3, no. 4 (1986): 391–408.

Flexner, Eleanor. *Century of Struggle: The Woman's Rights Movement in the United States.* Cambridge, Mass.: Belknap Press of Harvard University Press, 1975.

Forshey, Gerald E. *American Religious and Biblical Spectaculars.* Westport, Conn.: Praeger, 1992.

Fortune, Marie. "The Transformation of Suffering: A Biblical and Theological Perspective." In Brown and Bohn, *Christianity, Patriarchy, and Abuse,* 139–47.

Frankl, Razelle. *Televangelism: The Marketing of Popular Religion.* Carbondale: Southern Illinois University Press, 1987.

———. "Transformation of Televangelism: Repackaging Christian Values." In *Media, Culture, & the Religious Right,* edited by Linda Kintz and Julia Lesage, 163–89. Minneapolis: University of Minnesota Press, 1998.

Fraser, Nancy. "Rethinking the Public Sphere: A Contribution to the Critique of Actually Existing Democracy." In Calhoun, *Habermas and the Public Sphere,* 109–42.

Fraser, Peter. *Images of the Passion: The Sacramental Mode in Film.* Westport, Conn.: Praeger, 1998.

Frye, Northrop. *Anatomy of Criticism: Four Essays.* Princeton: Princeton University Press, 1957.

Frykholm, Amy Johnson. *Rapture Culture: Left Behind in Evangelical America.* Oxford: Oxford University Press, 2004.

Gilligan, Carol. *In a Different Voice: Psychological Theory and Women's Development.* Cambridge, Mass.: Harvard University Press, 1982.

Goldberg, Michele. *Kingdom Coming: The Rise of Christian Nationalism.* New York: W. W. Norton, 2006.

Goldzwig, Steven R. "A Rhetoric of Public Theology: The Religious Rhetor and Public Policy." *Southern Speech Communication Journal* 52 (1987): 128-50.

Goodnight, G. Thomas, and David B. Hingstman. "Studies in the Public Sphere." *Quarterly Journal of Speech* 83 (1997): 351-99.

Gorrell, Donald K. *The Age of Social Responsibility: The Social Gospel in the Progressive Era, 1900–1920.* Macon, Ga.: Mercer University Press, 1988.

Grant, Jacqueline. "Subjectification as a Requirement for Christological Construction." In Thistlethwaite and Engel, *Lift Every Voice,* 207-20.

Greenawalt, Kent. *Private Consciences and Public Reasons.* New York: Oxford University Press, 1995.

Grimké, Sarah Moore. *Letters on the Equality of the Sexes and the Condition of Woman, Addressed to Mary S. Parker, President of the Boston Female Anti-Slavery Society.* Boston: I. Knapp, 1838.

Gunn, Joshua, and David E. Beard. "On the Apocalyptic Sublime." *Southern Communication Journal* 65, no. 4 (2000): 269-86.

Gunton, Colin E. *The Actuality of Atonement: A Study of Metaphor, Rationality, and the Christian Tradition.* Grand Rapids: Eerdmans, 1989.

Guth, James L. *The Bully Pulpit: The Politics of Protestant Clergy.* Lawrence: University Press of Kansas, 1997.

Habermas, Jürgen. "The Public Sphere: An Encyclopedia Article (1964)." *New German Critique* 3 (1974): 49-55.

———. "Religion in the Public Sphere." *European Journal of Philosophy* 14, no. 1 (2006): 1-25.

———. *The Structural Transformation of the Public Sphere: An Inquiry into a Category of Bourgeois Society.* Cambridge, Mass.: MIT Press, 1989.

Halberstam, Judith. *Female Masculinity.* Durham, N.C.: Duke University Press, 1998.

Hall, Stuart. "Encoding/Decoding." In *Culture, Media, Language,* edited by Stuart Hall, Dorothy Hobson, Andrew Lowe, and Paul Wills, 128-38. London: Hutchinson, 1980.

Harrell, David Edwin. "Oral Roberts: Religious Media Pioneer." In

Communication and Change in American Religious History, edited by Leonard I. Sweet, 320–34. Grand Rapids: Eerdmans, 1993.

Hauser, Gerard A., and Chantal Benoit-Barne. "Reflections on Rhetoric, Deliberative Democracy, Civil Society, and Trust." *Rhetoric & Public Affairs* 5, no. 2 (2002): 261–75.

Hedges, Chris. *American Fascists: The Christian Right and the War on America.* New York: Free Press, 2006.

Hendershot, Heather. *Shaking the World for Jesus: Media and Conservative Evangelical Culture.* Chicago: University of Chicago Press, 2004.

Hicks, Darrin. "The Promise(s) of Deliberative Democracy." *Rhetoric & Public Affairs* 5, no. 2 (2002): 223–60.

Hoge, Dean R. *Division in the Protestant House: The Basic Reasons behind Intra-Church Conflicts.* Philadelphia: Westminster, 1976.

Holland, Shannon L. "The Dangers of Playing Dress-Up: Popular Representations of Jessica Lynch and the Controversy regarding Women in Combat." *Quarterly Journal of Speech* 92, no. 1 (2006): 27–50.

Hoover, Stewart M., and Lynn Schofield Clark. *Practicing Religion in the Age of the Media: Explorations in Media, Religion, and Culture.* New York: Columbia University Press, 2002.

Ignatieff, Michael. "The Myth of Citizenship." In Beiner, *Theorizing Citizenship*, 53–78.

Irving, Helen. *Gender and the Constitution: Equity and Agency in Comparative Constitutional Design.* New York: Cambridge University Press, 2008.

Jamieson, Kathleen Hall. *Beyond the Double Bind.* New York: Oxford University Press, 1995.

Jasinski, James. "Instrumentalism, Contextualism, and Interpretation in Rhetorical Criticism." In *Rhetorical Hermeneutics: Invention and Interpretation in the Age of Science*, edited by Alan G. Gross and William M. Keith, 195–224. Albany: State University of New York Press, 1997.

Kaplan, Jeffrey. *Radical Religion in America: Millenarian Movements from the Far Right to the Children of Noah.* Syracuse, N.Y.: Syracuse University Press, 1997.

Keith, William. *Democracy as Discussion: Civic Education and the American Forum Movement.* Lanham, Md.: Lexington Books, 2007.

———. "Democratic Revival and the Promise of Cyberspace: Lessons from the Forum Movement." *Rhetoric & Public Affairs* 5, no. 2 (2002): 311–26.

———. "Introduction: Cultural Resources for Deliberative Democracy." *Rhetoric & Public Affairs* 5, no. 2 (2002): 219–21.

Kelly, George Armstrong. "Who Needs a Theory of Citizenship?" In Beiner, *Theorizing Citizenship*, 79–104.

Kermode, Frank. *The Sense of an Ending: Studies in the Theory of Fiction*. New York: Oxford University Press, 1967.

Kohut, Andrew. *The Diminishing Divide: Religion's Changing Role in American Politics*. Washington, D.C.: Brookings Institution, 2000.

Kraditor, Aileen. *The Ideas of the Woman Suffrage Movement, 1890–1920*. New York: Columbia University Press, 1965.

Kuo, David. *Tempting Faith: An Inside Story of Political Seduction*. New York: Free Press, 2006.

Kymlicka, Will, and Wayne Norman. "Return of the Citizen: A Survey of Recent Work on Citizenship Theory." In Beiner, *Theorizing Citizenship*, 283–322.

LaHaye, Tim, and Jerry B. Jenkins. *Apollyon: The Destroyer is Unleashed*. Wheaton, Ill.: Tyndale House, 1999.

———. *Armageddon: The Cosmic Battle of the Ages*. Wheaton, Ill.: Tyndale House, 2003.

———. *Assassins: Assignment: Jerusalem, Target: Antichrist*. Wheaton, Ill.: Tyndale House, 1999.

———. *Desecration: Antichrist Takes the Throne*. Wheaton, Ill.: Tyndale House, 2001.

———. *Glorious Appearing: The End of Days*. Wheaton, Ill.: Tyndale House, 2004.

———. *The Indwelling: The Beast Takes Possession*. Wheaton, Ill.: Tyndale House, 2000.

———. *Left Behind: A Novel of the Earth's Last Days*. Wheaton, Ill.: Tyndale House, 1996.

———. *The Mark: The Beast Rules the World*. Wheaton, Ill.: Tyndale House, 2000.

———. *Nicolae: The Rise of Antichrist*. Wheaton, Ill.: Tyndale House, 1997.

———. *The Remnant: On the Brink of Armageddon*. Wheaton, Ill.: Tyndale House, 2002.

———. *Soul Harvest: The World Takes Sides*. Wheaton, Ill.: Tyndale House, 1998.

———. *Tribulation Force: The Continuing Drama of Those Left Behind*. Wheaton, Ill.: Tyndale House, 1996.

Leff, Michael. "Textual Criticism: The Legacy of G. P. Mohrmann." *Quarterly Journal of Speech* 72 (1986): 377–89.

Lerner, Michael. *The Left Hand of God: Taking Back Our Country from the Religious Right.* New York: HarperSanFrancisco, 2006.

Lewis, Justin. *The Ideological Octopus: An Exploration of Television and Its Audience.* New York: Routledge, 1991.

Lewis, Justin, Sanna Inthorn, and Karin Wahl-Jorgensen. *Citizens or Consumers? What the Media Tell Us about Political Participation.* Issues in Cultural and Media Studies. New York: Open University Press, 2005.

Longenecker, Dwight, and David Gustafson. *Mary: A Catholic-Evangelical Debate.* Grand Rapids: Brazos, 2003.

Macquarrie, John. *Mary for All Christians.* Edinburgh: T&T Clark, 2001.

Maddux, Kristy. "*The Da Vinci Code* and the Regressive Gender Politics of Celebrating Women." *Critical Studies in Media Communication* 25, no. 3 (2008): 225–48.

———. "Faithful Political Rhetoric." *Rhetoric & Public Affairs* 11, no. 1 (2008): 133–55.

———. "Feminism and Foreign Policy: Public Vocabularies and the Conditions of Emergence for First Lady Rosalynn Carter." *Women's Studies in Communication* 31, no. 1 (2008): 29–55.

———. "When Patriots Protest: The Anti-Suffrage Discursive Transformation of 1917." *Rhetoric & Public Affairs* 7, no. 3 (2004): 283–310.

———. "Winning the Right to Vote in 2004: *Iron Jawed Angels* and the Retrospective Framing of Feminism." *Feminist Media Studies* 9, no. 1 (2009): 73–94.

Marsden, George M. *Fundamentalism and American Culture: The Shaping of Twentieth Century Evangelicalism: 1870–1925.* New York: Oxford University Press, 1980.

Marty, Martin E. *Righteous Empire: The Protestant Experience in America.* New York: Dial, 1970.

Mattson, Kevin. "Do Americans Really Want Deliberative Democracy?" *Rhetoric & Public Affairs* 5 (2002): 327–29.

McGinn, Bernard J., John J. Collins, and Stephen J. Stein, eds. *The Continuum History of Apocalypticism.* New York: Continuum, 2003.

McKerrow, Raymie E. "Critical Rhetoric: Theory and Praxis." *Communication Monographs* 56 (1989): 91–111.

McMinn, Lisa. "Y2K, the Apocalypse, and Evangelical Christianity: The Role of Eschatological Belief in Church Responses." *Sociology of Religion* 62, no. 2 (2001): 205–20.

Mellow, Muriel. *Defining Work: Gender, Professional Work, and the Case of Rural Clergy.* Montreal: McGill-Queen's University Press, 2007.

Meyers, Robin. *Why the Christian Right Is Wrong: A Minister's Manifesto for Taking Back Your Faith, Your Flag, Your Future*. San Francisco: Jossey-Bass, 2006.

Moberg, David O. *The Great Reversal: Evangelism and Social Concern*. Philadelphia: Lippincott, 1972/1977.

Montgomery, Maxine Lavon. *The Apocalypse in African-American Fiction*. Gainesville: University Press of Florida, 1996.

Morley, David. *The Nationwide Audience: Structure and Decoding*. London: British Film Institute, 1980.

Morris, Aldon. *The Origins of the Civil Rights Movement: Black Communities Organizing for Change*. New York: Simon & Schuster, 1986.

Mountford, Roxanne. *The Gendered Pulpit: Preaching in American Protestant Spaces*. Carbondale: Southern Illinois University Press, 2003.

Murphy, John M. "'Our Mission and Our Moment': George W. Bush and September 11th." *Rhetoric & Public Affairs* 6, no. 4 (2003): 607–32.

Murphy, Troy A. "Deliberative Civic Education and Civil Society: A Consideration of Ideals and Actualities in Democracy and Communication Education." *Communication Education* 53, no. 1 (2004): 74–91.

Nickoloff, James B. "Introduction." In *Gustavo Gutiérrez: Essential Writings*, edited by James B. Nickoloff, 1–22. Maryknoll, N.Y.: Orbis Books, 1996.

Olasky, Marvin. *The Tragedy of American Compassion*. Washington, D.C.: Regnery Gateway, 1992.

O'Leary, Stephen D. *Arguing the Apocalypse: A Theory of Millennial Rhetoric*. New York: Oxford University Press, 1994.

Olson, Carl E., and Sandra Miesel. *The Da Vinci Hoax: Exposing the Errors in The Da Vinci Code*. Fort Collins, Colo.: Ignatius, 2004.

Orchard, Helen C. *Courting Betrayal: Jesus as Victim in the Gospel of John*. Sheffield: Sheffield Academic Press, 1998.

Palmer, Phoebe. "Tongue of Fire on the Daughters of the Lord." In *Phoebe Palmer: Selected Writings*, edited by Thomas C. Oden, 31–56. New York: Paulist, 1988.

Parry-Giles, Shawn J., and Trevor Parry-Giles. "Gendered Politics and Presidential Image Construction: A Reassessment of the 'Feminine Style.'" *Communication Monographs* 63, no. 4 (1996): 337–53.

Peach, Lucinda J. *Legislating Morality: Pluralism and Religious Identity in Lawmaking*. New York: Oxford University Press, 2002.

Peck, Janice. *The Gods of Televangelism: The Crisis of Meaning and the Appeal of Religious Television*. Cresskill, N.J.: Hampton, 1993.

Pezzullo, Phaedra C. "Resisting 'National Breast Cancer Awareness Month': The Rhetoric of Counterpublics and Their Cultural Performances." *Quarterly Journal of Speech* 89, no. 4 (2003): 345–65.

Phillips, Kevin. *American Theocracy: The Perils and Politics of Radical Religion, Oil and Borrowed Money in the 21st Century.* New York: Viking, 2006.

Pocock, J. G. A. "The Ideal of Citizenship since Classical Times." In Beiner, *Theorizing Citizenship,* 29–52.

Prothero, Stephen. *American Jesus: How the Son of God Became a National Icon.* New York: Farrar, Straus & Giroux, 2003.

Putnam, Robert D. "Bowling Alone: America's Declining Social Capital." *Journal of Democracy* 6, no. 1 (1995): 65–78.

———. *Bowling Alone: The Collapse and Revival of American Community.* New York: Simon & Schuster, 2000.

Rawls, John. "The Idea of Public Reason Revisited." *University of Chicago Law Review* 64 (1997): 765–99.

Ray, Angela G. *The Lyceum and Public Culture in the Nineteenth-Century United States.* East Lansing: Michigan State University Press, 2005.

Rich, Adrienne. *Blood, Bread, and Poetry: Selected Prose 1979–1985.* New York: W. W. Norton, 1986.

Rosen, Elizabeth K. *Apocalyptic Transformation: Apocalypse and the Postmodern Imagination.* Lanham, Md.: Lexington Books, 2008.

Rosenthal, Michele. " 'Turn it off!': TV Criticism in the Christian Century Magazine." In *Practicing Religion in the Age of the Media: Explorations in Media, Religion, and Culture,* edited by Stewart M. Hoover and Lynn Schofield Clark, 138–62. New York: Columbia University Press, 2002.

Ruddick, Sara. "Maternal Thinking." In *Mothering: Essays in Feminist Theory,* edited by Joyce Trebilcot, 213–30. Totowa, N.J.: Roman & Allanheld, 1983.

Ruether, Rosemary Radford. "Eschatology and Feminism." In Thistlethwaite and Engel, *Lift Every Voice,* 129–42.

Ryan, Mary P. "Gender and Public Access: Women's Politics in Nineteenth-Century America." In Calhoun, *Habermas and the Public Sphere,* 259–88.

Schaefer, Nancy A. "Y2K as an Endtime Sign: Apocalypticism in America at the *Fin-De-Millennium.*" *Journal of Popular Culture* 38, no. 1 (2004): 82–105.

Schudson, Michael. *The Good Citizen: A History of American Civic Life.* New York: Martin Kessler Books, 1998.

———. "Good Citizens and Bad History: Today's Political Ideals in Historical Perspective." *The Communication Review* 4, no. 1 (2000): 1–19.

Schultze, Quentin J., ed. *American Evangelicals and the Mass Media*. Grand Rapids: Academie Books, 1990.

———. *Christianity and the Mass Media in America: Toward a Democratic Accommodation*. East Lansing: Michigan State University Press, 2003.

———. "Keeping the Faith: American Evangelicals and the Media." In *American Evangelicals and the Mass Media*, edited by Quentin Schultze, 23–25. Grand Rapids: Academie Books, 1990.

Selby, Gary. "Framing Social Protest: The Exodus Narrative in Martin Luther King's Montgomery Bus Boycott Rhetoric." *Journal of Communication and Religion* 24, no. 1 (2001): 68–93.

———. *Martin Luther King and the Rhetoric of Freedom: The Exodus Narrative in America's Struggle for Civil Rights*. Waco, Tex.: Baylor University Press, 2008.

Shugart, Helene A. "On Misfits and Margins: Narrative, Resistance, and the Poster Child Politics of Rosie O'Donnell." *Communication and Critical/Cultural Studies* 2, no. 1 (2005): 52–76.

———. "Reinventing Privilege: The New (Gay) Man in Contemporary Popular Media." *Critical Studies in Media Communication* 20, no. 1 (2003): 67–91.

Silk, Mark. *Unsecular Media: Making News of Religion in America*. Urbana: University of Illinois Press, 1995.

Skocpol, Theda. "How Americans Became Civic." In Skocpol and Fiorina, *Civic Engagement in American Democracy*, 28–80.

Skocpol, Theda, and Morris P. Fiorina, eds. *Civic Engagement in AMerican Democracy*. Washington, D.C.: Brookings Institution, 1999.

———. "Making Sense of the Civic Engagement Debate." In Skocpol and Fiorina, *Civic Engagement in American Democracy*, 1–24.

Smith, Rogers M. *Civic Ideals: Conflicting Visions of Citizenship in U.S. History*. New Haven, Conn.: Yale University Press, 1997.

Smolinski, Reiner. "Apocalypticism in Colonial North America." In McGinn, et al., *The Continuum History of Apocalypticism*, 441–66.

Snitow, Ann. "A Gender Diary." In *Conflicts in Feminism*, edited by M. Hirsch and E. F. Keller, 9–43. New York: Routledge, 1990.

Sobrino, Jon. *Christ the Liberator: A View from the Victims*. Maryknoll, N.Y.: Orbis Books, 2001.

Solomon, Martha. "Stopping ERA: A Pyrrhic Victory." *Communication Quarterly* 31, no. 2 (1983): 109–17.

Sproule, Michael. "Oratory, Democracy, and the Culture of Participation." *Rhetoric & Public Affairs* 5, no. 2 (2002): 301–10.

Stanton, Elizabeth Cady. *The Woman's Bible*. New York: European Publishing Company, 1895.

Stark, Rodney. *What Americans Really Believe*. Waco, Tex.: Baylor University Press, 2008.

Stein, Stephen J. "Apocalypticism Outside the Mainstream in the United States." In McGinn, et al., *The Continuum History of Apocalypticism*, 493–515.

Stout, Daniel A., and Judith M. Buddenbaum. "Genealogy of an Emerging Field: Foundations for the Study of Media and Religion." *Journal of Media and Religion* 1, no. 1 (2002): 5–12.

Thistlethwaite, Susan Brooks, and Mary Potter Engel, eds. *Lift Every Voice: Constructing Christian Theologies frim the Underside*. Maryknoll, N.Y.: Orbis Books, 1998.

Townsend, Kathleen Kennedy. *Failing America's Faithful: How Today's Churches Are Mixing God with Politics and Losing Their Way*. New York: Warner Books, 2007.

Wallis, Jim. *God's Politics: Why the Right Gets It Wrong and the Left Doesn't Get It*. San Francisco: HarperSanFrancisco, 2005.

Walzer, Michael. "The Civil Society Argument." In Beiner, *Theorizing Citizenship*, 153–74.

Wander, Philip. "The Ideological Turn in Modern Criticism." *Central States Speech Journal* 34 (1983): 1–18.

Weber, Eugen. *Apocalypses: Prophecies, Cults, and Millennial Beliefs through the Ages*. Cambridge, Mass.: Harvard University Press, 1999.

Wilcox, Clyde, Sharon Linzey, and Ted G. Jelen. "Reluctant Warriors: Premillennialism and Politics in the Moral Majority." *Journal for the Scientific Study of Religion* 30, no. 3 (1991): 245–58.

Wilson, J. Matthew, ed. *From Pews to Polling Places: Faith and Politics in the American Religious Mosaic*. Washington, D.C.: Georgetown University Press, 2007.

Wuthnow, Robert. "Mobilizing Civic Engagement: The Changing Impact of Religious Involvement." In Skocpol and Fiorina, *Civic Engagement in American Democracy*, 331–63.

———. *Saving America? Faith-Based Services and the Future of Civil Society*. Princeton: Princeton University Press, 2004.

Yates, Melissa. "Rawls and Habermas on Religion in the Public Sphere." *Philosophy and Social Criticism* 33, no. 7 (2007): 880–91.

Young, William P. *The Shack*. Newbury Park, Calif.: Windblown Media, 2007.

Zaeske, Susan. "Little Magic: Martin van Buren and the Politics of Gender." In *Before the Rhetorical Presidency*, edited by Martin J. Medhurst, 44–62. College Station: Texas A&M Press, 2008.

———. *Signatures of Citizenship: Petitioning, Antislavery, and Women's Political Identity*. Chapel Hill: University of North Carolina Press, 2003.

INDEX